Twenty Years Later
Kibbutz Children Grown Up

Dr. Albert I. Rabin is Professor of Psychology at Michigan State University, where he has taught since 1948. He is a former Director of the Psychological Clinic and a recipient of the Distinguished Faculty Award of that institution. Dr. Rabin also served as Professor of Psychology at the City University of New York and as Visiting Professor at the Hebrew and Bar-Ilan Universities (Israel) as well as at the University of Aarhus (Denmark).

Dr. Rabin has authored or edited some ten books, chapters in some 25 other books, and about 150 articles, reviews, and other publications, including *Growing up in the Kibbutz* (1965), *Kibbutz Studies* (1971), and *Assessment with Projective Techniques* (1981).

He has had a lifelong interest in personality dynamics, development, and assessment and was the recipient of the Distinguished Contribution Award from the Society for Personality Assessment in 1977.

Dr. Benjamin Beit-Hallahmi is Senior Lecturer in Psychology at the University of Haifa, where he has taught since 1973. He has also been affiliated with the University of Michigan, the University of Pennsylvania, the Hebrew University, Tel-Aviv University, and Central Michigan University, holding clinical, research, and teaching appointments.

Dr. Beit-Hallahmi has also coauthored (with Michael Argyle) *The Social Psychology of Religion* (1975) and has edited *Research in Religious Behavior* (1973) and *Psychoanalysis and Religion: A Bibliography* (1978). In addition, he has contributed some 75 chapters, articles, and reviews to professional publications.

His research interests include personality development, the psychology of religion, and the history of psychology.

Twenty Years Later

Kibbutz Children Grown Up

A. I. Rabin

Benjamin Beit-Hallahmi

SPRINGER PUBLISHING COMPANY
New York

Springer Publishing Company, Inc.
200 Park Avenue South
New York, New York 10003

82 83 84 85 86 / 10 9 8 7 6 5 4 3 2 1

Library of Congress Cataloging in Publication Data

Rabin, Albert I.
   Twenty years later.

   Includes bibliographical references and index.
   1. Children–Israel–Longitudinal studies.
2. Kibbutzim–Israel–Longitudinal studies. 3. Family–
Israel–Longitudinal studies. I. Beit-Hallahmi,
Benjamin. II. Title.
HQ792.I75R3   305.2'3'095694   82-821
ISBN 0-8261-3310-X   AACR2
ISBN 0-8261-3311-8 (pbk.)

Printed in the United States of America

Contents

v

Preface

This is an intensive psychological study of two groups of adults, examining for the first time the long-range psychological effects of communal child rearing. These two groups were first studied, as children and adolescents, by A. I. Rabin in 1955, in the research that served as the basis for the book *Growing up in the Kibbutz* (New York: Springer, 1965). Twenty years after the original study, the same individuals became the subjects of a follow-up research, aimed at looking at the effects of their childhood experiences on their adult lives. The subjects are divided into two groups: those who had grown up in a kibbutz communal system, and a control group, made up of individuals who had grown up in nuclear families in a moshav, a rural noncommunal community in Israel. The moshav served as an appropriate control group, because of its overall similarity to the kibbutz and, simultaneously, its dissimilarity in relation to the crucial variable of child rearing.

The original study has been quoted widely and has been used to revise notions about the nature and the effects of kibbutz child rearing. It has often been relied upon as a source of information about the kibbutz and about alternative approaches to child rearing. The wide attention given to the original study and its findings and the unusual interest in the kibbutz on the part of psychologists and of social scientists in general led to the follow-up study.

The decision to carry out the follow-up stage of the study was influenced both by practical and theoretical developments. With psychology as a discipline coming of age, psychologists have become more interested in life span psychological development and have realized the need for more longitudinal research. Theoretical developments have emphasized the notions of development and change in personality beyond childhood and adolescence. However, longitudinal studies are often not carried out because of practical considerations. They involve more expenses and more practical efforts than any other kind of study with human subjects. The practical opportunity for starting the follow-up work presented itself when the second author accepted a position with the University of Haifa in 1973. The first ideas about the follow-up research were discussed in East Lansing in the summer of 1973, after A. I. Rabin had written a brief memorandum outlining the aims of such a project. The initial discussions were tentative and general. Many practical problems were regarded as difficult to solve: financing, tracking down the members of the original groups, and selecting the instruments to be used.

During 1973 and 1974, preparations for the study were continuing. Progress was made in tracking the members of the original group and in preparing the research instruments. By the end of 1974, the tasks of locating the subjects and preparing the instruments had been completed. In early 1975, twenty years after the original research had been done, the interviewing process was started, and it continued until the summer of 1977. The follow-up study included 85% of the original subjects, who were studied intensely by means of a structured interview and a number of psychological tests. Data from these instruments have been analyzed and the two groups compared in several areas of psychological functioning. The findings offer a perspective on these adults in terms of their overall adjustment to society and their accomplishments, their relationships with parents and peers, and their expressions of satisfaction and dissatisfaction with themselves and with the world around them.

This book presents the findings of our follow-up study, but it also attempts to provide a perspective on the kibbutz as a social phenomenon and as a changing historical reality. Much too often psychological studies done in natural settings ignore important aspects of social realities. We have tried to maintain a broad perspective and to provide the reader with a broader view of the phenomenon under study. Thus, this book aims at making a contribution to psychology, but also to the area of kibbutz studies.

In the framework of the present project we have not looked at some very intriguing psychological questions, which have to do with the internal consistency of personality over time, because our aim has been limited to a comparative study. The questions of personality consistency and personality development over time will be addressed in a separate monograph.

Acknowledgments

A great number of individuals, and several institutions, have contributed significantly to the completion of this project.

First and foremost, there are the 146 men and women who served as the subjects in our study. They offered us cooperation and hospitality, and they shared with us the details of their personal experiences and their private lives. Their friendliness and cooperation not only made the study possible but also made it much richer.

Several of our colleagues shared with us all the stages of this project, from data collection to final analysis and formulation. They are recognized in several of the chapters as coauthors. Ruth Sharabany contributed invaluable help in data collection, organization, analysis, and the formulation of our findings. Hanna Kaminer and Noga Engelstein collaborated in all stages of the project with devotion and offered refreshing viewpoints and ideas. Baruch Nevo offered us generous help in administration, data collection, and data analysis and got us out of various difficulties. Eliyahu Regev had a significant impact on the study through his ideas and his pratical help.

At the interviewing stage, in addition to individuals named already, we enjoyed the help of Yehudit Harel (who also prepared the final form of the Personal Interview), Tamar Neuger, Rachel Neuger, Varda Gilad, Arie Rothstein, Rivi Ben-Ari, Baruch Ashkenazi, Benjamin Gal, Yaacov Koren, and Israel Oz.

At the analysis stage we enjoyed the help of Carmela Rim, Hefziba Berman, Menucha Birenbaum, John W. Condon, William D. Crano, R. Karen O'Quin, Lawrence Messe, Eileen Thompson, and Tirtza Assor.

When we reached the writing stage, we had the benefit of review and advice from several colleagues, whose comments did much to make our ideas clearer. Robert A. Zucker, Albert Aniskiewicz, and Alexander Z. Guiora shared in this task. Many other colleagues and friends served as sounding boards for ideas and formulations and have often presented us with new ideas and insights.

The Institute for Research on Kibbutz Education facilitated our work by allowing us to carry out the work in the various kibbutz federations. We have also received permission from the research committee of the Ha-kibbutz ha-Meuhad federation and cooperation from several individual kibbutz secretariats.

Financial support was received from the Social Science Research Committee at the University of Haifa. The Israel National Academy of Sciences offered us a grant in 1976, which had to be declined for technical reasons. The College of Social Science at Michigan State University awarded the senior author a leave for research in the Spring of 1977 and covered much of the computer expenses for data analysis. The department of psychology at Michigan State University offered this project a home during its final stages, and the University of Haifa granted the second author a sabbatical leave in 1978/79 to complete work on it. We consider ourselves fortunate to have had so much help and support, without which the project would not have been completed.

And last, but not least, Constance Ryamond, Gnani R. Moses, Susan Pavick, and Julie Garanty did the typing of several versions of the manuscript faithfully and competently.

1

Introduction: Purpose and Context

This book is an attempt to evaluate the long-term effects of childhood experiences as they are reflected in the lives of adults, looking for the shadows of childhood events as they emerge in the broad daylight of adult life. It is an intensive study of two groups of adults, aiming at an assessment of the relationship between their particular childhood environments and their adult personality functioning. Taking advantage of a natural situation, the study can be conceived of as an experiment. One group in the study experienced childhood in a communal setting, while the members of the other group are products of traditional nuclear family rearing. The overall strategy is one of comparing the "experimental group"—the kibbutz-raised adults—to the "control group"—the moshav-raised adults. Mead (1966) suggested the use of the term "contrast group" in this particular case. We will use the terms interchangeably. The group of kibbutz-born adults we are looking at is part of what has become known as the kibbutz "second generation." This second generation is made up of the children of kibbutz founders and is thus the first generation to grow up in the kibbutzim. This is the first psychological study that has looked at these children as adults.

Our design, relying on the good fortune of historical and social circumstances, allows us to have a control group, so that everything except one crucial variable is held relatively constant. That crucial variable is the nature of the child-rearing system, and because we are interested in the specific effects of childhood experiences, this design is ideal for our purposes. Our experiment is an experiment of nature, but, as it will be clear when we reach our conclusions, the fact that the experiment is natural, and that it has occurred in a human society, also means that it is historical, that is, nonrepeatable, and that the variables involved are changing over time. The adults we have studied are products of the kibbutz child-rearing system as it existed in the 1940s and 1950s. If we consider the first six years of life as the most crucial and formative, then we can point to the fact that all the members of our study group had reached the age of six by 1960, and a majority were well into their teens or twenties by then. By studying adults who were children and adolescents in the kibbutz of the 1950s and the 1940s, we are studying the kibbutz child-rearing system of those times, and not of today. There have been many significant changes since then, both in the child-rearing system and in the kibbutz as a whole.

Another feature of our study is that it is a follow-up study. Members of the two groups had been studied before, and this is the second systematic look at them. Thus, they have their own special history. This group of kibbutz and moshav children and adolescents, first studied by A. I. Rabin in 1955, became known to readers of literature dealing with the kibbutz (Rabin, 1965). Like several other kibbutz groups that were the object of studies, members of the study were the center of much attention, without being aware of it in most cases. Undoubtedly, there were many readers of the original study and of reports about it in secondary sources who have asked themselves what has happened to members of the group. The original study reached several conclusions that were widely quoted. Some readers have undoubtedly asked themselves whether these conclusions have held true over time. The members of the study groups have moved on to different life stages. How were they coping with new life tasks? How did they manage as adults? There have been no psychological studies of the kibbutz-born as adults, although there have been several studies dealing with kibbutz children and adolescents. One reason for that was obvious: as long as the kibbutz was a young phenomenon, there were no adults who had been raised in kibbutzim. With the passage of time, the kibbutz-born have become adults, and the kibbutz has become multigenerational. In the early years of the kibbutz movement, the number of children was small. With growth and stability came more children, bigger and stronger families, and then grandchildren. Some kibbutz-born men and women are now grandparents in their own right.

The changes in the kibbutz over time and the expected changes in the members of the study groups led to the realization that a follow-up study would be important. With the kibbutz becoming an established reality, the time has come to look at the adults it had produced. The original study in the 1950s was not planned as a longitudinal one. There were many reasons for what, with hindsight, looks like a lack of a wider perspective. The researcher involved in a pioneering study is naturally more concerned with immediate pressures and difficulties than with looking twenty years ahead. The original design was based on a theoretical frame of reference that emphasized the importance of early childhood for personality development. The concern with childhood events seemed to make looking further almost unnecessary. The practical difficulties were undoubtedly equally important in the original conception of the study as an early cross-sectional development research.

In some ways, a cross-sectional study cannot tell us the whole story of personality development. A longitudinal or follow-up study, by focusing on the same subjects, can give us a more complete picture of development and adjustment. A follow-up shows us how development continues and life changes leave their marks. The original study (Rabin, 1965) reflected an emphasis on the importance of the early years of childhood in personality development. A follow-up may reflect a change in focus from the early years to later development, but it may also be tied to the original emphasis. In other words, if the early years are crucial, their influence should continue to be felt as the personality moves through the later stages of development. If indeed the early influence is what is crucial in personality development, then these influences should be discerned further down the road, after the passage of the years.

The present stage of the research was a follow-up, not a follow-through. The members of the study groups were left on their own, so to speak, between 1955 and 1975. When we went back to interview them after twenty years, we were interested both in determining how far and in what direction they had traveled between the two points in time and in the point they had reached at the later date.

The overall history of the wider social group was shared by members of both groups. In the years between 1955 and 1975, they all experienced the same political changes, economic changes, war times and peaceful times, together with the other inhabitants of Israel. The twenty years between 1955 and 1975 were times of significant historical change there, both internally and externally. The country was involved in three outbreaks of undeclared war, in 1956, 1967, and 1973, and in long periods of border fighting. Internally, there was an ideological and political change, with the Zionist–socialist ideology, which had been dominant in the early years of the state and was especially strong in both the kibbutzim and the moshavim of 1955, being replaced by a more procapitalist attitude. This process did have serious implications for the way kibbutz members viewed themselves, especially vis-à-vis the larger society. The prestate view of the kibbutz as the vanguard was replaced by the view of the kibbutz as integrated with the rest of society, both in economics and in ideology.

Both groups are second generation groups, that is, the children of the founders of their communities. All the communities involved are quite well off economically and considered middle-class to upper-middle-class in terms of the whole society. Rosner et al. (1978) provide an informative and general review of the kibbutz second generation, dealing with ideological commitments and general world view. We are dealing with the same generation, but we are interested in the psychological questions of personality functioning and self-image on the individual level. We did not examine the ideological character of kibbutz second generation members in our study. We did not assess their commitment to the kibbutz ideology, or their feelings about the kibbutz as a community. We were concerned with them as individuals. It was decided to look at several areas of adult functioning as a measure of normal adaptation. A large number of measures, all related to theoretical concerns and to the areas of functioning we considered important, was used in the study. Some of the time we had specific hypotheses or hunches about differences between the two groups, but at other times we were essentially checking for possible differences.

This study is an observation by professional researchers on

the lives of people in a social setting different from their own. Thus, the observer's viewpoint has to be considered. Researchers in many studies of adult development show a natural blindness to what is specific to their own culture, assuming that the unique is universal, and that their own culture represents the whole human experience. In the present work we have tried to avoid such blind spots, and it was indeed easier to do so. By looking at two kinds of communities that had such unique features when compared to similar Western groups, we obtained a natural salience of cultural differences. Both the moshav and the kibbutz are communities that are proudly self-conscious of their ideological bases. The kibbutz is not only an intentional community, it is a self-conscious and a self-critical community. The tradition of self-criticism in the kibbutz is typical of utopian experiments and revolutionary movements. The fact that most of the self-consciousness and self-criticism is recorded in writing makes our job in understanding the kibbutz easier. We discover that the first generation of kibbutz founders was quite sophisticated in terms of asking important psychological questions and being aware of the possible conse-quences of various social arrangements. One could not avoid seeing how the fundamental ideology was reflected in all areas of life. As a researcher, one became conscious of unique influences in the community, just as the community was trying to emphasize its cultural and iedological uniqueness. At the same time, awareness of cultural influences created a more difficult task of differentiating between the effects as a social-psychological factor and the effects of ideology on personality development. The latter were con-sidered to be working through the influences of early childhood experiences. The former are at work throughout the individual's life.

The observer's viewpoint is an issue in any case of cross-cultural research. There is always a danger of distortion as a result of the researcher's ethnocentrism and natural cultural biases. The typical cross-cultural research study is done in the context of a non-Western culture by a Western observer, who is a complete outsider attempting to decipher patterns of culture with the aid of informants and through some direct experience. The history of research on the kibbutz includes several cases of researchers who made cross-cultural observations as complete outsiders, without any knowledge of the language or the general culture. Bettelheim (1969) is the best-known case in point. At the same time, an insider's viewpoint could also be validly criticized, since it may involve significant ethnocentrism and cultural biases, just as the outsider's viewpoint. The present investigators, while being outsiders in the sense of not being kibbutz or moshav members, also had several significant advantages through their direct and intimate knowledge of the history and ideology of the moshav and kibbutz movements. It also included many previous personal and professional contacts with kibbutz and moshav members.

THE KIBBUTZ SETTING

Since the beginning of the nineteenth century, various attempts have been made to found utopian communes that would presumably serve as building blocks for the ideal society for the future. Most of these enterprises have involved little more than isolated groups of fervent believers whose efforts ended in failure, following brief periods of existence. So far, the most successful attempt at building a utopian commune has been the Israeli kibbutz. No wonder Martin Buber (1958) called the kibbutz "an experiment that did not fail." The considerable interest shown by social scientists in the kibbutz has been similar to that shown in other social experiments that combined changes in social institutions, including child rearing, such as those in China and Cuba.

The history of the kibbutz intentional community extends over 70 years. There were a few turning points and changes during this period. The first kibbutz communities, started in the second decade of the century, were independent Zionist agricultural enterprises struggling for survival. The subsequent decades saw a high level of agricultural development in the kibbutzim, and around 1950 the movement toward industrialization began.

There were particular circumstances that made the kibbutz such a success. Actually, it was an ideal solution to the problem of colonizing Palestine in the years before the founding of the State of Israel. Settling the land with groups of young, vigorous, and idealistic individuals having attachments only to the collective was more practical and logical than settling through the traditional way of family homesteading. This form of settlement was also militarily more defensible, a fact worth considering given the hostile environment into which Zionist settlements entered. The kibbutz differed from its predecessors in utopianism in that it was a part of a social national revival movement and one growing out of larger social groups that supplied its members. The idea of a voluntary membership commune grew out of a combination of nationalist and socialist ideologies, the same combination that had led the Zionist–socialist movement to the founding of the State of Israel. Agricultural work was seen as the way to changing the abnormal social structure of Jews in the Diaspora, and thus agricultural settlements became the instruments for resolving not only national problems but also human ones.

Beyond the particularistic ideals of national revival and reconstruction, the kibbutz movement shared in the universalistic ideals of returning to nature and rearing a new type of human being. The movement believed in the perfectability of human nature, or at least in its possible amelioration. There was a strong belief in the changes that a revolutionary way of life would bring about in what seemed like persistent and undesirable human qualities. In a truly egalitarian commune, people would be less selfish, more secure, and more generous. The change in social structure was expected to lead to a psychological change in every individual. And if there were doubts about far-reaching changes in the first generation of kibbutz founders, who had been brought up in bourgeois society, then the aim of education for the kibbutz-born was defined as the creation of the new human being. Here, in forming a new child-rearing system, the kibbutz founders had a chance to make their children in the desired image of the collectivist, egalitarian, work-oriented person (Leon, 1969).

The kibbutz founders followed a comprehensive ideology that sought to change the Jewish people and human society in general. It was based on an interpretation of the past and a vision of the future. The high point in terms of the political and social position of the kibbutz was in the 1930s and 1940s, with the population of the kibbutzim reaching 7.5% of the Jewish population in Palestine in 1957. Since 1948, when the State of Israel was founded, the kibbutzim have been declining in political and social power but have gained enormously in terms of economic power and success. The current situation of the kibbutzim within Israeli society can be summarized in a few figures. As of 1980, there are 253 kibbutz communities, with a total population of 110,000, making up 3.3% of the Jewish population of Israel. They hold 33% of all cultivated land in Israel and produce 40% of the food supplies. Together with their part in industrial production (11% of national production), they are responsible for more than 7% of the gross national product. Kibbutz industry, which did not exist before 1950, now includes 300 industrial plants, with some kibbutzim having more than one plant. There are only 25 kibbutzim, as of January 1980, with no industrial plants. Most are also involved in regional plants, hotels, and farms held jointly by several kibbutzim. There are 110 such regional concerns. What these figures indicate is considerable economic success, which may be tied to changes in many facets of kibbutz life. Historically, most kibbutzim were part of one of three distinct federations: the "rightist" (Ihud Hakibbutzim, with 92 member kibbutzim in 1979), the "moderate" (Hakibbutz Hemeuhad, with 65 member kibbutzim in 1979), and the "leftist" (Hashomer Hatzair, with 80 member kibbutzim in 1979).* The ideological distinctions that gave rise to the three federations, and that concerned their commitment to socialism, are much less pronounced today. In the summer of 1979, formal steps were taken toward unification of the "rightist" and the "moderate" federation, leading to a "superfederation" of 157 kibbutzim. Again, it is important to emphasize that these ideological labels are of historical interest only. By today's standards, most kibbutz members could not be viewed as politically committed to a radical socialist world view.

THE CONTEXT OF THE KIBBUTZ CHILD-REARING SYSTEM

One way of starting our presentation is looking at the various misconceptions people have of kibbutz child rearing. Misconceptions have a way of highlighting selected aspects of reality, and misconceptions of the kibbutz usually concentrate on child rearing and ignore other aspects of the kibbutz system. One of the most popular misconceptions about the kibbutz child-rearing system is that of viewing it as a modal system in Israel, assuming that every Israeli child goes through this system or at least spends some time in it. Another common misconception is that the system is government-controlled, and that children and parents are assigned to it by the government. In reality, of course, the kibbutz system is atypical in Israel almost as much as it would be atypical anywhere else. Laymen and professionals have had similar misconceptions when they failed to see how kibbutz child rearing was related to other

*Note: a few kibbutzim belong to a small religious federation.

aspects of kibbutz life. Mainly, they failed to see how child rearing was related to economics and to ideology.

Child rearing has been a subject of intense discussion since the early days of the kibbutz. Hand-in-hand with the new practices, a new ideology emerged that sought to create a theoretical base for the roles of both parents and teachers. In terms of the definition of childhood and the meaning of childhood in the kibbutz, we have much evidence to support the view that the kibbutz is a child-centered and an education-centered community. The child was seen as fulfilling the ego-ideal of the parents and the community. Through hindsight it may be claimed that the new child-rearing patterns were a practical necessity on which an ideology was later imposed, in keeping with the overall ideology of the kibbutz movement. Whether the practice or the ideology came first will be determined by historians, but the fact is that kibbutz child rearing has been accompanied by an ideology that sought to rationalize its practices and served as a significant force in affecting parents and educators. There were two significant principles, with considerable psychological consequences, in the kibbutz child-rearing ideology.

The first stated that communal child rearing would work against individualism and identification with the family unit. The second stated that experts in child rearing could inculcate the ideology of the kibbutz with greater ability and objectivity than could the parents. Almost every person can become a parent, but not every person can become an effective socializer. The socializer had to educate the child according to an ideal that should go against contemporary social realities. This explicit ideology led to relegating the parents to second place as socializing agents. The major socializing agents became the nurses, the teachers, and the peer group. Since the parents were no longer the sole representatives of authority, children's attitudes toward them, and especially toward the father, were expected to become more positive.

Historically, the first kibbutzim had a family-based child-rearing system. The four oldest kibbutzim, established before 1918, still retain this system. The kibbutzim founded after World War I reflected a movement toward radical collectivism, emanating from groups of young, unattached new pioneers. These newer kibbutzim established the communal system that became then the norm for every kibbutz.

What went into the creation of a new child-rearing system was more than just the positive vision of a better future generation.

There was also the more negative element of rejection of what had been regarded as the traditional way of family life. One must remember that the founders of the kibbutz were in open rebellion against their own parents, a rebellion sometimes taking the form of a total rejection of the institution of the family. In the first years of the kibbutz, this attitude culminated in the absence of any formal marriages. The rebellion against traditional family patterns included a move toward equality of the sexes and the abolition of traditional sex roles, especially in the area of work. The ideal of the equality between the sexes and the breakdown of traditional sex roles has been one expression of the struggle against the traditions of an unjust and declining world. Thus, the emphasis was put on the dismantling of the traditional bourgeois family, with its close mother–child ties, which was perceived as promoting selfishness and individualism. Communal child rearing was seen, since the earliest days of the kibbutz movement, as a major task for the whole community.

THEORETICAL OVERVIEW

Views and Research

The kibbutz as a "natural laboratory" has aroused the interest of two groups of researchers: psychodynamically oriented psychologists (Rabin, 1957a; Rapaport, 1958) and anthropologists of the "culture and personality" school (Spiro, 1958). The first systematic observation of child rearing in the kibbutz appeared in the literature of the early 1950s (Irvine, 1952; Spiro, 1953). Since then, the number of social science publications on the topic has grown immensely (Rabin, 1971; Sharabany, 1975, Shur et al. 1981), and their findings cannot be easily summarized. The phenomenon of multiple care-taking in childhood is neither in itself unusual in human societies, nor associated with social disruption or parental neglect. Mead (1966) found that multiple care-taking was actually typical of societies that showed a great deal of concern for children, rather than neglect. In a cross-cultural view, caretaking by the mother alone was often associated with neglect. Barry and Paxson (1971) surveyed 186 societies with regard to child-rearing responsibilities. Their findings showed that while the mother was the primary caretaker of infants in 46.2% of the cases, almost 40% of the cases showed infants subject to multiple caretakers. In the time of early childhood, in less than 20% of the societies was the mother rated as the principal caretaker; 20% of the societies had young children spend most of their time away from their mothers. The kibbutz is unusual in the early involvement of other caretakers during infancy and in the involvement of nonfamilial caretakers.

The anthropological approach to the kibbutz regards it as a different subculture, related to a different personality type. In the kibbutz, several social institutions, especially the handling of economics and the family, were different enough from those of other societies to designate it as a separate culture. At the same time, the kibbutz offered the advantage of being a part of Western culture, in the usual sense of the term, and its members could be easily communicated with.

Some writers have described the product of kibbutz child-rearing in the following terms: "egocentric and envious with little capacity for affective relationship, a good deal of mistrust and a good deal of mutual contempt" (Kardiner, 1954). More recently, another anthropologist has presented a "psychohistorical analysis" of kibbutz "personality dynamics" (Diamond, 1975). In it, the author, whose conclusions are allegedly based on Rorschach projective data, describes the second generation kibbutz person as demonstrating "poor inner productivity, scanty emotional life; restricted capacity to relate effectively to other people; to give of oneself; general lack of personal dynamism or fluidity; formal stereotyped attitudes; inhibition and resistance to the function of thinking 'abstractly'; low initiative; lack of pretension; exaggerated petty focus on isolated parts of reality to the neglect of the whole, etc." (p. 14). The problem encountered by those concerned with the possible effects of kibbutz child rearing upon personality development is that the basis for the pronouncement by Kardiner, mentioned above, is unknown. No data of any kind are reported in support of the conclusions. In the case of Diamond, for some reason, the conclusions are offered some 25 years after his original field study; and the Rorschach data upon which much depends are not available to public scrutiny. They seem to remain private privileged information rather than public scientific documents.

The more systematic "participant observer" results of Spiro's study (1958) of a single kibbutz are pretty well known to those interested in the topic of kibbutz rearing and personality. The product of collective education was described as introverted, insolent, hostile, and insecure. Bettelheim's clinical report (1969) regarding children and adults in a kibbutz observed by him for several weeks are interesting and insightful. However, the impressionistic mode and the absence of systematic supporting data for the alleged "flatness" of the affect of the kibbutz-reared, his/her incapacity for intimacy, the "collective superego," and other intriguing notions concerning the kibbutz personality dictate the need for more systematic, data-based examination of these "conclusions."

A general observation regarding the foregoing is that in most of the instances the authors' characterizations are in absolute terms. Kibbutz-reared people are emotionally "flat," have low initiative, are hostile, and so forth. These traits imply an important comparison with a standard group of people who are *not* hostile, who are *not* flat, and so on. The standard or control group with which the product of collective education is compared is not specified. Is it that the control group—the backdrop against which the authors draw their portraits—are members of another culture whose modal characteristics they implicitly employ in the comparison?

In 1955 a group of 92 kibbutz children from ten different kibbutzim was systematically studied by means of several psychological techniques; the results were reported and are open to public scrutiny (Rabin, 1965). Moreover, the kibbutz children were compared on a number of relevant variables with a control group from rural Israel. Thus, the control was explicit, and the comparisons were made between two subgroups within the same culture. The major difference was in the modes of child rearing; the control group consisted of children reared in the more conventional individual, nuclear family setting. Essentially the results that were reported were at variance with those listed above. Kibbutz children were not that much different from children reared in the ordinary family setting. There were some variations in the developmental tempo of the children, differences in a number of socially conditioned attitudes (as to sex, selection of identification models, and so forth), but none of those serious characterological and behavioral defects mentioned by some of the authors who have reported before and since the 1965 publication summarizing our results.

It is this apparent discrepancy between the views of different writers and observers that served as a stimulus for us to return some 20 years later—in 1975/76—and have another look at the former children from the kibbutz and from the control setting.

THE PRESENT STUDY

As we noted in the previous section, past researchers have raised many questions and presented us with different findings and views of kibbutz-reared children and adults. In addition to the cross-sectional findings reported in 1965 and earlier, we are now in a position to introduce the temporal dimension via a follow-up investigation.

The effects of variation in child rearing on adult functioning and personality and the effects of a special childhood environment on later behavior are the general questions in our society. Such a research project involves several areas of psychological investigation and theory. In a follow-up study of children we are dealing with both the effects of childhood and the development of adult personality structure. We will deal with several specific areas of personality functioning, together with some areas of interpersonal relations. "If dynamic psychology had demonstrated anything at all, it is the power of childhood events to produce lasting personality states" (Aronoff, 1967, p. 170). Our central hypothesis is that childhood experiences are crucial to the development of the adult personality, through the development of specific conditions in childhood. It is no longer sufficient to assume that early experience does make a difference in later development. We should now specify more clearly the particular effects of differences in early experiences. If we believe that early childhood experiences leave their mark on the individual's personality and have long-term consequences, then we should be able to measure the effects of child rearing on adult personalities.

Beyond the more general question of the effects of early childhood experience on life-long behaviors, there is the question of specific effects of parenting and the nature of parenting. What happens if traditional parenting is limited and socialization by caretakers and peers takes its place? Another set of questions has to do with the effects of this special variation in child rearing on general processes in personality development, such as the separation from parents and the formation of identity. We are trying to correlate antecedents, in this case early childhood experiences, and consequences, in this case adult functioning. There are two kinds of antecedent conditions in our study—the traditional family child rearing system and the communal child rearing system. The question is whether these two clearly distinct antecedents would lead to two equally distinct styles of adult functioning and how adult products of the two systems would differ.

Several theoretical perspectives are possible in approaching the study of the communal child-rearing system: the psychodynamic personality development approach, the object relations approach, and the culture and personality approach. What they all have in common is a psychodynamic orientation that assumes both the existence of consistent and internal motivation patterns and a complex relationship between motivation and behavior. Developments in psychodynamic theory since the original study was carried out have affected our conceptions of communal child rearing and its psychological outcomes. While our viewpoint has remained psychoanalytic, our emphasis has shifted, along with that of many others, more to an object-relations approach. Object-relations theory emphasizes early human relationships and their internal representations, which determine long-range personality development and psychopathology.

Much of the modern psychology is focused upon developmental issues. For the most part, until recent years, development was conceived within a relatively narrow framework: the period from infancy through adolescence. More recently the interest of writers and investigators has been extending through the life-span. The concept of development encompasses the lives of persons and is not confined to evolution and involution in childhood and ageing, respectively. We have become aware of a "life beyond adolescence" and have, albeit still rather tentatively, discerned stages, sequences, or "eras" in persons' lives (Levinson et al., 1978). But, strictly speaking, this book is not concerned with development and with the distillation of general principles that characterize the histories of humans in general. Although ours is a *follow-up* study, it is not a longitudinal study in the more accepted and conventional sense of the word. Longitudinal studies commence with cross-sectional assessments of young children and subsequently, at various nodal points in their lives, reassess them and compare the individuals with *themselves* as they grow and develop. Change patterns in individuals are evaluated, and the extraction of general more universal principles concerning development is attempted.

The present study begins with two contrasted populations examined more than twenty years ago. Certain modal characteristics differentiated the two groups of children in 1955 (Rabin, 1965). Our follow-up is concerned with the modal characteristics of these two groups in young adulthood (ages: 20–38), differences and similarities between the groups, and how they compare with the modal patterns detected in the children twenty years earlier.

We were curious to see how the children of 1955 have turned out as adults. And, again, we wished to study and compare the two groups with respect to attitudes, personality, and character; with respect to their life-course as they moved into young adulthood. To this end we approached these people with a number of standard methods and techniques that would allow a systematic examination of similarities and differences.

In a recent discussion of personality development in children, Lois Murphy (1981) states that "there was a time in the field of child development, psychology, and psychiatry when all behavior, competent and incompetent, deviant and 'normal' was attributed to the earliest relationship between mother and child—as if heredity and constitutional elements—the genes had nothing to do with behavioral development." This warning of oversimplification with respect to causality underlying child behavior and personality may be extended, even more so, to adult behavior and personality. Moreover, the years between early infancy, in which child-rearing procedures are maximally contrasted, and adulthood are not devoid of unique experiences that leave their mark as well, granted the unique genetic and constitutional characteristics.

Yet, being cognizant of individual differences in genetics and organism, which may be randomly distributed, the two groups we studied were exposed to important variations in early experience of the interpersonal milieu, which according to developmental theories should make a difference. It is this possible overarching difference—fact or phantom—that we intended to pursue in this work. However, differences are not to be pursued at all costs. The absence of differences, the presence of similarities in attitudes and characteristics are just as significant, for they provide a test of some time-honored theories with respect to the antecedents of the adult personality and its development.

In her review of *Growing Up in the Kibbutz* (Rabin, 1965) Margaret Mead (1966) characteristically raises an important and practical question with respect to the kibbutz-reared second generation. She mentions the utopias built by some protestant sects, such as the Hutterites, and wonders whether children being "enveloped in a tightly closed system" have developed sufficient flexibility and capacity for adapting to other social settings. She comments that "the children are superbly fitted to carry on the small tight Utopias their parents or their great-great-great-grand-parents once built, and unfitted for any other sort of life." The issue, therefore, is to what extent the kibbutz-raised are handi-capped by their upbringing when it comes to living outside the confines of their kibbutz system. We expect to glean a partial answer to this question from a subsample, rather small to be sure, of the original kibbutz group that now lives outside the kibbutz system, in cities and other noncommunal settings.

A comparison of the present study to the original one (Rabin, 1965) would uncover a great number of significant theoretical and methodological differences. The theoretical framework of the present study is broader, its concepts different, and its research instruments not identical to the ones used in the original work. These changes are inevitable. Without them the present work would indicate just stagnation and insulation from all the significant changes in psychology in the past 25 years. There have been marked changes in our theories of personality development and in our view of the individual personality within society. The psychology of today is more a psychology with a social context and a social face. We are looking at personality as reflecting social structure and changes in personality as related to changes in social structure. We have tried in the present study to aim at a broad historical and social perspective, within which psychology looks at individuals and their individual life histories.

It is quite clear that we are studying the interaction of societal influences and individual personality. But it is not enough to acknowledge that culture, history, and present social institutions affect the life of the individual. It is necessary to specify influences and consequences. We are not assuming here the existence of a "kibbutz personality." We are only trying to correlate antecedent variables with consequences in the adult personality. As with any other social structure, the communal child-rearing system of the kibbutz translates the needs of the social structure into modifica-tions in personality structure, or at least attempt this translation.

The "culture and personality" school offers a general concep-tion of the relationship between social structure, child-rearing methods, and personality structure, which can be illustrated in the following diagram:

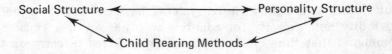

Social Structure ←————————→ Personality Structure
Child Rearing Methods

In the case of the kibbutz, this relationship between the three factors in the diagram is openly presented and actually pursued. Unlike the case in many "primitive" cultures, the visiting anthropologist in the kibbutz does not have to discover the relationship. It is discussed, recognized, and aimed at by most kibbutz members. One has only to look at the enormous literature on the aims of communal child rearing, written by kibbutz members, to realize that. Since there are such clearly declared aims, we may also inquire about the extent to which those aims have been achieved.

There have been two extreme and broad views regarding the effects of the kibbutz child rearing system. The internal view, formed by the theorists of kibbutz education, not too surprisingly, expected the kibbutz child-rearing system to produce a new, improved human being. The critical view formulated by outsiders such as Kardiner (1954) regarded the kibbutz system as such a deviance from normal patterns that it should bring about only negative consequences in the form of grossly deficient human beings. In contrast to the old views of kibbutz child rearing, which emphasized what was lacking in it, we offer another view, which examines what is in it, and what possible psychological consequences it might have. Once the early views about the kibbutz child-rearing system as an example of institutional child care or "maternal deprivation" (Bowlby, 1951) had been laid to rest (Rabin, 1965), a more fruitful approach should be looking at the constituent elements of the system. What is the kibbutz child-rearing system based on? The major characteristic of the system, from a psychological viewpoint, is the involvement of non-familial caretakers and the early group existence. The infant starts his life as a member of a group, and he has to relate to this group, to the caretakers, and to his family. This early experience of a great number of significant others, under the special constraints of interacting with each of the subgroups (family, peers, and caretakers), is the major determinant of psychological development in the communally raised child. Our aim in this book is to examine the long-term consequences of this early psychosocial environment.

In the following chapters we will present the research setting, history, design, and instruments (Chapters 2, 3, 4), and then the findings of the follow-up study (Chapters 5, 6, 7, 8). The last chapters of the books are devoted to an analysis and summary of the findings.

2

The Research Setting

THE KIBBUTZ CHILD-REARING SYSTEM

This detailed description of the communal child-rearing system, as it has existed in the formative years of the members in our research group, that is, between 1945 and 1965, is based on material presented by Rabin (1965). Since 1965 there have been many changes in the kibbutz and in the communal child-rearing system (Beit-Hallahmi & Rabin, 1977; Gerson, 1978), some of which will be discussed later on.

Several days after the birth of a kibbutz baby, which takes place in the maternity ward of a regional hospital, mother and infant return "home"—to the kibbutz. The mother returns to her own quarters, which she shares with her husband, while the infant is placed in the "infant house." Henceforward, the child is, with rare and exceptional interruptions, primarily in the company of his peers until he graduates from high school, at the age of eighteen, and becomes eligible for adult membership in the kibbutz. As we shall see, the separation from the parents is only partial. The infant- and child-rearing process passes through several stages, which we describe in some detail.

Infancy

Ordinarily the infant house is equipped to accommodate between 18 and 20 children from the first week of life to about 15 months. The building is made up of two separate sections: one for the very young, another for those who have been weaned. The younger babies are placed in two large rooms, five to six in each room. In each of the large rooms there is also a corner for bathing and caring for the physical needs of the child. Every infant has his own crib and toys. In the room there are also chairs for mothers who breastfeed their babies. The section for the weaned infants also accommodates six children in a room, with a corner for the necessary services, such as heating food, folding laundry, and so on. There is room for crawling and playing. A porch with a separate entrance is used for placing playpens, with two to three children in each. These playpens for the older infants are much larger than those of the younger ones and offer ample opportunity for crawling, trying to walk, and for other ventures in exercising newly-acquired mastery and coordination. The kibbutz usually attempts to make these houses as attractive as possible. The walls are painted in appealing colors and are often adorned with pictures, curtains, and flowers. An attempt is also made to place the house in attractive physical surroundings.

Demand feeding is the rule in the kibbutz. Thus, during the first six weeks of the life of the infant, the mother is available whenever needed. Breastfeeding is encouraged. Mothers, however, who do not breastfeed also take care of all the feedings during the first six weeks following confinement. They do not have to return to work during that period. After the first six weeks, a feeding rhythm is established, and the mother feeds the infant at about four-hourly intervals, five times a day. The feeding itself lasts about 20 minutes, but the time of contact is usually extended to about 45 minutes or an hour. In addition to feeding, the mother also changes diapers, carries the infant, plays with him, and finally puts him to sleep. In some instances the mother may be permitted to sleep in the infant house for several weeks, especially if late-night feeding is necessary. If the child wakes up in the middle of the night, the night watchwoman may give him something to drink to pacify him. Only in exceptional cases is the mother awakened to come and attend to the infant's needs. Once the infant is six weeks old, the mother resumes working on a half-time basis until he reaches about four months of age. During that period she continues her breastfeeding (or bottle feeding) and caring for the infant during several periods of the day. Once the infant is four months old and the mother has returned to full-time work, the number of feedings is gradually reduced, and the child is weaned to the bottle and solid foods by the time he is five to six months old. This is a very gradual process, and the timing may differ from individual to individual. The mother continues to have the major part in the care of the infant until he is about nine months old. The evening feeding and putting the child to bed is still the mother's prerogative until he is about a year old.

The literal meaning of the word *metapelet* (plural: *metaplot*) is "the one who takes care" of the child—the nurse. The metapelet is in charge of the infant house and its inhabitants. She is responsible for the house, its order and cleanliness. She also follows, carefully, the health of the child, washes him and bathes him, takes care of any additional food he requires, weighs him regularly, and serves as liaison with the physician who makes his visits from time to time. She keeps close watch over the infants when the mothers are not around and keeps notes concerning the behavior and any special reactions of the children. She also guides the younger and inexperienced mothers in the process of feeding and taking care of the infants during their period of contact.

The metapelet is available to the child when he cries or is restless; she comforts him and plays with him in the absence of the mother. She does this increasingly as the infant gets older and the time of contact between mother and child decreases. Ordinarily there is one metapelet for every five to six children. During the period of earliest infancy, the metapelet may have charge of a larger number of infants, since the mothers do have a good deal of the work involved. When the infant is about six to nine months old, his group of four to six infants gets a "regular" (permanent) metapelet, who stays with the group for approximately the following four to five years—through the toddler stage until, and sometimes after, they enter the kindergarten. The regular metapelet of infants in the second half of their first year is with the children from morning until the middle of the afternoon, about 2:00 p.m. Her assistant is there when the children wake from the afternoon nap, at around 3:00 o'clock. She picks the children up, dresses, them, gives them their milk, and plays with them until the parents come to pick them up for their daily visit from about 4:30 to 6:30 in the evening. Then, when the parents return the infants to their house, the regular metapelet is back again, feeds the children, undresses and bathes them, and puts them to bed.

In addition to the contacts that the biological mother maintains with her infant during the early months, there is also some contact with the other parent and with the biological siblings. Weather permitting, the family may take out the infant for a short visit (half an hour) when he reaches three months of age. During the latter part of the first year of life the length of the visit may extend to as much as two hours. In addition to the parents, siblings are also present during those visits. Visiting is after the regular working hours of the parents. They are, therefore, completely "at the service" of their children during that period.

Parents' or siblings' visits to the infant house are usually not encouraged except when they pick up the child or return him. Unexpected or irregular visiting tends to upset the routine of the children as well as of the metapelet, who usually has her hands full.

The Toddlers

As mentioned above, the infant house keeps children until they are about 12 to 15 months old. At this time each group of infants of five to six children is transferred, as a group, to the toddlers' house. Ideally, kibbutz planners advocate a toddlers' house for two groups of six children each, divided into two units. However, in reality the physical arrangements differ. Many toddlers' houses are larger and include more children and more units. The house in which the toddlers remain for approximately three years is equipped to meet their needs and development. In addition to bedrooms— often, still, with four to six children per room—service areas, and porches, the houses have playrooms with many toys for the increasing activities of the toddlers. A dining room is also included. Another feature of the toddlers' houses is the play yard surrounding them or adjacent to the porches. The yards are enclosed, but within them there is freedom of activity; they contain a sandbox, simple "jungle gym" equipment, and other materials appropriate for the small groups of toddlers.

The regular metapelet who has taken over the care of the

group of infants during the last several months in the infant house accompanies the group when it is transferred to the toddlers' house. The role of the mother in caring for the infant had already become considerably reduced during the latter part of the first year of life. In the toddlers' house, the metapelet "takes over," fully and literally. She is responsible for the rearing of the toddlers in her group. The responsibility is entirely and completely hers. Training in self-feeding and eating habits, toilet training, and other habits of cleanliness are directly handled by the metapelet. She helps the children to learn to dress and undress and get ready for bed. She supervises play. When the children are around three years of age, group play is introduced for short periods. Here the metapelet aids in the transition from the individual, spontaneous play to more organized and cooperative types of activity. In addition, she takes the children for short walks, leads them in exercises and rhythmic games, teaches them songs, and tells them stories. The metapelet is with the children for most of the day. The exception is the "visiting period," when the children go or are taken to the parents' quarters after work for a couple of hours daily and for longer periods on Saturdays and holidays.

The pattern of family contact established at the beginning of the toddler period is followed through the kibbutz child's eighteenth year, after which he begins to be considered an adult, enters the army, and becomes a full-fledged kibbutz member. As mentioned above, official contact with the parents and siblings is confined to the two to three hours of daily visits with the family following work hours, in late afternoon and early evening. After the visit, the toddler is usually returned to his house by his parents. The daily parade of parents returning children to their houses at about 6:30 or 7:00 in the evening is a familiar sight in every kibbutz.

Upon their return to their house, the toddlers are met by the metapelet, who has in the meantime returned from her own quarters and, probably, from a visit with her own children. She feeds the children and then puts them to bed. In some kibbutzim the parents put the children to bed. This procedure is sometimes quite a trial for children and parents alike. Imagine several children and several pairs of parents, crowded into one bedroom, trying to put them to bed, to say goodnight to them, tell them stories, sing songs, and engage in a variety of other quieting methods. In many instances separation for the night is quite difficult and becomes expressed in temper tantrums, "new games," and a variety of other subterfuges on the part of the children. Once the children have been put to bed, the duties of the metapelet are over until the following morning. The night watchwoman takes over until then. Usually she makes the rounds to different children's houses, infants to preadolescents. Her job is not an easy one, for a great many problems need to be faced and dealt with. In one house, a child may wake up and start crying; soon he may be joined by the members of his group, in a wailing chorus. In another house, a child may suddenly fall ill, feel pains, or need a drink or some reassurance about his fears, nightmares, or anxieties. The watchwomen usually attempts to pacify the children, to reassure them and comfort them. This is not always effective, and one or more children in a group may spend a sleepless night. Further discussion of the role of the night metapelet, with the possible implications of still another figure in loco parentis, will be found later.

The Kindergarten

Generally the children remain in the toddlers' house through their fourth year of life, and somewhat beyond. At the age of four to five, they become members of the peer group known as the kindergarten. Whereas the groups during the infant and toddler period were small, not more than six children, the new grouping, in the kindergarten, consists of about 18 children, combining three groups transferred from the toddlers' house. The kibbutz concept of the kindergarten is different from the conventional one. The kindergarten stage covers a period of about three to four years and includes the equivalent of first-grade school work. Thus the children remain members of the kindergarten until approximately the age of seven. Upon leaving the kindergarten, they become second-graders. The kindergarten is housed in a building of its own; the building contains bedrooms, a play and work room, a dining room, showers and toilets, as well as porches. There is a large yard around it, equipped with suitable articles for gymnastics and different types of play and recreation. Some work tools are available. Small gardens and enclosures for animals are also provided. A reduction of the number of children per bedroom takes place at this stage. About three to four children in each bedroom is the usual arrangement. The bedrooms also have special "corners" for toys and books, so that the child has an opportunity to follow his own interests beyond the group activities of the kindergarten. The group activities are part of the formal program, but time is allowed for informal individual and spontaneous play as well.

Personnel for the 18-child kindergarten consists of a teacher and two metaplot. Thus, the ratio of children per metapelet increases from 6:1 to 9:1, approximately. The metaplot are assisted with some of the household chores and during some necessary absences and weekends by less regular workers. For most of the morning, the children in the kindergarten are in the charge of the teacher whose function it is to conduct group activities and help each individual child develop his creative potential to a maximum. A short period in the afternoon is set aside for formal, organized activity. The number of hours under the direction of the teacher increases with the years that the children spend in the kindergarten.

During the kindergarten period, the children begin to get acquainted with the kibbutz workaday world. The teacher takes them on tours of the various branches of the kibbutz economy; they visit fields and the gardens, stables and chicken coops, packing houses and small factories. These visits serve as topics for prolonged discussion with the teacher, who explains and answers the numerous questions. At this time, the children also begin "working" themselves. In addition to taking care of the small garden outside their building and of the small animals that they may keep nearby, the children make their own beds, set the table at mealtime, and do a few additional small chores as part of the day's routine.

The last year, before entering the second grade, is called the "transition kindergarten." The children, usually in their seventh year of life, are now taught the fundamentals of the three R's in group and classroom instruction. But they still receive a good deal of individual attention. An attempt is often made to help a particular child in acquiring these skills, according to the level of his maturity and development. Since "outside" teachers are rarely employed in the kibbutz, the teachers who are also members of the kibbutz are expected—and are available—to spend longer hours with their pupils than is customary in the conventional school systems. During this last year in the kindergarten, there is an increased emphasis on group activities in every area, on mutual aid, on discipline, and, generally, on greater social interaction and integration.

In discussing the toddlers, we have indicated that the pattern of visits and visiting time to the parents' quarters, established during that period, is maintained throughout childhood. In the parents' room there are usually "corners" or closets for each child, containing some toys that are the child's "very own." The child is not expected to share them with anyone else. If there are several children in the family, each has a corner with his "personal" belongings, suitable to his age level and interests. During visiting hours it is not an unfamiliar picture to see each child turn to his corner and check on his belongings, play with them, and try to draw one or both parents into his activities. This is especially true with the younger children—the older toddlers and those in kindergarten. Expressions of sibling rivalry and competition for the attention of the parents during the visiting period are not altogether uncommon, especially when the siblings are close to each other in age. Toward the end of the kindergarten period, as the children get more involved in group activities, their visits in the parents' quarters become spontaneously shortened. It is not an infrequent complaint of parents that the child just breezed in and left quickly because he was "too busy" with group and peer activities. Nevertheless, the children rarely give up or avoid such visits completely. They wish to spend some time "with the parents."

The Children's Society: Primary-School Years

Following the years in kindergarten, the child is transferred to the elementary school, the pupils of which also constitute the younger "children's society." Since work, equivalent to that required in the conventional first grade, has already been done in the kindergarten, the school proper starts with second grade and ends with sixth grade. The elementary school group thus ranges in age from seven to twelve years. The second-graders move from the kindergarten into a new building, which is a combination of dormitory and classroom. The building usually accommodates 20 to 25 youngsters. Three or four youngsters sleep in each bedroom. The classroom is usually quite large and serves a variety of purposes in addition to instruction. It is often used for recreation, as a general meeting place for the group, and as a party room. Similar buildings are available for the other four grades in the elementary school system. In the more prosperous, well-established, and well-planned kibbutzim, this group of buildings forms a somewhat separate cluster. Adjacent to it are outdoor sports facilities and a small farm and gardens worked by the children themselves under the guidance of older children and adults. Each grade that enters the school acquires a new metapelet and a teacher–counselor. Both stay with the group through the elementary-school period, until age 12, when the children enter the Mosad or institute, which is equivalent to a combination of junior and senior high school in the United States.

The role of the metapelet becomes less significant from now on in the life of the youngster. She takes care of the physical needs, cleanliness, food, and order in the dormitory; in addition, her function tends to become that of a "housemother" in a dormitory or fraternity. The teacher, who is often a man, now becomes a dominant figure of influence in the life of the children. His responsibilities go far beyond subject-matter instruction. He is teacher, counselor, work supervisor, and the conscience of the group, all wrapped up into one. He is the one who is responsible for the morale of the group and for the development of its social consciousness, for setting up the complex organizational network within it, and for making it an integral part of the "children's society" (which will be discussed later). In the elementary school the child spends four to six hours daily, six days a week, on his studies. The first two grades—second and third graders—spend only four hours; fourth and fifth graders, five hours; and in sixth grade this is increased to a full six hours of study a day. Most of the classes are generally conducted in the hours before noon.

The group or the grade is set up as a cooperative rather than a competitive unit. The same level of achievement is not required of everybody. There is full recognition of individual differences in the talents and abilities of the children despite the complete equality of opportunity in the egalitarian society of the kibbutz. Every child is encouraged to follow his interests and do the best he can in contributing to the group effort. Consonant with this approach there is, of course, no grading system, and "promotion" is assured for everybody. This arrangement demands a tremendous amount of devotion and individual work on the part of the teacher. His duties are far from over at the end of the more formal instructional period.

THE GROUP

From early infancy onward, the kibbutz child lives in a group. At first he is in the company of several other infants in the same room; this is not a "group" in the full meaning of the word. "Groupiness" or cohesiveness between several young infants cannot be expected. Attachments between infants are, however, often formed very early in life. Any metapelet can relate episodes of some infant "falling in love" with the infant in the next crib. The infant may watch his friend practically during all his waking hours, babble at him, and become extremely upset and morose when his friend happens to be moved to another room. Such separations have been known to cause loss of appetite and a run-down physical condition, which improved upon reunion of the "twins."

In the nursery or in the toddlers' house the children are grouped by room and by the metapelet who is in charge of them. There are attempts to organize group activities for the three- and four-year olds and to evolve a group morale involving group censure and group approval. However, at this level, mutual help and the respect for the rights of other members of the group are most important.

When the children are transferred to the kindergarten, there is a temporary loosening of the old ties. There is a new group formation, and the groups are somewhat larger. Often the children who belonged to the same toddlers' group may form a cohesive "group within a group." Attempts are usually made by the organizers of the kindergarten to avoid such divisiveness. During the three years in kindergarten, the group concept and group responsibility are not yet fully developed. There are cooperative activities of the entire kindergarten, to be sure, but little self-government of the group and, what is even more important, little if any formal or official relationship with other groups of children. This changes considerably when the child enters the second grade in school. The group that becomes the second grade ordinarily remains stable for the following ten to eleven years—until the children graduate from high school at the age of 18. The principle of closeness in age is adhered to. The spread in age is, on the average, about six months. The group is a "living unit" as well as an educational grade. The group resides in the same dormitory, has the same metapelet and teacher, takes care of its house with the help of the adults, and takes care of its garden. Every group conducts a series of autonomous and "internal" activities. It organizes hikes and outings, attends the theatre and movies as a unit, and demonstrates via exhibitions and via a variety of "end of the year" events its achievements during the past year to parents and to the entire kibbutz. Private parties as well as birthday parties, to which the parents and siblings of the child are invited, are also arranged by the group.

As a study unit, or school grade, it completes a certain number of topics during the year. Informal activities, such as the hikes, parties, and exhibitions, are frequently interwoven and related to the classroom material. With the guidance of the teacher, and as a result of continuous sharing and living together collectively, there develops a "group conscience." Any deviation of the individual from proper behavior and any neglect of duty, whether work or academic, comes immediately to the attention of the rest of the group. At meetings of the group, which may sometimes take place daily, under the guidance of the teacher and at times without him, the offender may be brought to task. The group demands discipline and responsibility from the individual. The very knowledge of accountability to the group becomes a strong deterrent to deviant behavior. The individual is loath to incur group disapproval; "public opinion" of the group becomes most important in the life of the primary school child.

THE CHILDREN'S SOCIETY

Although the kibbutz sees considerable advantage in the like-age smaller group, it is cognizant of the advantages that might accrue from contacts between younger and older children. The "children's society" was created to fulfill this function. It is essentially a federation of the primary grades 2 to 6, including all the children between the ages of seven to twelve.

Socially as well as geographically, the children's society forms a semi-autonomous unit within the larger kibbutz society, as mentioned earlier. The entire organization is governed by a children's "secretariat," consisting of representatives of each group or grade, with the participation of one of the teachers. The activities of this larger society are numerous, involving the work and care of an independent "farm," sports, editing a paper, cultural activities, and so forth. These activities are directed by committees selected at the general meetings of the society, which take place periodically, several times a month. Each committee also includes a teacher among its members. Nearly every week there is a general party of the entire children's society. On such occasions each of the groups, constituting the society, participates actively in preparing a portion of the program, which may consist of music, songs, readings, dances, or plays.

This complex organization provides a multitude of opportunities for interaction between the younger and older children. The latter are frequently helpful in tutoring the younger children and in training them in sports; on many other occasions, they function as older siblings. The children's "farm" deserves special notice. It belongs to the children. It is a sort of miniature farm introduced into the educational system in order to establish early work habits and to get the children acquainted with the agricultural life, for at that level they do not yet participate substantially in the adult agricultural and economic enterprise. To a degree, the farm compensates for the discontinuity between children's roles and those of the adult world. The farm includes chickens, goats, rabbits, and pigeons as well as small areas for planting and for grazing. In the work the children are guided and supervised by the teachers and, sometimes, by other adult kibbutz members. Care is taken to rotate the children in their farm work. The younger children are rotated fairly frequently—every week to a new activity. The older ones may spend one or two months on some particular job. The rotation is designed to maintain the interest of the child as well as to offer him a greater variety of experiences in the different branches of the miniature economy. In their house or dormitory the children are expected to do most of the chores involved in keeping the house in order. They sweep, clean, make their own beds, and so on. The total amount of house and farm work expected increases with age, from about half an hour daily for the younger children to about one-and-a-half hours a day for the older ones.

THE "TEENS" IN THE KIBBUTZ

Ages 12 to 18 are represented by still another social organization within the kibbutz, the older children's society—the society of adolescents. The organization has many features similar to those of the children's society, but some differences in structure and content do exist.

The last six grades constitute the high school. At approximately the age of 12 the children "graduate" from the sixth grade and from the children's society. The group as a whole is transferred to the final educational stage.

Physically and geographically, the high school is more definitely a separate entity; it is usually built apart from the kibbutz. Regional high schools may be built halfway between two kibbutzim. In addition to the individual grade–dormitory–classroom buildings, similar to those in the primary grades, there is a central dining room for pupils and teachers, similar to those available for the regular kibbutz members. As in the kibbutz, the dining room is the cultural and social center of the adolescent society. It serves as a meeting place for the entire high school. There, parties are held, holidays are celebrated, and gatherings of a less formal nature take place. A library and reading room, a teachers' room, a music room, and physics, chemistry, and biology laboratories are some of the other public buildings.

In the average high school, there are around 200 pupils and a staff of about 20 or more teachers, counselors, and metaplot. The grade size is the same or slightly larger than the primary level. Two parallel curricula are offered: the "humanistic" and the "realistic." The former encompasses subjects such as literature, sociology, history, and economics; the latter is based on the sciences: physics, chemistry, and biology. Both curricula offer instruction in Arabic and English, mathematics, drawing, music, physical education, and shop.

The adolescent society is organized pretty much along the lines of the children's society of the primary grades. Here, too, we have a federation of smaller groups: the educational, social, and living units of the adolescents, corresponding to the academic grade levels. The same type of democratic organization of the group under the tutelage of the adult teacher-guide also prevails. The functions of the teacher and metapelet, however, are not quite so prominent in the guidance of the adolescent group as in the younger group. The adults function more in an advisory capacity, whereas the group, with its committees and democratic institutions, becomes dominant. This is especially so in the last two years of the high school, when the children are 17 and 18 years old.

An important supplement to the educational curriculum and social program of the adolescent society is the network of "circles." These are informal voluntary groups formed by the youngsters.

One evening a week is usually devoted to meetings of the different circles, which are concerned with literature, arts and crafts, dramatics, music, agriculture, and so forth. The circles give children with special interests the opportunity to work and develop special knowledge in the subject areas of their choice. The circles are led and instructed by teachers and, sometimes, by other kibbutz members who have achieved some expertise in that particular field of endeavor.

The adolescents, like the younger children's society, maintain their own farm. This establishment is on a somewhat larger scale, more diversified, and requiring a good deal of work and skill on the part of the youngsters. The farm may include sizeable areas for vegetable gardens, feeds, and other kinds of plants, as well as several hundred chickens, goats (for milking), a couple of horses, and even a small tractor as an aid in cultivation. The younger children work from one to two hours daily on their farm, whereas some of the older ones may serve as instructors or be in charge of a particular branch of the venture. In many respects, a miniature kibbutz economy, agriculturally and administratively, is represented by the farm and its management. The oldest children who are not engaged in the supervision of the younger ones become involved in the regular adult kibbutz economic enterprise. They are expected, approximately from the ages 16 to 18, to spend about three hours daily working in the various branches of the kibbutz economy. At first they may spend about three months in each branch; later, six months or longer in one particular area of agricultural specialization. Thus, the youngsters serve a sort of limited apprenticeship, which prepares them to become fairly versatile future members of the kibbutz. Whereas the children's farms are designed as educational or preparatory workshops, the work with the kibbutz adults during the last two years is the "real thing."

The organization and administration of the work program in high school is in the hands of a committee consisting of representatives of the different age groups. An older student (eleventh- or twelfth-grader) is the responsible functionary in charge of the execution of the work program, advised and aided by one of the teachers or metaplot.

Although the adolescent society is still a federation of smaller groups, the children tend to become involved more and more in the larger collectivity and its functions. Moreover, intimate relationships between fewer persons, in smaller groups, tend to develop and to detract somewhat from the importance of the like-age school grade group. Besides, as we pointed out, the homogeneity of the groups may also be disturbed by changes in their composition.

KIBBUTZ COEDUCATION

Consonant with the general ideological orientation of the kibbutz, complete equality of the sexes is a cherished ideal. This ideal is reflected in the equal and nondifferential treatment of boys and girls in the educational system—in "collective education." In the kibbutz setup, coeducation reaches the ultimate. It is not confined to school activities, that is, boys and girls having classes together; both sexes actually live together, from infancy to maturity.

After leaving the toddlers' house, the boys and girls continue to share sleeping quarters until they graduate from the Mosad at the age of 18. There is no separation between the sexes in the dormitories, or even in the shower room. Boys and girls shower together—theoretically, until adulthood. In practice, however, the pubescent girls, especially those who have developed fairly obvious secondary sexual characteristics, maneuver to take their showers when the boys are not around and develop a good deal of modesty with respect to their body.

Leaders in kibbutz child rearing or in collective education have always insisted upon this principle of what we might call absolute coeducation. They feel that it creates a healthy relationship between sexes; removes the mystery from sexual differences and from the appearance of the body of the opposite sex; and, in general, takes care of "sex education" in an informal and, presumably, effective manner.

Although the adolescent boys and girls may share sleeping rooms and shower facilities, most of the time they manage to avoid self-exposure. Going to bed at different times, undressing in the dark, showering at different times are some of the techniques that have developed in the service of modesty and sexual segregation.

It may well be that the modesty that develops is in the service of defense against the instinctual drives that are intensified during adolescence. Despite the "freedom" with respect to viewing the body of the opposite sex, kibbutz taboos and prohibitions with regard to sex play and sexual contacts are strict and unrelenting.

These taboos apply primarily to members of the peer-group, with whom the contact is continuous for many years. The taboos are not unlike the brother–sister taboos in the conventional family. It is probably due to this fact that there are no marriages between members of the same group in the kibbutz. Such "incestuous" relationships are avoided by marrying outside the group, often into another kibbutz or by importation of a spouse from the city.

The official attitude of the kibbutz movement as well as that of the youth movement toward premarital intercourse or sex play is negative. "Friendships" with the opposite sex are encouraged; sexuality without love is discouraged and considered base and degrading. The attitude is that the capacity to experience "true love," of which sexuality is only a part, is reached upon maturity and not before then. If maturity is reached and true love is achieved, then marriage is the natural consequence (Golan, 1961).

KIBBUTZ CHILD REARING: A PSYCHOLOGICAL ANALYSIS

The analysis that follows will deal with the topics that cut across the different age levels that have served as reference points in our description.

Significant Figures: Adults and Children

The first and foremost issue that needs careful treatment is that of the early and continuous interpersonal relationships of the child. Here we are particularly concerned with those persons who are in a position to exert an important influence upon the growing youngster due to their specific roles in relation to him.

During the early formative years the adults are of particular significance as sources of affection, nurturance, and security, and as agents of socialization and transmitters of the cultural values. We shall review the sequence of adults in the life of the child, with some attention to the temporal dimension.

The mother is in close and almost continuous contact with the infant during the earliest period of life—the first four months or so. During that period her relation to the infant does not differ from that of a mother in the nuclear family setting. The main exception is that the mother is usually not available to the infant during the night. Between the ages of four to nine months, the mother's contact with the child is reduced considerably as she returns to full-time work. Breastfeeding may be confined to twice daily, and a gradual transition to solids, which is not handled by the mother as a rule, takes place. Contacts, therefore, between mother and child are reduced to two periods, of one or one-and-a-half hours each, in the morning and late afternoon or early evening when the mother may put the infant to bed for the night. Following the ninth month—or often two to three months later—the mother's contacts are further reduced to a daily after-work visit with the child, usually in the parents' quarters; for longer periods on rest days. At such times the mother and father are entirely "at the service" of the child, or of the children in the case of the child who is not the oldest or who is not an only child This pattern of contact continues throughout the life of the kibbutz child. As he grows older, of course, the frequency and duration of such contacts are increasingly under his own control.

Contacts with the father during the first year of life are during brief visits in the infant house, usually after working hours. Subsequently, the visits follow the same pattern as with the mother.

The metapelet is, of course, a very significant figure. We should speak of her in the plural, metaplot, for the child has several during his childhood and adolescence. The first metapelet is the one who cares for the infant during the first nine months of life. During approximately the first half of this period, the metapelet merely supplements the care given the infant by his biological mother. She takes care of the infants between the feeding periods, when they are asleep a good deal of the time. From the fifth month on, the metapelet begins to come into focus as a "socializing" agent. She introduces the infants to solids and takes over many of the functions, in addition to feeding, that were hitherto within the domain of the mother. After this partial transition from mother to metapelet has taken place, still another switch occurs. The infants' metapelet relinquishes her duties when the infants are weaned (she starts another group of newborn infants) and passes on her functions to a "regular" or permanent metapelet, who takes over for the next several years.

The permanent metapelet sees the children through the toddler period and often well into the kindergarten. She is the one who carries the burden of the most important socialization functions in early childhood. She teaches them self-feeding, bowel and bladder control, some rudiments of group living and mutual respect, and many other habits that are part of the civilizing process. The functions of the permanent metapelet are probably the most important from the point of view of the personality formation of the children. They are more important than the functions any other metapelet will have.

When the child reaches kindergarten, or sometime thereafter, his group may acquire a new metapelet. From now on, however, the metapelet is shared by the larger, combined kindergarten group consisting of twelve to eighteen children. The focus begins to shift away from the metapelet. She continues with the physical care of the children, but the force of leadership and a good deal of authority are lodged in the person of the kindergarten teacher.

Subsequently, through the grades and in high school, the youngsters may have a succession of metaplot who are included in the over-all educational planning but are involved largely in house-keeping and technical functions. Group leadership becomes the prerogative of the teacher–educator–counselor (all one person) when the children join the children's society.

The teacher generally accompanies the same group of children for several years, through the sixth grade. Not only does he or she teach the subject matter (via projects), but he also serves as counselor, guide, and general adult authority. He is available to the children not only during the hours of instruction, but during evenings and sometimes weekends as well. He settles disputes among the children in the group meetings and aids in the further socialization process. He is a representative of the kibbutz and imparts its morality and ideology to the youngsters during the latency period. In high school a new group leader–educator is appointed. He, too, is a teacher, usually of one or two subjects.

He may teach these subjects to his group as well as to other grade groups. However, as regards guidance, leadership, and authority, his functions are confined to one group only. The adolescents view him as a representative of the adult world and come to terms with that world under his tutelage.

The role of the teacher in the kibbutz is more inclusive and more "parental" than that of the teacher in the moshav or in the city. It is significant that the kibbutz teacher is known as "educator," a generic term for all non-familial agents involved in child rearing beyond the kindergarten years.

The young leader is also an effective mediator between

adolescence and adulthood. In age he is close to his group and probably understands its members better than does the adult. Yet he is usually sufficiently mature to influence the adolescent in the direction of adult morality and ideology, which he represents. He can identify with the adolescents' needs more easily and serve as leader, companion, and "father confessor" with greater facility than the adult, who may be regarded as a member of another generation.

In the life of the kibbutz child there are figures that have group significance. He often refers to the metapelet as "ours" (the group's); however, the parents are referred to as "mine." This distinction is created early and is maintained as additional adult figures enter the child's life.

Children who are members of the group in which the kibbutz youngster grows up are also significant figures in his life. He shares with them most of his waking hours and sleeps in the same room or the same house with them. Later they are members of the same grade, work on the same projects, and are under the watchful eye of the same teacher. In many ways they are like siblings, or probably more like twins, for the age differential characteristic of siblings in the biological family is lacking. Often, close friendships and patterns of identification between individuals are observable.

Peer Socialization

The group has something that goes beyond the individuals who comprise it. From the very beginning, collective education is geared to group life and group upbringing, in preparation for later sharing and living together in the collectivity or the communal society that is the kibbutz.

The kibbutz child is born into, and spends the rest of his childhood with, the peer group. The group is viewed not as a mere collection of individuals, but as an entity in its own right. Around the third year of life, in the toddlers' house, the emphasis on group living commences. The sharing of food, toys, and goodies, group activities, respect for the rights of others receive their rudimentary emphasis. As the child progresses through kindergarten and the grades, it is group rather than individual achievement that is stressed. As an individual he is judged by the group on the basis of his effort and contribution to the group endeavor. In school, too, he contributes his share to the project that is a group activity. His failure to perform the functions placed upon him, be it performing at a party of the children's community or keeping his room clean, is viewed as a betrayal of the group. Judgment and reactions come swiftly, and group ostracism may be quickly felt. Group disapproval and ostracism is to be avoided at all costs. Group pressure and group opinion are powerful influences in keeping each child in line. On the other hand, group cohesiveness and solidarity give him a feeling of strength and security. As he grows up, he may often have difficulty in imaging himself alone, acting on his own entirely, without his peers watching over his shoulder.

Education

Since each grade—in kindergarten, in primary school, in the Mosad—is also a group and living unit, the physical arrangements are designed correspondingly. Each group has its own building, consisting of living quarters for all members of the group and a classroom–clubroom combination. Generally, these houses are well equipped. Children come first and are given the best the kibbutz can afford.

Youth Culture

Kibbutz children are reared exclusively in groups composed of their age peers. Their contacts with the biological parents are relatively limited. Other adults interact with kibbutz children primarily in their capacity as cultivators of the children's societies or of what might be termed the youth culture. The peer group has a central role as a socializing agent in the kibbutz, but it is closely guided and monitored by adults.

The school-age children of the kibbutz are divided into two "societies"—the children's society (primary school) and the adolescent society. Each society is a federation of several smaller groups that correspond to the classroom grades. All of the activities of the children take place in their world, in their societies, but not in the adult's world or in his society. The main reference point of the child is the group of peers rather than the family consisting of adults and other children of different ages. There is an age range within the societies of the children, for each spans about five to six years of the child's life, but the same age prevails in the intimate smaller groups that make up the federated society.

Work and training for work is part of the childhood experience, but the kibbutz child does not, until the later teens, become involved in the work of the adult. Almost until he becomes an adult himself, he works on the children's farms for relatively short periods of time every day. These are rather "make believe" farms, since nobody depends upon their income and productivity; they represent only a "dress rehearsal" for adult living. There is no integration with the workaday world of adult society, its worries, cares, anxieties, and aspirations. The children remain distant from this world and are shielded against it through the network of childhood institutions—through the youth culture.

Home for the kibbutz child means not just the parents' apartment, but the whole community. It includes the children's house, the general dining room where all major events take place, the school facilities, or even some of the work branches that he likes to visit because his father works there. The kibbutz child-rearing system is a coherent part of the kibbutz community. It cannot be understood without taking into consideration the overall qualities of the kibbutz as an integrated community, with relationships that are less alienated and less specific than in the outside society. The close proximity in which all members of the community live, and the fact that they all share in several roles, create a greater degree of involvement and mutual responsibility.

What is unique about the kibbutz is that in addition to the formal importance of nonfamilial socialization agents there is an informal socialization network and a general feeling of responsibility for "our children." Since the earliest days of the kibbutzim, the infants and children were always housed in the best available buildings. This use of physical resources underlined the nature of the kibbutz as a child-centered society.

BASIC PSYCHOLOGICAL THEMES IN KIBBUTZ CHILD REARING

The following characteristics of the kibbutz child-rearing system, gleaned from the description so far, can be viewed as the basic psychological themes that affect children growing up in it.

Multiple "significant others"

The number of significant others who are in contact with the child during the first year of life—and later—is much greater in the kibbutz than in the traditional family. The mother, who is naturally a permanent object, spends much time with the baby during the first weeks of life, but this interaction changes over time.

The child–adult ratio

In the communal child-rearing system, every adult has more children under his care than in most nuclear families. The metapelet, being the main socializing agent, spends most of the day with a group of up to six children under her primary care.

Continuity in adult–child interactions

The question of continuity of the significant other—usually the mother—is crucial in parent–child contacts (Bowlby, 1951). This continuity can be construed in several ways. It may be a continuous contact between adult and child during the day or daily contacts at regular times with the same adult. In the kibbutz the biological mother is a continuous figure from day to day, though only for a limited time period each day. The metapelet is a discontinous figure, because she will change several times during childhood. The kibbutz situation can be described as "intermittent mothering" or "concomitant mothering" (Rabin, 1965).

Specificity and warmth in emotional contacts
between adult and child

There is a high degree of emotional relatedness in the interaction with the parents, especially in early childhood. The metapelet, on the other hand, is instrumental and nonspecific in her reactions. In her dealings with the children she does not make distinctions among children, but in general she is warm and not always "objective." Theoretically, the nonspecific reactions of the metapelet coexist with the specificity of the parents' reactions. There have been suggestions that the kibbutz system leads to an exaggerated expression of positive feelings during the parental visits (Bettelheim,

1969; Spiro, 1958). At the same time, it is safer to assume, with Kaffman (1965), that there is a great deal of variance in parenting, from love and acceptance to rejection, so that it does not seem fruitful to describe typical kibbutz parenting, but only typical kibbutz arrangements for parenting.

Acceptance and support

Acceptance and support for the children seem more prominent in the kibbutz system, because parents are not usually involved in disciplining their children. The metapelet is a source of acceptance and reward, but also of discipline and punishment.

Stress reduction and need satisfaction

In this area there is a clear difference between the nuclear family and the kibbutz system. In the nuclear family there is a possibility for the immediate gratification of needs. The gratification may come in a "magical" way, without much effort in the child's part, and without frustration. In the kibbutz the situation is different. The mother is not continuously present in the infants' house, and the metapelet, with several children in her charge, cannot respond immediately to expressions of need. At night the situation is even more extreme, because the mother and metapelet are absent, and the night worker is a stranger. The child receives immediate gratification only during parental visits. During these periods the child is at the center of attention and does not have to compete for it with peers.

Richness and social stimulation

In the traditional nuclear family, parent–child interactions constitute "constant stimulation" (Goldfarb, 1955), but not so in the kibbutz. During most of the time the social stimulation is less intense and varied, while during parental visits it is most intense.

Variance in stimulation

In the children's groups the child has to follow structured stimulation, dictated by the needs of the organization. The structure is less stereotyped when the child is with the parents.

The above analyses of parent–child interaction in the kibbutz show that it is quite different from the interaction in the traditional nuclear family, and also different from patterns of institutional child rearing, but in some respects similar to both. The communal child-rearing system is characterized by the fluctuations of the child's interactions with adults in early life. These fluctuations occur daily in the child's life as a result of the "multiple mothering" pattern (Rabin, 1965) in the communal system. Kibbutz children and infants have experiences similar to those of children in the traditional family only for a short period during the day. The differences are not only quantitative, but, most importantly, qualitative. During the short period of intensive interaction with the parents, the child is likely to be treated with acceptance, warmth, and love, but during most hours of the day, and especially the night, the interaction with caretakers is less warm and non-specific. The child in the kibbutz has to adjust from early on to two separate social worlds, one the family, the other the infants' and children's houses. It is important to note that these houses are not "institutional" in their treatment of children, and that the metapelet is usually a warm mother figure. Nevertheless, the kibbutz child has to experience frequent transitions from family to peer-group and metapelet. He has to learn to change his expectations and reactions according to the two worlds of his social environment. This duality is not limited to early childhood but continues until adulthood, and it must have an effect on personality development (Rabin, 1965).

What is most important from a psychological point of view is the presence of multiple caretakers at an early stage in the children's development. This characteristic, and especially the limited contact with the mother, has raised several questions regarding its possible effects. Should the multiple caretaking be conceived as a form of maternal deprivation, maternal substitution, or multiple mothering? On the basis of available research, which will be covered later, we may conclude that the latter formulation is correct. The psychological characteristics of child rearing in the kibbutz can be summarized as follows: The number of significant others interacting with the child is higher than in the traditional family, but the relationships with some of these figures are nonexclusive and not continuous. The metapelet (caretaker) takes care of a group of children and is likely to be changed several times during childhood. In the infants' and children's group, the child is exposed to a uniform, less personal treatment, and his needs are satisfied less readily than in the traditional family. As the child grows older and becomes an adolescent, his age group becomes more and more a central part of his physical and psychological world. The function of age groups (Eisenstadt, 1956) has always been to attempt to overcome the influence of the family in terms of revolutionary change. The emphasis in the communal system on the peer-group and on the children's society reflect this attempt to undermine traditional family influences. Eisenstadt (1956) describes life in the kibbutz age groups as centered on formal education, work, and social activities. He emphasized two aspects of group life: total self-government through committees, and total participation of members in all activities. Many group activities parallel those of adult kibbutz members but are completely independent.

Since the child has to divide his attachments between these two worlds and among a large number of human objects—parents, teachers, and peers—one may ask whether this spread of feelings weakens the dependency on one significant figure, reduces the intensity of feelings toward parents, reduces the ambivalence toward parents, or diffuses identification over many objects. Rabin (1957, 1965) hypothesized that these conditions of reduced attachment and dependence would lead to a diffusion in identification, a reduction in ambivalence toward parents, and a reduction in sibling rivalry. Regev (1977) summarized these hypotheses into two: the moderation hypothesis and the diffusion hypothesis. The moderation hypothesis states that the kibbutz child has more moderate feelings toward objects in his environment, and the diffusion hypothesis states that the kibbutz child divides his attachment among a greater number of objects. Indications of moderation and diffusion have been cited by kibbutz educators as an indication of the success of kibbutz child rearing in creating a personality that is better suited for kibbutz life (Golan, 1961).

THE KIBBUTZ AND THE MOSHAV

One of the problems in research on the kibbutz is finding an appropriate "control group." What we selected as a control group in this study is another form of rural settlement in Israel, which shares much with the kibbutz in terms of history and ideology.

Both the kibbutz and the moshav were started as planned, intentional communities (Weintraub, Lissak, & Azmon, 1969). The importance of ideology and planning is quite evident in the two systems. Both the kibbutz and the moshav were part of the Zionist settlement effort and were designed to facilitate the effort. One part of Zionist–socialist ideology, which gave rise to both, was the attempt to change the social structure of the Jewish people by creating an agricultural working class. This was a deliberate attempt to turn an urban population into agricultural workers living by their own labor. This can be regarded as an intentional downward mobility. In both cases, the second generation, made up of the children of the founders, was expected to grow up as workers on the land and to stay where they had grown up.

Both the kibbutz movement and the moshav movement were part of the national pioneering elite (Weintraub et al., 1969). And both the kibbutz and the moshav share the common colonizatory values of national ownership of lands, pioneering, productive employment, manual labor, and simplicity of life. The moshav as a community settlement pattern appeared later than the kibbutz, and the moshav movement was initially smaller than the kibbutz movement. By 1948 there were only 58 moshavim, compared to about 150 kibbutzim, but today there are about 350 moshavim and 250 kibbutzim. The moshav is legally defined as a cooperative organization with limited liability of members, established to promote farming as the only source of income for its members. The typical moshav is made up of about 100 nuclear families, and the family is the basic economic and social unit. Production, consumption, and socialization all take place within the family, but there is also a considerable amount of mutual solidarity, as well as cooperative economic enterprise, such as marketing, supply, and credit arrangements. There is an equality in the means of production, namely, land and other capital, but there are no attempts to maintain exact equality in living standards.

The moshav was described by Weintraub et al., (1969) as an attempt to combine the family farm ". . . with the pioneering values and strong community solidarity and cooperation of the collective" (p. 125). The moshav was planned to realize goals that parallel those of the kibbutz (Weintraub et al., 1969, pp. 125–128):

1.   The common goal of all pioneering groups: the three-fold ideal of productivization, nonexploitation of others, and national service . . .

2.   The creation of a family-farm culture . . . , and
3.   The establishment of a *Gemeinschaft.*

The moshav founders wanted to create a cooperative agricultural community, but they differed from the kibbutz founders in their emphasis, from the beginning, on the central role of the family. The moshav was defined as a community of families, with the family farm being the unit of production, consumption, and socialization.

The kibbutz pattern was relatively known when the moshav was being planned as a form of settlement. The moshav was planned historically as an alternative and a reaction to the kibbutz. One of the objections the moshav founders had to the kibbutz was that of communal child rearing. The moshav founders were older men, with established families who ". . . were suspicious of communal encroachment upon the domestic domain and unwilling to risk the sacrifice of family ties for an experiment whose success was by no means assured" (Weintraub et al., 1969, p. 125). There was a deliberate decision in most kibbutzim to delay the birth of children and the role of parenthood. Quite the contrary was true of the moshav, where children were part of the community from its earliest beginnings.

It is important to recognize that there are kibbutz and moshav movements, in the sense of organized political groups or federations of kibbutzim and moshavim, offering both political and economic advantages but also providing a coherent ideology. From the point of view of the individual, there is always an identification with the movement in addition to the identification with a particular community. The role of "kibbutz member" or "moshav member" is generalized across the whole movement. Unlike other communal and cooperative settlement experiments and communities, a moshav or a kibbutz was always a part of a larger movement that provided economic, social and psychological support, and directed policy, including policy on education and child rearing. The two groups share in the same wider culture: in the language, geographical location, background of parents, school curriculum, the economic base of the community and living standards, ethnic origins, and general ideology.

Comparing the kibbutz and the moshav, Eisenstadt (1956) states that "many of their social and economic characteristics may be treated as almost totally equivalent" (p. 178–179). At the same time, Eisenstadt states that ". . . yet they differ very markedly, both in their family organization (and the place of the family within the total community) and in the prevalence of formalized age groups" (p. 179).

The similarities and the differences between the social settings of the kibbutz and the moshav are summarized in Table 2.1.

Table 2.1

Characteristics of the two communities

Trait	Kibbutz	Moshav
community type	rural	rural
community size	small	small
economic base (in the 50s)	agricultural	agricultural
ideology	communal Zionist-socialist	cooperative Zionist-socialist
production unit	communal	family
socialization unit	communal	family

The differences between the two child-rearing systems may be defined in terms of the number of *significant others* surrounding the child and the quality and quantity of interactions with them. Since it is assumed that interaction with significant others has a major effect on personality development, we can expect differences in the former to lead to differences in the latter.

Avgar et al. (1977) found a greater similarity in socialization technique between the kibbutz and the moshav than between the kibbutz and the city. They found that kibbutz-raised children showed a greater readiness to help each other than did moshav-raised children, but the difference was smaller than that found between the kibbutz-raised and the city-raised. Given all this, we can assume that the similarity between the two groups is greater than the dissimilarity, and the crucial difference is indeed in child rearing. The similarities between the kibbutz and the moshav let us concentrate on the crucial variables that separate the two systems, and let us attribute any differences found between the two groups to the influence of these crucial variables, namely, differences in the relationship with the parents in the early years.

The kibbutz and the moshav can be viewed as two sub-cultures within the larger, and complex, Israeli society. They share many characteristics of the overall social system, as shown above, and they differ in the emphasis on the role of the family in the community and in the degree of economic cooperation. Nevertheless, there is much community feeling within the moshav subculture. In reference to children and grown-up children, one may find many expressions of a communal attachment in the kibbutz; a kibbutz member may, for example, refer to a youngster, or an adult who grew up in the kibbutz, as "our child." The relationship between the kibbutz and its children may be expressed in the following sentence: "Novelist X is the child of kibbutz Y." However, similar expressions, though less frequent, may be found in the moshav subculture, with an adult referring to "General V, a child of moshav Z." These are reflections of a community feelings that differs quantitatively between the two subcultures but is in existence in both.

3

From 1955 to 1975: The Original Study and the Follow-up

The aim of the present chapter is to make the connection between the original study, carried out in 1955 and reported in the literature between 1957 and 1965 (Rabin, 1957b, 1961a, 1961b, 1965), and the present one. Originally, this was not designed to be a longitudinal study. The original was planned to stand on its own. Nevertheless, there are obvious continuities between the first stage and the follow-up stage, which will be briefly explored below. Several topics will be covered.

THE RESEARCH SAMPLE

Consonant with the attempt to obtain representative samples, the research on the children spread to a number of different kibbutzim and moshavim. In contrast to the method of the anthropologist who may, following residence and "participant" observation in a single village, make generalizations about the entire culture or subculture, we attempted to cast a wider net for our tests and observations. The varying ethnic backgrounds, economic statuses, and unique modifications of common practices make it questionable, if not hazardous, to generalize from one kibbutz to all others. Thus we sampled kibbutzim of different ages; some were veteran kibbutzim, around 30 years old in 1955, while others were "middle-aged," founded around 15 to 20 years previously. Still others were of more recent origin. The sample included children whose parents had come from a variety of national origins—from Hungary, Poland, Russia, and so forth--though belonging to the general culture area of Eastern European Jewry. Details of this procedure may be found in chapter 4 of *Growing up in the Kibbutz* (Rabin, 1965).

In addition to the concern with representativeness—although we have not undertaken a systematic sampling procedure—were also some practical considerations. Since the original design of the study had called for groups of children of different ages—infants, 10-year olds, and adolescents—it was necessary to study kibbutzim of different ages. Young, or very old, kibbutzim were visited, for only they had a sufficient number of second- or third-generation infants, and "middle-aged" and older kibbutzim were visited in order to obtain the school-age youngsters and adolescents. Thus, a total of ten different kibbutzim were visited and sampled.

Basic to the design of the study of kibbutz children was the employment of a parallel "control" group, with which they were to be compared. The notion of comparing these children with an American group of similar age was out of the question, for it would have introduced a great many contaminating cultural and other factors. It was imperative that we select a group of children from the same broader Israeli culture, with parents of similar backgrounds, residing in rural settings, with which the "experimental" kibbutz group was to be compared. The moshav setting was deemed most appropriate because the founders—and parents —of the moshavim were similar in background (ethnic-national), in general culture (modern, secular, Israeli) and occupations and settings (rural, agricultural) to those of the kibbutzim. Thus, with some of these variables "controlled," we were able to focus on family life and child-rearing conditions, in which the experimental and control groups differed markedly and which, according to the discussion below, were focal to our theorizing and hypothesis generation.

The final groups of children who were individually interviewed and tested consisted of 92 kibbutz and 79 nonkibbutz children, for a total of 171 examinees. There were 24 kibbutz and 20 nonkibbutz infants between the ages of 10 and 17 months, from five different kibbutzim and four moshavim; 39 kibbutz and 34 nonkibbutz ten-year olds were drawn from six kibbutzim and four moshavim, while the 30 kibbutz and 25 nonkibbutz adolescents (ages: 16.7–17.9 years) came from four different kibbutzim and three moshavim. As with the kibbutzim, the moshavim were selected on the basis of age of the settlement and the origins of its adult membership. The data concerning the samples in the original study are summarized in Table 3.1.

Table 3.1

The Groups of Children in the Original Study

(Numbers)

	Kibbutz				Moshav			
	M	F	T	Mean age	M	F	T	Mean age
Infants	13	11	24	13.4*	10	10	20	13.0
Children	27	11	38	10.2	21	13	34	10.2
Adolescents	17	13	30	17.5	14	11	25	17.6

*Age of infants, in months; children, in years.

It may be noted from the table that although the infant groups and adolescent groups are nearly evenly divided as to sex, there was an imbalance in the ten-year-old groups. Here the males exceeded markedly—in the kibbutz more than twice—the numbers of females. In this instance, "representativeness" is flawed.

QUESTIONS, HYPOTHESES, AND VARIABLES

The major questions regarding personality development that were considered were of substantial importance to the follow-up project, for they offered some guidelines for further predictions and developmental expectations during adulthood. They helped us address the issue of personality continuity and the possible stability of group differences when comparing the "modal" kibbutz and nonkibbutz personality.

Essentially, the general question raised was the one regarding the possible effects of the kibbutz child-rearing system on the development of the child's personality. It was hypothesized, on the basis of a detailed analysis of the child-rearing conditions, that the kibbutz child is exposed to a setting that can be placed roughly between the nuclear family home and the traditional institution or orphanage. It was further speculated that although the conditions were not such as to bring about "maternal deprivation" (Bowlby, 1951) or "psychological deprivation" (Goldfarb, 1955) to the extent described by several investigators, some deprivation was present nevertheless. In comparing the kibbutz setting with the child's environment in the ordinary family, we noted a few differences. There is a larger number of children per adult in the kibbutz setting, somewhat less continuity in the adult–child interaction, and perhaps lesser "specificity of adult–child emotional response." We considered this a state of "partial deprivation," due to the discontinuity and intermittency of the contacts of the child with his or her biological mother.

In relation to this partial "maternal deprivation" several general questions were posed regarding the possible developmental characteristics of kibbutz children as compared with those reared under ordinary, intact family conditions.

First was the general question of competence. Is the kibbutz child's social and intellectual development, his adaptative capacity, comparable to that of children reared in more conventional family settings?

Second was the question of "homogenization." Does the kibbutz child tend to show less originality and creativity, less imagination and uniqueness than the control child?

Third in our concerns was the question of the comparative capacity for impulse control, the "normal capacity for inhibition," and delays of gratification—an important function in ego development.

Fourth, concern with the capacity for forming and maintaining close interpersonal relationships—including intimacy—was an additional area of investigation.

Fifth, and finally, we wished to learn something about the capacity to experience guilt, which, of course, may be related to the issue of "controls from within" mentioned in the third item under the rubric of capacity for inhibition and impulse control.

As we mentioned before, under extreme maternal deprivation various investigators have observed defective intellectual-conceptual ability, poor impulse control, difficulty in forming genuine inter-personal relationships, and deficiency in superego formation. However, whether such pathological developments follow less extreme "deprivation" conditions was a central question of concern. To be sure, we were dealing with children whose personalities had not yet crystallized; they were still "in process," so to speak. These questions become even more pertinent when we look at adult personality status and development.

In addition to the questions raised above, several specific predictions, based on psychodynamic theory, were made regarding the kibbutz children. It was expected that kibbutz children

1.   will show evidence of low Oedipal intensity;
2.   will show identification "marked by a greater diffusion of objects";
3.   will exhibit little ambivalence toward their parents;
4.   will not evidence as intense sibling rivalry as will the controls.

We may readily note that these predictions are not completely discrete and independent entities, but are theoretically and clinically very closely related. If we start with the observation of the greater diffusion of attachment to objects in the environment in the kibbutz child-rearing setting, then everything else seems to fall into place. With cathexes less concentrated and spread to several important figures—biological mother, metapelet, peers, and so forth—the intensity of relationship to the parents of the opposite sex (Oedipal) is reduced, identification as a consequence is more diffuse, parental roles are less threatening and there is, therefore, less ambivalence in relation to them, and, finally, the siblings are not so threatening for the kibbutz child's "cathectic eggs" are not all in the parental basket. Besides, unlike in the case of the child in the ordinary family, there is no well-established "king" (oldest child) and no usurper, no late arrival who threatens the kingdom. Kibbutz children arrive on the scene in the infant house and, later, in the toddler house in multiples of 3, 4, or more, and there is no priority that is threatened by late-comers.

Personality variables beyond those alluded to in the preceding paragraphs were also of interest to the comparative study of person-ality development in kibbutz and moshav children. We have not confined ourselves solely to these parameters predicted from theory but frankly engaged in exploration as well. We attempted to exploit the richness of the data obtained with numerous techniques and add some qualititative and content characteristics related to the structural variables, which might point further to differentiation between the groups.

THE ORIGINAL FINDINGS

Since our original research concerned three groups of children at different age levels—infancy, school age, and adolescence—and since the same variables could not be assessed at every age and different methods of assessment had to be employed at the different ages, treatment of results needs to be equally subdivided. Findings related to the infants will be followed by the results with the ten-year olds and, then, with those of the adolescents.

Infancy is a very interesting period, but psychology has not developed many adequate and standardized assessment procedures and objective observational methods that do justice to its rich potentialities. More than twenty years ago, the investigator's armamentarium was even much more limited than it is now. In recent years, more complex and sophisticated methods of infant assessment have been introduced (such as Uzgiris & Hunt, 1975, Yarrow et al., 1975). However, in our study we limited ourselves to two standard assessment methods then available, in addition to some informal observation and history-taking. The Vineland Social Maturity Scale, based on information obtained from adults, and the Griffith Mental Development Scale administered directly to the child yielded some clear-cut and fairly consistent results.

1.   On both scales, kibbutz infants obtained lower scores than their nonkibbutz peers.
2.   A special deficiency of the kibbutz group was noted on the "personal–social" subtest of the Griffith, while no significant differences were noted on the "locomotor" tasks, or on "speech and hearing" and "eye and hand" coordination subtests.

We speculated at the time that the "multiple mothering" experience of the kibbutz infant is frustrating and anxiety-arousing, for the infants have difficulty in making rapid transitions from one mother figure to another. This experience brings about a withdrawal, for a time, which affects his adaptative process. We stated (Rabin, 1965) that "this withdrawal tends to reduce identification and interferes with the orderly learning and developmental process which becomes reflected in lower achievement, especially in the personal–social sphere . . . (p. 111)."

No attempt will be made to review the variety of methods employed in the assessment of personality with the school-age (ten-year-old) children and adolescents. Such a description or even an enumeration is not essential in the present context, for our focus is primarily that of the results obtained, especially in relation to the particular variables listed in previous paragraphs.

With the ten-year-olds the obtained findings can be summarized as follows:

1. Intellectually, a reversal of the trend observed with the infants has apparently taken place. ". . . the kibbutz children are at least as well developed as, and to some extent surpass, the nonkibbutz children" (Rabin, 1965), p. 144).
2. Measures of ego strength, adjustment, and emotional maturity tend to favor the kibbutz children as compared to their controls.
3. With respect to the dynamic hypotheses or predictions, the findings were what was expected from theory:
   a. Kibbutz children do show lower oedipal intensity in their attachment to parents than do nonkibbutz children.
   b. They also evidence greater diffusion in their objects of identification, which includes parents, peers, and unrelated adults.
   c. Although they exhibit a more positive attitude toward the family unit, at a more unconscious level there is greater hostility toward parental figures. Furthermore, at a more conscious level, the attitudes of kibbutz boys seem to be more favorable to the mother figure and the attitudes of the girls less positive to the mother figure than in the nonkibbutz boys and girls.
   d. There was support for the hypothesis of lesser sibling rivalry in the kibbutz group.

Addition results not predicted originally included:

1. There is a minor tendency toward greater anxiety in the kibbutz group.
2. There is evidence of greater guilt (superego anxiety) in the nonkibbutz group.
3. There is evidence of less narcissism in "object choice" among kibbutz children.
4. Kibbutz youngsters tend to stress short-term goals as compared with the more extended and future time perspective in the nonkibbutz peer group.

As far as the adolescents are concerned, some continuity with the earlier variables may be stressed, but several new parameters of personality were considered. The findings may be summarized succinctly in the following lines:

1. As far as intellectual development is concerned, the results tend to confirm the shift that had taken place from infancy to later childhood. The "kibbutz adolescents function at least as well and perhaps somewhat better than the controls" (Rabin, 1965, p. 179).
2. Although there was no particular measure of homogeneity of content, the great variability noted in the various fantasy productions showed no differences in range of fantasy between the two groups.
3. There is evidence of less intense affective involvement of kibbutz adolescents with members of their family and lesser experience of conflict in relation to them.
4. No differences in overall "adjustment" were obtained.
5. Kibbutz adolescents show greater repression of sexuality.
6. With respect to drive, generally the kibbutz group evidenced greater control and sublimation of primitive drives.
7. While the nonkibbutz adolescents tend to fantasize aggression more often and assume the role of aggressor, the kibbutz adolescents see themselves more often the victims of aggression, from without or self-directed.
8. Although no differences in the level of anxiety were discerned, there are differences in the mode of handling anxiety in that the kibbutz group tends to attack its source head on, whereas the nonkibbutz adolescent more frequently tends to seek help or withdraw.
9. Compared with controls, kibbutz respondents show less evidence of guilt.

10. Finally, in contrast with the controls, the kibbutz group does not exhibit personal career ambitions, yet is interested in personal self-development and growth.

Needless to say, in highlighting the group differences we have neglected to point out the similarities. Some were noted in the summaries. However, the similarities between the groups were more numerous than the differences. When reviewing the comparison between the adolescent groups we could find no marked differences with respect to intelligence or on a number of aspects of the self-concept. The Rorschach test findings indicated no marked differences in personality structure between the two groups. Levels of anxiety and affectivity, and of overall "adjustment," were quite similar for both groups, not indicating any extreme deviations or psychopathology. Both groups were seen as consisting of competent, coping, and integratively functioning individuals. Yet by focusing on personality differences and relating them to differences in antecedent child-rearing conditions, we can hopefully throw some light on the processes that underlie them.

FROM CHILDREN TO ADULTS

A comparative study of kibbutz and nonkibbutz adults can be defended as worthwhile in its own right. Of course, the question of selecting the relevant variables may be rather vexing. In the present follow-up study, after an intervening period of twenty years, the problem of relevant personality variables is partially obviated. We may select those parameters that have been proved particularly effective in differentiating between the groups. Do the differences observed in childhood persist in adulthood, as we might predict from the viewpoint of consistency of personality? Consonant with the earlier findings on the children and adolescents, one might expect the following:

1. There will be no marked differences in psychosocial competence between the two general groups—kibbutz and nonkibbutz.
2. The less intensive involvement of kibbutz offspring with their parents will persist through adulthood.

3. The general level of "adjustment" and ego strength will not differ markedly.

4. Repression of sexuality will show little difference upon reaching adult status, although earlier (in adolescence) it was most marked in kibbutz youngsters.

5. There will be a persistence of differences in defensive strategy between the two groups. This will include evidence of greater intropunitiveness in the kibbutz group.

6. Although changes in the kibbutz attitudes toward higher education have taken place, it may still be expected that personal career ambitions are less salient in kibbutz than in nonkibbutz subjects.

Although, on the basis of an earlier work, the above expectancies may be reasonable, we should not confine ourselves to these alone. A number of other authors have examined and analyzed the kibbutz child-rearing system and have made a number of diagnostic as well as prognostic statements. To the extent that our methods of study and examination can yield information about these issues, we shall attempt to address them as fully as our own predictions. Naturally, when examining the large amount of data we accumulated on both samples, we shall not confine ourselves to findings stemming from theory and prediction. Other expected or seredipitous results are not to be neglected and are grist to our mill.

4

The Follow-up Study: Design, Instruments, and Procedure

The follow-up project was not just a continuation of the original study. It had to come to its own in terms of aims, psychological research instruments, and procedures. This chapter will describe the development and implementation of the follow-up study from the first general ideas to the completion of data-gathering.

RATIONALE AND DESIGN

To check for the representativeness of the two groups, they were compared to larger populations, of which they were samples. The kibbutz group in our study was compared to the population of the kibbutz second generation, studied by Rosner et al. (1978), and it was found that the group was highly similar to the whole population. The demographic profile of the second-generation population shows an average age in the late twenties, a higher percentage of males, a high school education, a majority being married, and about a third who have left the kibbutz. The study group fits closely with this profile. Detailed biographical findings presented below (Chapter 5) should remove any doubts about the representativeness of the sample.

One question in the design of the follow-up was that of handling the three age groups, of subjects who were now 22 to 23, 30 to 31, and 37 to 38 years old, respectively. We felt that treating each group separately would create both statistical and conceptual difficulties, and we decided to emphasize what all three groups had in common at this stage. What they had in common is that they have become adults, at different stages of adulthood, but still having reached independence from their parents. The whole group can be defined as a group of "young adults," aged 22 to 38, according to the description offered by Levinson, et al. (1978). They have all passed the "transitional state" of entry into adulthood and have all established themselves as adults. Possible differences among the three age groups were examined in relation to most variables. In most cases there were no differences, and the three groups were then combined. We decided to look at features of psychological functioning and malfunctioning that are typical of the two samples, and not at the differences among the three age levels. An important argument in favor of combining the three groups is that we have no reason to expect that this age range affects the variables we are looking at.

Sex differences in the findings are reported when relevant to the psychological meaning of the findings. In most cases, the sex differences we have found indicated the construct validity of our measures, that is, there were sex differences that could have been expected on a theoretical basis and showed that our measures were in accordance with other studies.

LOCATING THE MEMBERS
OF THE ORIGINAL STUDY GROUPS

The basis for locating the members of the original study was the original list of subjects, kept since 1955. The list contained the following information: name, place of residence, age group (infants, children, or adolescents). In some cases there was also the name of the age group (kibbutz age groups often bear "totemic" names of animals, plants, and so on) or the name of a metapelet. The original locations included ten kibbutzim and six moshavim, and these places were the starting points for the research. After checking the list, it was found that the names of two subjects were lost (one from the kibbutz group and the other from the moshav group), and this reduced the number of subjects to 169 out of the original 171 in the two groups.

A preliminary attempt to locate some members of the group was carried out in 1973 by A. I. Rabin. Through the use of several well-placed informants in three kibbutzim and one moshav, information was obtained on the whereabouts of 24 kibbutz subjects and 35 moshav subjects. The information was in many cases quite general and could not be checked without additional efforts. The best information was in the cases of those who had stayed in their original communities, but the information was less reliable about those who had left. What this attempt made clear, however, was that locating the members of the original group was feasible.

A systematic strategy for locating the original subjects was developed and put into action in 1974. It involved the use of additional informants, seeking information from official community sources, and using telephone directories. The search was sometimes hampered by insufficient information in the original list, similar or identical names (two subjects in one location had the same name), and name changes. While name changes for women as a result of marriage are to be expected in any follow-up study, a phenomenon almost unique to Israel is the prevalence of name changes for both men and women as the result of national ideology. The adoption of Hebrew names to replace foreign names as an expression of nationalism has been common among Zionists since the beginning of this century. This created an obvious problem in tracing persons who had adopted a new name and identity during the previous twenty years. These difficulties, however, were minor compared to some of the special advantages we had in tracing the subjects. What made the search easier was the fact that we were trying to find people who had come from relatively small communities in a small country, and most of them still resided in small communities. It was not difficult to find informants who knew about most people in their communities. In the case of the kibbutzim, the average size of the community was around 500. In the case of the moshavim, it was higher, but still the average was around 1200 persons in a community. Every kibbutz has a central register of present and past members and their children, which is used for a variety of purposes. Once the knowledge and the resources of several kibbutz informants had been exhausted, official letters were sent to several kibbutzim, asking for information from their registers. Using these resources of informants and kibbutz records, we were able to ascertain the whereabouts of 70 members of the original group and to obtain leads related to several more. We also found out that two members of the original kibbutz group had died; one had been killed in the 1967 war, and another had died of leukemia. In locating the rest of the members, we used the help of relatives, using various leads and doing an amount of detective work.

The summary of the tracing operation, as shown in Table 4.1, indicates our success in locating the vast majority of the members of the 1955 study groups. Out of the original 171 subjects, only 12 were unaccounted for. Excluding the four who were deceased, we had 155 subjects to work with in the interviewing stage, 83 (out of 92) from the kibbutz group and 72 (out of 79) from the moshav group. In terms of geographical distribution, the subjects were living in 51 localities in Israel, including 24 kibbutzim, 13 moshavim, and 14 cities and suburbs. Six subjects were temporarily or permanently away from Israel. In this first stage of the follow-up project, that of locating the members of the study group, we had succeeded in finding 90% of the members of the 1955 study group, and we thus avoided the problem of sample depletion that is common in many follow-up studies.

Table 4.1

Locating the original sample
(In percentages)

Original group	Total	Deceased	Not located	Located	Participants
Kibbutz	92 (100%)	2 (2.4%)	7 (7.6%)	83 (90%)	78 (85%)
Moshav	79 (100%)	2 (2.6%)	5 (6.4%)	72 (91%)	68 (86%)
Total	171 (100%)	4 (2%)	12 (7%)	155 (91%)	146 (85%)

SELECTING THE RESEARCH INSTRUMENTS

Our general aim was to learn as much as possible about the lives and personalities of our research subjects, using psychological instruments characterized by reliability and validity. We tried to use standard psychological tests as much as possible, in order to avoid too many methodological and theoretical tangles. The differences between the age of the respondents in the original study and in the follow-up stage also dictated some differences in instruments. Some of the instruments in the original study were especially designed for children. Dealing with adult respondents necessitates a different relationship and a different way of collecting information.

During the process of selecting the instruments we were also guided by consideration of *practical* issues: how much time and money would an instrument call for? How simple was the administration? How were our subjects likely to react to a certain instrument? These practical considerations are mostly self-explanatory. Any large-scale research project is hampered by practical limitations of manpower, time, and budget. Because the voluntary cooperation of our respondents was so crucial, we had to take special care in selecting instruments that would be inoffensive and easy to complete. We were planning to have our subjects take an active part in the study, leaving them the responsibility of filling out and mailing us some of the instruments. Thus, the instruments had to be as simple and as attractive—or at least nonthreatening—as possible.

Our study was a field research project, in the sense that we were looking at people in the natural setting of their lives and literally entering their homes and private lives. We tried to maintain a degree of openness with our respondents, to the extent that this was possible, and our openness was reciprocated. Our instruments were self-explanatory. Since we did not use any projective materials, our purposes in asking most questions could be clear to the respondents, which encouraged an atmosphere of trust and acceptance.

We selected five research instruments, varying in what they require of the respondents and of the researchers, and in the areas of behavior they were trying to assess.

The final battery of instruments selected included the following:

1. the Personal Interview Schedule, for a face-to-face interview with each member of the research groups; administration time: 2 to 4 hours (see Appendix I);
2. the MMPI—a Hebrew version of the MMPI, standardized on an Israeli sample by Butcher and Gur (1976) and including 566 items; administration time: 2 to 3 hours;
3. a Semantic Differential Schedule, including 8 concepts to be rated on 20 scales; administration time: up to 20 minutes;
4. Sentence Completion Blank—this instrument is identical to the one used by Rabin (1965); administration time: up to 20 minutes;
5. Biographical Questionnaire—prepared and standardized in Israel by Nevo (1976) and including 80 items; administration time: up to 45 minutes.

Items 2, 3, and 5 were to be filled out by the respondents on their own and mailed to the researchers. Total time invested by the respondents might have been up to eight hours. Our final battery includes three kinds of instruments: the structured interview is the most elaborate, and involves a face to face interaction. Two instruments, the MMPI and the Biographical Questionnaire, are self-report instruments, and the other two, the semantic differential schedule and the sentence completion blank, can be regarded as projective or semiprojective. As is the case with most studies, no amount of advance planning could assure us of the usefulness of our instruments. Some of them turned out to be disappointments, providing us with little important information or ideas for further analysis. Other instruments provided us with both information and stimulation in the form of new ideas.

In data analysis, each instrument was treated separately, but areas of personality functioning and personality traits were defined across instruments. For instance, attitudes toward the parents, an important variable in comparing the two groups, were assessed according to data from the interview, the Sentence Completion Test, the MMPI, and the semantic differential. Thus, there were multiple measures of every variable. There were different numbers of subjects in the two groups for the statistical analyses of data because of differences in the number of respondents who completed the various instruments. Thus, the Sentence Completion test was filled out by 66 members of the kibbutz group and 60 members of the moshav group. The semantic differential schedule was filled out by 63 members of the kibbutz group and 57 members of the moshav group, the MMPI was filled out by 61 members of the kibbutz group and 59 members of the moshav group. The Personal Interview was administered to 77 members of the kibbutz group and 68 members of the moshav group, and the Biographical Questionnaire was filled out by 78 members of the kibbutz group and 68 members of the moshav group. Furthermore, for various technical reasons, such as lack of an answer for a particular item, incomplete answers, and so on, there are varying numbers representing the two groups in the detailed presentations of the findings below. Therefore, the numbers of subjects may be inconsistent from one table to another.

A more detailed description of the five instruments, including both technical and nontechnical aspects, follows.

Personal Interview Schedule

The structured Personal Interview was our main instrument in assessing the respondents as fully functioning adults. Through a personal face-to-face contact, we attempted to learn as much as possible about the respondents' lives and personalities. The interviewer asked the person himself to describe the major components of his life structure: his marriage and family life, his occupation and work, his feelings about himself, his roles in various social contexts, his reaction to conflicts. This was an opportunity to gather information and to form impressions, to ask about actions, events, desires, and feelings. We asked our respondents what they had done in the previous twenty years, what they remembered of their childhood, and what they intended to do in the future. We asked them about their daily work, their sex lives, what they remembered of their parents in early childhood, and how similar they were to the parents. The Personal Interview Schedule (Appendix I) was partly based on the interview schedule used by Kagan and Moss (1962), from which 96 of the 125 items were taken, with 29 added questions contributed by Albert I. Rabin, Eliyahu Regev, and Benjamin Beit-Hallahmi. The original items were translated into Hebrew and changed as necessary to account for cultural differences. The following areas of behavior were covered in the Personal Interview:

1. vocational performance and vocational aspirations—questions on actual work experiences and desired work experiences;
2. present family and marriage—the respondent as parent and spouse;
3. social relations—patterns of friendship and preferences in friendships; interest in intimacy outside the family;
4. sexual behavior, pre- and post-marital;
5. sex-role attitudes—questions about advantages and disadvantages of sex roles;
6. self-esteem—direct evaluation of the self, and questions on positive and negative qualities in the self;
7. psychosomatic symptoms—a list of 20 symptoms, which was read to the respondent;
8. achievement attitudes; wishes to succeed or excel;
9. attitudes toward parents; similarity in own parenting to the parents;
12. dependency behavior; turning to others for help and advice;
13. hostility; expressions of anger and aggression in various situations.

The interview was divided roughly into two parts. The first part dealt mostly with the individual's public life: work history, career expectations, and social relations. The second part dealt with more intimate aspects of life: marriage and sex, relations with parents and siblings, emotional problems, and so forth. This structure was intended to facilitate cooperation and minimize anxiety, with a gradual transition from the more public to the more private aspects of life.

The main advantage of the interview was that it enabled us to gain a large amount of significant information directly from the respondents; the main disadvantage was its length, which averaged two-and-a-half hours.

As expected, the interview provided us with a wealth of material, which was analyzed by breaking it down to the subject areas and using a variety of scales. Scales were constructed from groups of related items and were aimed at achieving quantitative measures in the various areas of behavior covered.

Minnesota Multiphasic Personality Inventory (MMPI)

The Minnesota Multiphasic Personality Inventory (MMPI) needs no introduction to the readers of psychological research literature. The MMPI is a self-report inventory that includes several measures of psychopathology, anxiety, and defensiveness. As Butcher and Tellegen (1978) pointed out, its popularity can be explained on the basis of several of its characteristics: its administration is simple and easy; objective scoring is available, as well as objective interpretations; its validity as a criterion measure is well established.

Our aim in using the MMPI in this study was to have a general measure of personality functioning and psychopathology that would be objectively scored and easy to administer. The MMPI seemed the most suitable instrument for this task because of the considerable experience in using it obtained in thousands of studies. Since most studies using the MMPI have been done in the USA, the question arises whether it can be profitably used in Israel. A Hebrew version of the MMPI, developed by Butcher and Gur (1967) and standardized on a group of 373 Israelis, has been in existence since 1974. The modal member of the standardization group (Butcher & Gur, 1976) was a college student in his twenties, born in Israel and residing in a large city. This was considered a representative sample of native-born young Israelis and is an especially good comparison group for our research sample. We have used the norms developed on the basis of the work with the Israeli standardization sample reported by Butcher and Pancheri (1976).

According to the suggestions by Butcher and Tellegen (1978) regarding the correct use of MMPI scores in research, we have used the following rules:

1. Non-K-corrected t scores were used. Since the validity of scale K as a "suppressor" could not be assumed, it is being used as a separate indicator, while clinical scales normally corrected by K scores are left as they are.
2. We used both non-K-corrected t scores and raw scores in comparing the two groups. As will be shown below (Chapter 8) the results obtained using the two sets of scores were essentially similar.
3. In addition to using the standard clinical scales and a group

of research scales, we have also used a list of "critical items" to investigate further the meaning of the responses to items.

The MMPI scale scores and profiles were used in several ways: first, as a general measure of adjustment and symptomatology; second, specific scales were used as indicators of psychological functioning in several areas. Thus scale Si was one of the measures of sociability, scale R was used to measure the variable of Repression versus Sensitization, and scale ES was used as a general measure of ego strength.

Semantic Differential (Appendix I)

The semantic differential is one of the most popular instruments in psychological research. It was developed by Osgood (1952) for the evaluation of concepts through ratings on a set of bipolar scales, defined by two opposite adjectives. Thus the respondent is asked to rate a concept on a semantic scale, with seven possible scores from one to seven. Figure 4.1 shows a part of the semantic differential rating schedule used in our study.

We used a semantic differential schedule including 20 scales. Our respondents were asked to rate 8 concepts on these 20 scales. The ratings for each concept can be expressed graphically as a profile. Every rating reflects a choice among several alternatives, and it locates the concept in semantic space. A factor analysis of

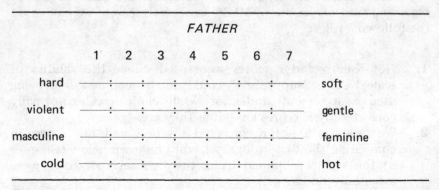

Figure 4.1

Semantic Differential ratings scales

semantic differential ratings produced three independent factors: Evaluation, Potency, and Activity. These are considered the three basic dimensions of "connotative meaning" (Osgood, Suci, & Tennenbaum, 1957), but the Evaluation factor (positive–negative dimension) is considered the most important. Factor analyses done in various cultures (Osgood, 1971; Wylie, 1974) showed that the Evaluation factor explains most of the variance in all cultures tested. The Potency and Activity factors were second and third, respectively. The semantic differential ratings have a test–retest reliability, as reported by Osgood et al. (1957), of .85. The reliability of semantic differential ratings collected in our study was similarly high, with an alpha coefficient of .86.

The semantic differential as a psychological measurement instrument should be regarded as a controlled associations test. Many of the adjectives and the scales cannot be applied to the concepts literally but can only be used methaphorically. Our respondents, for example, were asked to rate the concept *THE FUTURE* on a seven-point scale between "thick" and "thin" and on a seven-point scale between "dull" and "sharp." These scales relate to the concept only metaphorically and supply us with an indirect way of obtaining affective responses from the respondents, which otherwise would not have been produced.

We have used the semantic differential in this study to examine the ways in which our respondents, members of the two research groups, see themselves, their parents, their friends, their past, and their future. The semantic differential schedule was given to the respondents following the personal interview. They received an explanation on how to fill out the schedule, and it was left with them to be mailed later. The eight concepts rated by our respondents were: *MY CHILDHOOD, MY BEST FRIEND, FATHER, ME, MOTHER, ME AS I WOULD LIKE TO BE* (ideal self), *THE PLACE WHERE I GREW UP, THE FUTURE*.

The Sentence Completion Test (Appendix II)

This particular sentence completion form was devised by Sacks & Levi (1950), adapted and translated into Hebrew (Rabin, 1965), and employed in our original study with children and adolescents. This is a fairly structured projective technique in the sense that the stimuli (incomplete sentences) place certain restraints on the response; but the method is "response-free" (projective) nevertheless, for a wide choice of responses is available to the respondents.

The instruments consisted of 51 incomplete sentence stems. Respondents were asked to complete the sentences as best they could. Completions were written on the forms provided for the purpose.

Thirteen different areas were covered by these sentence stems. There were four incomplete sentences for each area (with the exception of one for which there were only three items). Among the areas of concern were: father, mother, family, future, past, and so on. Examples of the sentence stems and completions (in parentheses) in the first three areas are as follows:

I think that my father . . . (is a good man)
My mother . . . (is getting old)
Most families I know . . . (are full of strife)

Scoring was based on the range of the actual responses obtained. Following an inspection of the entire array of completions to a particular stem, a classification was devised for the purpose of group comparison. For the most part, the attitudes implied were placed into three categories—positive, neutral, and negative. The three completions quoted above illustrate these categories. The first one views father in a positive light ("good man"); the second completion is factual and noncommittal with respect to the mother ("getting old")—neutral. Finally, the third completion is seen as negative ("full of strife").

The Biographical Questionnaire

This is a detailed questionnaire, including 80 items and dealing with all aspects of the respondent's life: family background, education, military service, work experience, marital status, hospitalizations, psychological problems, and psychosomatic symptoms. It is easy to fill out and provides an additional source of information and means of validating interview data. It covers mainly facts and experiences and includes a few items asking for feelings and preferences. It was developed and standardized in Israel by Nevo (1976).

CONTACTS WITH SUBJECTS
AND INTERVIEWING PROCEDURE

The first stage of our contact with the subjects was that of informing them of the study and its procedures and eliciting their cooperation. The second stage was that of interviewing and leaving them with additional questionnaires. The third stage involved mail contact regarding the return of the questionnaires, and the fourth stage letters of thanks and feedback from us to the members of the group.

The first contact for most subjects was a brief letter mentioning the 1955 study, telling about the follow-up stage, and asking for cooperation. A form was enclosed with this letter, on which the respondent was asked to indicate the time and place most convenient for him for an interview. The form then had to be mailed back to us. The response to the initial mailing was quite positive. There were no cases of outright refusal, although some people indicated that scheduling the interview would be difficult. The next step was a question of logistics—coordinating the schedules and locations of interviewers and interviewees. The subjects were now located in 51 different localities in Israel, in all parts of the country. Attempts were made to schedule more than one subject living in the same area for one day of interviewing, in order to save travel time. In all, about 10,000 miles were traveled in two years of interviewing.

In the case of subjects being out of the country, a special attempt was made to have them fill out as many of the research instruments as possible. In two cases the structured interview questionnaire, with some modifications, was mailed to them, and they filled it out. In one case the interview was conducted in New York City. In all of these cases contact was maintained by mail and telephone, and excellent cooperation was achieved.

When subjects did not respond to the initial mailing by returning the form, another letter was sent and additional telephone calls made. At this stage, and later on in the process of collecting data, we tried to elicit complete cooperation from the respondents by emphasizing the importance of the study and the need for a complete sample and a complete set of data from each respondent. The interviewer's task was not just to obtain data but also to ensure continued cooperation. This was especially important since the respondent was asked to complete and mail back to the researchers three psychological instruments that were left with him at the end of the interview. Before and after the interview, the purpose of the study and the different procedures had to be explained and many questions answered. The structured interview itself took between an hour and a half and three-and-a-half hours. It was clear that some respondents were looking at this form of "catharsis" and used the interview to talk about themselves freely. Others were more reticent.

In general, the Personal Interview stimulated considerable personal openness. Many individuals responded with a great deal of highly personal and emotional material. The statistical analyses of the material do not seem to do justice to the richness and deeply human quality of what our respondents were telling us. Many of them shared with us the most intimate experiences of their lives, painful past experiences together with their secret hopes and aspirations for the future. Several respondents cried during the interview, when the material was especially painful. The raw material of responses written on the mimeographed Personal Interview forms is moving and impressive, as life stories unfold through a variety of anecdotes and memories. Because we are interested in group comparisons rather than individual profiles, most of this material is reported only indirectly.

In almost all cases the interview took place in the homes of the respondents. The interviewers had to exercise skill, tact, and good judgment in obtaining the best conditions for the interview and ensuring complete cooperation. Conducting an interview at the respondents' homes introduced a number of practical problems that had to be solved: How to ensure privacy and confidentiality? —How to deal with the presence of children?—What to do about a spouse who wants to sit in and listen? The interviewers had to convince the respondents and their families of the importance of keeping uniform arrangements, privacy, and confidentiality, Spouses presented the most difficult problem, being jealous of their right to hear whatever their mate had to tell the interviewer. Due to the respondents' cooperation and the interviewers' tactfulness, these problems were resolved. The respondents as a group showed a great deal of cooperation and hospitality. The interviewers were treated as welcome visitors and offered refreshment and sometimes meals. Only two interviews took place in offices, for reasons of convenience.

Following the end of the structured interview, the respondent was asked, in most cases, to respond to a Sentence Completion form, which was handed to him on the spot. Once the form was completed, which took just a few minutes, the respondent was given an envelope containing the additional instruments—the

MMPI, the biographical questionnaire, and a semantic differential schedule. Detailed instructions were given and questions were answered about the three instruments. An envelope left with the respondents was stamped and addressed to the investigators. They were expected to mail it as soon as possible, but no time limit was given.

Those who returned the completed questionnaires received a form letter expressing our thanks. Those respondents who had not returned the questionnaires one year after the interview were contacted by letter and asked to return the materials as they were, either partially filled out or blank. The eventual rate of return for the questionnaires by mail was around 75%, which was high enough to enable us to use the data in a meaningful way. It is estimated that each respondent had to spend about ten hours in answering both the structured interview and the additional questionnaires. In view of this considerable personal sacrifice, the respondents' cooperation seems outstanding.

There were 13 interviewers, who conducted between two and twenty-five interviews each. They included one of the investigators (BBH), five graduate students in psychology, and seven holders of BA degrees with a psychology major. Training of interviewers included going over all research instruments and procedures, interviewing persons who were not members of the study group, and then sitting in on at least one research interview with one of the more experienced interviewers. Although 90% of the interviews were conducted by the more senior members of the research staff, feedback from interviewees and the overall high level of cooperation seem to indicate that all interviewers performed well in their demanding and delicate role.

Members of the study group were assured of the confidentiality of the information provided by them. The interviewers made a point of not mentioning names of classmates and friends who were in the study group, as a way of demonstrating their discretion. As indicated above, however, some members of the study groups communicated with each other and thus knew about each other's participation. Confidentiality was indeed one of the concerns expressed by the respondents following the interview. As indicated above, there was a great deal of variance in the respondents' reactions during the interview. Some were reluctant to answer questions about personal matters or expressions of feelings. Others treated the interview as an opportunity for ventilating feelings and concerns and admitted that the interview was stimulating and rewarding. Some regarded the interview as an occasion for taking stock of their lives so far. Some showed an amazing degree of openness about personal problems and even asked for advice. It had been expected that a long interview, covering every aspect of the respondent's development and difficulties, would lead some respondents to regard it as a therapeutic exercise, especially when done under the aegis of a university psychology department. Interviewers limited their role to information gathering, listened sympathetically, and when explicitly asked for help referred the respondent to community agencies.

A report containing a general description of the study and most of the findings in Chapter 5 was sent to all participants after the start of the final data analysis. A second report, containing a summary of the findings, was sent to the participants at the conclusion of data analysis.

PARTICIPANTS AND NONPARTICIPANTS— LEVELS OF COOPERATION

Of the 155 members of the study group who had been located, 146 participated in the follow-up study and completed either the whole battery or a part of it. Participants were defined as those who completed the interview or at least one other research instrument. Actually, there was only one case in which a participant did not complete the interview but completed another instrument. Thus, 145 participants were interviewed, 85% of the members of the 1955 study group and over 90% of those members that had been located. The rate of completion for interview and questionnaire contacts was 94% (completion rate equals $\dfrac{\text{interviews}}{\text{eligibles}} \times 100$). The outright refusal rate was 1.3% (only 2 refusals out of 155 eligibles).

The question of cooperation and motivation suggests itself in the cases of those nine members of the study group who were located but did not participate. In three cases the person involved was known to be in a foreign country, but his exact address could not be obtained. In six cases the person was contacted by letter and telephone but chose not to cooperate. Though their number is small, we should look at these cases in the light of any information we have obtained about them. There were four such cases in the kibbutz sample. One was living in Europe as an artist, apparently doing very well, and did not respond to repeated mailings. The second was living in a city, working as a professional, having left the kibbutz a few years earlier. Despite repeated attempts to get in touch with him, he seemed to be actively avoiding the research staff and was described by his neighbors as a "strange character." The third was a kibbutz member, quite active in community affairs, and an army reserve officer who was held in high respect in his unit. Despite our repeated attempts, this man responded with an outright refusal of our requests for cooperation. A fourth member of the kibbutz group was described to us as a diagnosed mental patient who spent most of his time in hospitals and was incapable of cooperating with us.

There were two such cases in the moshav group. One was a man, now living in a large city, extremely busy in an entrepreneurial line of work. He expressed readiness to cooperate, but repeated attempts to schedule him failed. His wife reported on the telephone that he was busy with work. The second case involved a woman, now living in a city, who never responded to our mailings. She was described by members of her former community as a woman who had been dealt hard blows in life, suffered from a serious ailment, and encountered many other difficulties. When we had learned about her problems, we stopped our attempts to contact her, because we did not want to intrude or add to her difficulties.

5

Life Progress
and Psychosocial Adaptation:
Biographical Data

We chose to start our comparison of the two groups by looking at their general adaptation to adult life roles. Examining the biographical data available to us will tell us the story of what has changed in the lives of the respondents during the previous twenty years, since we had last seen them as youngsters. This is one way of assessing psychosocial adaptation. Following Phillips (1968), we will make a distinction between two areas of functioning in which social adaptation can be expressed. They are: "(1) the impersonal world of technological and socioeconomic activities, in which the person acquires an education, develops work skills, and insures the well-being of himself and his dependents, and (2) the world of personal relationships, of intimate contacts with others, which require an abundance of sensitivity and awareness of human motives and an intuitive grasp of the subtleties of human relationships" (p. 4). In this chapter we will report on the two groups in terms of the first area of functioning, the area that is impersonal, or at least relatively impersonal, compared to the second area of functioning, which will be reported on in later chapters. The

Note: This chapter was prepared by Benjamin Beit-Hallahmi, Baruch Nevo, and Albert I. Rabin.

question of "impersonal" psychosocial adaptation involves fulfilling social expectations presented to the individual by his culture. Since in this case we are dealing with two separate subcultures, we should remember that the expectations and their fulfillments are different.

LIFE PROGRESS

The life histories of our subjects since 1955 have developed in the framework of the history of their society, which has involved them in wars and economic and social changes, and the life of their communities, whether kibbutz or moshav, which has affected their individual life histories by determining opportunities for work, education, and marriage. Historical events are reflected in individual experience. Our respondents have taken part in wars and have been wounded, crippled, or widowed as a result. They have taken part in all aspects of the life of the smaller and the greater community and have been involved in all facets of adult life. We found some information on life progress of our subjects in the mass media of Israel, as they contributed to cultural events and cultural productions. Two of our respondents were involved in the translation of well-known books from English to Hebrew. Another got into trouble for writing what was considered by some to be obscene materials. Some of our respondents are looked up to by members of their communities as leaders and heroes. Others lead quiet lives and are mostly followers.

Most of the biographical information presented here was gathered through the Biographical Questionnaire developed and standardized by Nevo (1976). The questionnaire included 80 items and covered basic personal information, information on the parents and their background, the respondent's formal education, work history and current occupation, military service, physical illnesses, and psychosomatic symptoms. It included items dealing not just with facts and life events, but also with feelings, satisfactions, and dissatisfaction with those facts and events. Additional information on life progress and psychosocial adjustment has been taken from the Personal Interview data. The findings reported below present what might be called the "life progress" of individuals in both groups, that is, the extent to which they have moved on to fulfill roles culturally appropriate for their age and sex and their success in coping with both normal and unusual life tasks. The mean age for the kibbutz group was 29.6 and for the moshav group 30.0. There are 47 men (out of the original 57) and 31 women (out of the original 35) in the kibbutz follow-up group, and 40 men (out of 45) and 28 women (out of 34) in the moshav group. Findings in six specific areas are presented below:

1. Present place of residence

The first question involves the "loyalty" of both groups to the kind of community in which they had grown up. We can expect children as they grow up to move away from the communities in which they spent their childhood, and we can especially expect children who grow up in rural communities to move away to the cities. In the case of both the kibbutz and moshav, which are a part of a national settler movement, an effort is made through the educational system to keep children loyal to the communal (in the kibbutz) and the agricultural (in the moshav) ways of life. The problem of second generation "attrition" is considered a special problem in the kibbutz, which has to rely on the kibbutz-born to recruit new members. Our data, shown in Table 5.1, indicate that the two groups in our study have been stable in this respect, with 74% of the kibbutz group still in a kibbutz—but not necessarily the one in which they had grown up—and 66% of the moshav group still in a moshav, but not necessarily the one in which they had grown up. We were also able to ascertain that 41 of the 92 original kibbutz subjects were still living in the kibbutz in which

Table 5.1

Present (1977) and original (1955) place and type of residence for located respondents

Group	Total	Same place	Any kibbutz	Any moshav	City
Kibbutz	83	41	62	2	19
Moshav	72	38	1	47	24
Total	155	79	63	49	43

they had lived in 1955, and 38 of the 79 moshav subjects were still in the same moshav. All these findings seem to indicate a significant degree of stability in both groups.

Members of both groups who had left either form of settlement and now lived in cities were compared in terms of the time since their departure from the original community. No differences were found between the two groups.

The proportion of kibbutz-raised adults who had left the kibbutz in our research group is similar to the one reported by Rosner et al. (1978) in a survey of the second generation in all the kibbutzim. This may be seen as one indication of the representativeness of our sample.

2.   Marital status

In terms of marital status the two groups are almost identical, with the same rates of marriage. Less than a third in each group, mostly members of the youngest subgroup (22–23), are still single. Almost all those who have married, in both groups, are already parents. The average number of children for parents in the kibbutz group was 1.57, with a range of 1 to 4, and the average for the moshav group was 1.66, with a range of 1 to 6. A more extended discussion of marital status and marital life in the two groups is presented in Chapter 7.

3.   Education

There are some differences in the level of formal education achieved by members of the two groups, which can be attributed to historical differences in official educational policies. Formal education in the kibbutz is uniform, and graduation from high school is guaranteed. In the moshav there is a wider spread, with more cases being below 12 grades of school but also more university graduates. This can again be attributed to kibbutz policies in the past, which used to discourage higher education. The result is a slightly higher level of formal education in the moshav group, as shown in Table 5.2. When it comes to the parents' education as reported by their children, the situation is reversed. Kibbutz parents have a higher level of formal education, compared to the moshav parents. In the kibbutz group, 14 out of 78 fathers had some university education, whereas only 3 out of 68 moshav fathers had reached

Table 5.2

Educational attainment in the two groups

Group level	Kibbutz	Moshav
Did not graduate from high school	1	8
High school and postsecondary	69	42
Some university and university graduates	8	16
Unknown	—	2
Total	78	68

that level. This difference points to a historical paradox in the development of the kibbutz and its attitude toward education. The founders of the kibbutz were well-educated radicals who were interested in "downward mobility" for themselves and their children and discouraged formal education beyond high school for the kibbutz-born. While the kibbutz of the 1950s did not encourage formal education for its children, there was a definite emphasis on the value of knowledge and on informal education and cultural enjoyment. The moshav group can be compared to a more traditional rural group, with some upward mobility aspirations.

4.   Occupation and work history

Two separate items asked about satisfaction with one's occupation and about satisfaction with one's current job, which may not be identical with one's occupation. The kibbutz group reports a lower level of satisfaction with present occupation, although the overall rates are high. In terms of work history, differences between the two groups can be linked to differences in the work arrangements of their communities. The kibbutz subjects report a history that included a higher number of jobs compared to the moshav group (3.32 versus 2.47). This can be related to work assignment policies in the kibbutz, which are based on frequent job changes according to the needs of the system. It may lead to a greater degree of dissatisfaction with a present job in the kibbutz, and this is indeed the case, although overall levels of satisfaction are quite high. In the kibbutz group, 80% are satisfied with their present jobs, compared to 92% in the moshav group. We should expect differences in vocational satisfaction between the two groups, because the kibbutz historically has not viewed vocational choice as an individual issue but as a community decision.

Outside the kibbutz, occupation is the major determinant of income and status. The process of occupational choice in early adult development becomes an important or central component of one's identity. In the kibbutz tradition, occupational identity was considered marginal. Historically speaking, the kibbutz until the mid-seventies has not emphasized, and in fact deemphasized, the importance of an occupational identity for its members. The answer the kibbutz has prescribed for the question: "What do you want to do when you grow up?" has traditionally been "Be a kibbutz member." The role of kibbutz member played down occupational specialization. The member was to be ready to do any work necessary for the benefit of the collective. Only with the development of industry in the kibbutz and the general rise in living standards and economic production has this situation changed. But for most of the men in our study who had remained in kibbutzim, defining an occupational identity was not a major task. The young adult was socialized into being a kibbutz member, with an unspecified occupation, ready to take on any task needed by the collective. Our sample of kibbutz members had grown up under these conditions, so that occupational identity for them may not be as salient as for city residents. In a related finding, more members of the moshav group define themselves as professionals, but there are also more who define themselves as farmers. Despite the agricultural image of the kibbutz, it has become highly industrial in recent years, while the moshav has remained agricultural. Thus we have 25 members of the moshav group (including five women out of 68) who define their occupation as agriculture (about one third), while the corresponding figures for the kibbutz are 16 out of 78 (with no women), making up only 20% of the group.

When asked about the reasons that led them to choosing their current occupation (as part of the Personal Interview), there was a marked difference between the two groups. In the kibbutz group, occupation was not regarded as a matter of choice or self-expression, but rather as a result of circumstances. They were doing what the kibbutz had wanted them to do, in most cases, and they regarded this state of affairs as normal and unproblematic. In the moshav group, on the other hand, two kinds of responses were dominant. The first was an expression of taking over from the parents or carrying on the tradition, and this was true in all cases where the respondent was not taking care of the family farm. In a way, there was an implication of circumstances, rather than choice, in these cases, but references to the parents were frequent. There were no references to parental influence or parental occupations in the kibbutz group. The second pattern in the moshav responses was that of choice and individual interest. The aspect of continuity with the parents in occupational choice will be discussed below (Chapter 6).

The respondents were also asked, as part of the Personal Interview, to name what they thought was the ideal occupation for themselves. The results for the two research groups were in keeping with what we have already observed regarding the place of occupational identity in the personality of the kibbutz member. First, only 53 out of 77 kibbutz respondents named an ideal occupation, as compared to 61 out of 68 moshav respondents. This is the only item in the whole study on which we have fewer kibbutz responses. When the occupations by respondents were classified, the clearest difference between the groups emerged in the number of those who regarded agriculture as their ideal occupation, with 22 out of 61 in the moshav group and 11 out of 53 in the kibbutz group naming it (see Table 5.3).

Among those who had left the kibbutz, a variety of present occupations could be found. Very few were in business as entrepreneurs. Most were salaried workers at various levels of responsibility, such as a mechanic, an engineer, a physical education teacher, or a career army officer. Several were involved in university studies at various levels. There were quite a few entrepreneurs among members of the moshav group, both among those who have stayed in a moshav and among those who had left. Despite the basic equality in the historical moshav structure, a moshav farmer can engage in outside businesses and can get ahead of his neighbors by forming partnerships with outsiders. The only wealthy people among our respondents were present and former moshav members.

Table 5.3

Occupations listed as being "ideal" for members of the two groups

Occupations	Kibbutz	Moshav
Agriculture	11	22
Personal service (teaching, social work)	15	11
Technical— administrative	13	8
Artistic— academic	13	9
Medical	1	6
Other (housewife, athlete, driver, etc.)	0	5
Total	53	61

5. Future goals

The interviewees were asked about their goals in life and about their personal goals for the coming year (Items 48 and 49 in the Personal Interview Schedule, Appendix I). Examples for the answers to the questions on goals in life are presented below:

Participant 16, a 22-year-old woman (kibbutz group): "To actualize myself, working in a job I like, job I will identify with. Many children in a happy family. Good life with future husband. Changing the kibbutz in which I live now, and creating a just society."

Participant 2, a 38-year-old man (kibbutz group); "To live in the kibbutz, to have a good life, with a large family."

Participant 3, a 22-year-old woman (kibbutz group): "To have many children, to create a warm family, to have an interesting occupation."

The answers were classified in terms of four areas of accomplishment: self-actualization—being a better person, better educated, and so on—(Table 5.4), family role, economic success (Table 5.5), and contribution to society and community. There were clear differences between the two groups in two areas: self-actualization and economic success.

The same differences were found for the areas mentioned in the goals for the next year, with the kibbutz group more often mentioning self-actualuzation goals (p. $<.01$), and the moshav group more often mentioning economic success (p. $<.01$). These differences can be explained in terms of the ideological background and the current situation of the two groups. Many members of the moshav group can be defined at present as entrepreneurial farmers, and all are on their own economically. Most members of the kibbutz group are still kibbutz members, and, as such, are

Table 5.4

Self-actualization as life goal for the two groups

Group	Kibbutz	Moshav	Total
Mentioned	63 (82%)	45 (66%)	108
Not mentioned	14	23	37
Total	77	68	

Table 5.5

Economic success as a life goal for the two groups

Group	Kibbutz	Moshav	Total
Mentioned	3 (4%)	23 (34%)	26
Not mentioned	74	45	119
Total	77	68	

$\chi^2 = 19.99$

$df = 1$

$p = .000001$

unconcerned both ideologically and practically with economic success—since they enjoy unlimited economic security—and follow an ideology of equality among kibbutz members.

6.   Military service

The respondents were asked to indicate their military rank and their army assignment while in the service. Since in Israel military service is compulsory and most men serve in the military reserves, this could be regarded as a measure of performance in a universal social role. The differences between the two groups in this area are rather remarkable. If we take the rank distribution in the two groups (men and women combined), we find that in the moshav group 18 out of 68 were in the two lowest ranks (private, p.f.c.) while in the kibbutz group the figure is 3 out of 78. If we compare men in the two groups, we see that among kibbutz men 46% were officers and 65% reported holding a command position (that is, a position in which they held command over a group of soldiers either as commissioned or noncommissioned officers), while in the moshav group 27% were officers and 34% held command positions.

A significantly higher proportion of kibbutz men (34 out of 47) took part in actual combat as part of their military career as compared to the moshav men (18 out of 40); 9 out of 47 kibbutz men, and 7 out of 40 moshav men were wounded in the service; 2 kibbutz men and 1 moshav man won military decorations for exceptional valor in combat. When we look at the women in both groups, the picture is more balanced in terms of rank, but kibbutz women are overrepresented in combat units. Table 5.6 gives a detailed picture of military ranks for both groups. These findings are in accordance with other surveys on the performance of the kibbutz-born in the Israeli army (Amir, 1969). All previous surveys have shown kibbutz men to be overrepresented among officers and in combat units. According to Golomb and Katz (1970), kibbutz men (representing about 3% of the Israeli population) make up 25% of the men in volunteer combat units and 50% of fighter pilots in the Israeli Defense Forces. Rosner et al. (1978) reported that 30% of the men in their study of the kibbutz second generation were officers. What is clear in the case of our control group is that this group itself performs above the rate expected of the Israeli population in general. The moshav group seems to be

Table 5.6

Military rank for members of the two groups

| | Kibbutz | | | Moshav | | |
Group rank	Males	Females	Total	Males	Females	Total
Private, Pfc.	0	3	3	7	11	18
Corporal, Sgt.	18	24	42	16	9	25
Sgt. Major	7	1	8	4	1	5
2nd Lt., Lt.	16	0	16	9	5	14
Captain	5	0	5	1	0	1
Unknown	1	3	4	3	2	5
Total	47	31	78	40	28	68

above the population average in rank but is clearly outranked by the kibbutz group, as has been expected. (Table 5.7.)

When asked about what they liked or did not like in their military experiences, both groups seemed quite critical of several aspects of military life. Out of 62 kibbutz respondents who answered questions specifically, 16 found nothing positive in their army experience, compared to 15 out of 54 moshav respondents; 30 kibbutz respondents out of 62, and 20 moshav respondents

Table 5.7

Combat experience for men in the two groups

Group	Kibbutz	Moshav	Total
Present	34	18	52
Absent	13	22	35
Total	47	40	87

Corrected $\chi^2 = 5.62$

$df = 1$

$p < .05$

mentioned the experience of independence and the contact with new people among what they liked about military service.

What is most striking about the findings is that the two groups show a great deal of similarity in their overall functioning. If we look at such indicators as contact with the community that raised them, marital status, education, and work history, it becomes clear that members of the two groups represent what is regarded by their culture as well-functioning adults. They have grown up to fulfill the roles expected of them, and they are doing that with a great deal of competence.

Where we do find differences, however, we are able, in most cases, to relate them to differences in institutional policies and norms in the two communities that had socialized the two groups. The differences in performance in the military service can be definitely related to different group norms, although there has been an attempt to relate them to pysochological differences (Amir, 1969). What Levinson et al. (1978) call the early adult transition, between the ages of 17 and 23, is in Israel institutionalized by the culture, with universal military service being its major component. Almost every member of the study group (there are two exceptions, a kibbutz member rejected for psychiatric reasons and a moshav member rejected for a congenital heart defect) went through 20 to 36 months of military service between the ages of 18 and 22. The military service is both a separation from home and the first chance to prove oneself in the "real world." The role of the military in the life of the young Israeli adult can be compared to the role of college in the life of middle-class American young adults. The question with regard to the better performance of kibbutz men in the military, as measured by rank, is whether this can be explained by psychological and sociological factors. In other words, is there something in the personality of the kibbutz-raised man that makes him more successful in the military, or is it simply a matter of a strong group norm that pushes the kibbutz soldier to serve with distinction?

There are some elements of kibbutz education that may contribute to better adaptation in the military. The emphasis on group solidarity and group living and the experience of living together in a group should contribute to an easier adjustment in the army. Still, Yinon & Freedman (1977) found that city respondents rated higher than kibbutz respondents on measures of social approval and social responsibility. Their conclusion was that these factors cannot be used to explain the better performance of the kibbutz-raised in the military. Another explanation for the special involvement of kibbutz with the military is that it may be a substitute for the missing occupational identity in the life of a kibbutz man. Because the kibbutz does not expect young men to create occupational careers and occupational goals, achievement in the military, which entails reserve duty for long periods and becomes a "second career," may fill this void, and provide a partial identity and an area of individual achievement.* Gerson (1978) suggests that the army is an opportunity for "self-fulfillment" for men of the second generation in the kibbutz.

In trying to offer explanations for the performance of kibbutz men in the military, the context of the relations between the kibbutz and the wider society should be examined.

The kibbutz movement regards military service as the first encounter of the kibbutz youngster with the outside world, an encounter that may draw him away from the kibbutz and will expose him to a host of direct and threatening influences, from the community's point of view. One possible way of averting the risks involved for the kibbutz is through making the kibbutz soldier a representative of his movement and an outstanding serviceman. In this encounter with Israeli society, the only forum where kibbutz and nonkibbutz young men are going to interact so completely, the kibbutz proves its value as a community of the elite, and the kibbutz-raised soldier proves his superiority. In becoming an officer, the kibbutz man is setting himself apart as a model soldier and a representative of his community and thus reduces the forces that would draw him away from the kibbutz.

The findings above regarding the very mixed feelings of the respondents about their military experience seem to support this explanation. The army, in the eyes of the kibbutz-raised adult, is not seen as a major source of satisfaction but mainly as an unpleasant though necessary duty. It is the first chance to be away from home, but also the first opportunity to live in an authoritarian institution, regarded as a necessary evil despite individual success in handling its requirements. It is quite clear that we are dealing here with a multiple causation, and no single explanation can do justice to the phenomenon of the performance of the kibbutz-raised in the military. However, explaining the phenomenon itself is not our concern here. In terms of our study, we can draw two clear conclusions:

*We are indebted to Yoel Yinon for this explanation.

1.   Our group of 78 kibbutz-raised adults is typical and representative of the kibbutz-raised population in this respect, as in all others.
2.   The performance in the military is indicative of the overall effectiveness and adaptiveness of the kibbutz-raised.

The differences in formal education, with the moshav group rating a bit higher than the kibbutz group, are definitely related to the attitude toward formal education in the kibbutz prevalent during the 1950s and 1960s, in contrast to the policies in the moshav. Those differences that are to be expected on the basis of explicit variations in community standards and norms lead us to believe that the groups are indeed representative samples of their respective populations. The differences in formal education, for instance, or in military rank, which are so typical of kibbutz and moshav populations, lead us to assume safely that the two groups are typical in their social and psychological functioning, and that other differences, if obtained, will be related to typical attributes of the two populations. Thus, we may conclude that the two groups, in addition to being essentially made up of stable, well-functioning individuals, are representative of their two respective subcultures.

In the context of the overall study, the findings presented here seem to offer strong support both for the rationale and the findings of the earlier work (Rabin, 1965) on these two groups and for the rationale of the follow-up study. The logic of choosing these two groups for comparison holds up very well twenty years after the original field work. It was assumed back in 1955 that the kibbutz and the moshav presented essential similarities, together with the crucial difference in family functioning and child rearing. It was expected then that this crucial difference would bring about specified differences in personality functioning, but that overall personal effectiveness would be similar. The follow-up data presented here also give some support to the earlier (Rabin, 1965) findings, which showed the two groups to be more similar than dissimilar. χ^2 tests showed no significant differences on sex, age, marital status, and number of years away from original community for members of our two follow-up samples.

The groups are in actuality matched on the variables of sex, age, marital status, and education, as shown in Table 5.8, which enables us now to continue with our task of comparing them on a variety of psychological variables.

Table 5.8

Demographic characteristics of the two research samples

	Kibbutz	*Moshav*
N	78	68
Age (mean)	29.6	30.5
% male	60	56
% female	40	44
% single	30	27
% married	66	70
% widowed, divorced	4	3
Education (mean years)	12.6	12.3
Living in cities	24	31

6

Adults and Their Parents:
Past Memories
and Present Attachments

Looking at the relationships between grown-up children and their parents takes us necessarily beyond the boundaries of the present and the visible. Ties between generations carry within them memories and perceptions of the past, layers upon layers of accumulated experiences, feelings, and wishes originating at different points in intergenerational history. Thus the relationships between adults and their parents have to involve feelings about the whole family of origin, feelings about childhood, memories— pleasant and painful—of other times, and attitudes toward the role of the family and the role of parents, children, and siblings. The connections between childhood experiences and later family relations have not been widely explored, and studies examining the effects of socialization on the relations between generations usually focus on the period of childhood. There is still no systematic theory dealing with the effects of socialization practices on these relations. We have looked at the possible relationships between socialization practices in the traditional family and in communal child rearing, and certain aspects in the relations of grown-up children with their parents.

Note: This chapter was prepared by Ruth Sharabany, Hannah Kaminer, Benjamin Beit-Hallahmi, & Albert I. Rabin. Based in part on Kaminer (1979).

In the traditional family, the parents play a dual role: they are loving and nurturant and satisfy the child's needs, and at the same time limit, punish, and threaten the satisfaction of the same needs. The balance between the two functions leads to the attachment to the parents and to identification with them (Fenichel, 1945).

The kibbutz child lives in two separate and concurrent worlds. One is the family unit, where the child spends a short time during the day, in a personal and unique interaction. The other is the children's house, where the child is among peers and his interaction with adults is discontinuous, less personal, and less often unique (Rabin, 1965). This division of authority and responsibility in child rearing raises questions about the quality of interpersonal relations the child is likely to develop, especially with his parents. In this study we have had the first opportunity of its kind to examine the effects of communal child rearing on interpersonal contacts in adult life. In this chapter we will report on three aspects of the relationship with the parents: the perception of parents, the nature of attachment to parents, and the degree of identification with them.

The analysis and understanding of relations between parents and their grown-up children are informed by theories and studies dealing with the same relations in childhood. This clearly stems from our preliminary assumption that early experience determines to a large extent the nature of later interpersonal relations. This view, relying on psychoanalytic thinking, states that mother–child ties in childhood are a prototype of future relations, and traumas during the early period have a crucial effect on later functioning (Freud, 1915).

The comparison between the kibbutz-raised and the moshav-raised groups will enable us to see whether the special characteristics of parent–child relationships in the kibbutz do affect relations among parents and children in adulthood. First, we assume that kibbutz parents are more permissive in their contacts with their children, since other people take on the role of disciplinarians. The question is whether kibbutz parents have been perceived in this way, and what effect this perception will have on their relations with their children. If indeed kibbutz parents are more permissive and accepting, compared to parents in the traditional family, what kind of emotional ties would that create? The fact that the time spent with the parents is devoted to pleasurable activity, with the child at the center, may reinforce the ties between children and parents and lead to a positive perception of the parents. At the same time, transferring socializing functions to other individuals and the daily separation from the parents may lead to a feeling of distance, or may even be interpreted as a rejection, which could diminish the emotional ties between parents and children. In the moshav group, the fact that the parents are also the disciplinarians would create a more ambivalent perception, together with deeper emotional ties. An important issue is that of the possible effects of separating the socialization functions in the kibbutz on identification with parents. Will identification with the parents in adulthood be less intense because of the diffusion of relations over a large number of significant others? The evidence based on studying kibbutz children (Rabin, 1965) seems to answer this question in the affirmative.

EARLY ATTACHMENT AND IDENTIFICATION IN COMMUNAL CHILD REARING

Previous observations showed that during the first six months of the child's life, the kibbutz mother spends with her baby an amount of time equivalent to that of a city mother. The main difference is during the night, when the baby sleeps in the infants' house (Gewirtz, 1965). During these six months, the mother is a primary caretaker, but not the only one (see Chapter 2). After the age of six months, the metapelet is the primary caretaker, and contacts between baby and mother are limited to a few hours a day. The question is whether these conditions, under which the mother stops her intensive caretaking during a crucial period of infancy, will prevent a strong attachment from forming, or will at least disrupt the normal process of attachment. Will the nature of attachment be affected by the daily experience of separation? In an attempt to answer this question, Maccoby and Feldman (1972) carried out a study in which the quality of early attachment was tested. They hypothesized that kibbutz children aged 30 months would be less upset over being separated from their mothers than American children. The findings did not support this hypothesis. There was a great deal of similarity in the responses of children in the two groups, and kibbutz children did not display less attachment behavior in this case. Fox (1977) reported similar findings. In a study that was designed to examine the effect of multiple caretakers on emotional development, Fox tested reactions of kibbutz children between the ages of 8 and 24 months to separation and meeting with the mother and the metapelet, separately and together. The findings showed that for most children the mother and the metapelet were interchangeable attachment figures. The child's protest following separation did not differentiate between the mother and the metapelet. At the same time, a number of children were still troubled after being reunited with the metapelet. These two studies clearly indicate that the formation of attachment does take place, despite the diffusion in object relations. The question of the nature of the attachment and the effects of frequent separations still remains.

The discussion so far, regarding the nature of early attachment in the kibbutz, would lead us to believe that the nature of later attachments is going to reflect the complexity of the early situation. The division of attachments among several objects and the constant movement between the two social worlds of the kibbutz child may lead to what Rabin (1965) has suggested: a moderation and diffusion in all relationships, including those with the parents.

The fact that parents are no longer responsible for discipline removes the inevitable ambivalence usually directed at socializers. One might say, in agreement with Krasilowsky et al. (1972), that the kibbutz relieves parents of some of their responsibilities and actually assumes a parental role! The moshav structure does not relieve parents of any of their responsibilities, and thus the parental role in the moshav is more complex and more demanding. Arguments and conflicts around discipline are infrequent among kibbutz parents and their children, and the times spent together are usually pleasant and leisure-oriented (Talmon-Garber, 1954, 1970). The time periods spent with the children have a different quality in the kibbutz because of two factors (Gerson, 1966):

1.   during these times all activities are child oriented, and no other activity takes place;
2.   starting at an early age, the father is always involved and is active in taking care of the children.

Spiro (1958) reported that teachers and metaplot were perceived by children as the ones responsible for discipline, while parents are viewed as rewarding. Devereux et al. (1974), in a comparative study of socialization practices in the kibbutz and in the city, found that kibbutz children reported a lower involvement of their parents in discipline. The metapelet and the peer-group were the main disciplinarians. Teachers and parents were seen as supportive. Avgar et al. (1977), in a comparative study of adolescents in the kibbutz, the moshav, and the city, reported that kibbutz parents were seen as the most supportive and the most encouraging of autonomy in their children. Moshav parents were in the median point on the continuum between the kibbutz and the city but still less supportive than kibbutz parents.

The diagram in Figure 6.1 presents the differences between the traditional family and the communal child-rearing system in parental roles and the resulting expected differences in the processes of attachment and identification.

It is important to point out that the kibbutz does not discourage the formation of particular attachments to parents. Unlike in some fictional utopias (for example, Skinner, 1948) the children know quite early in life that the parents mean a great deal more than just adult members of the community. The attachment to the parents is encouraged by the arrangement of visiting hours. Interaction with parents may be quite intensive, despite its seeming limitation. During the two or three hours that parents and children spend together, the parents' total attention is devoted to their children. It is also possible that since physical care is the responsibility of other caretakers, the parents consciously become more concerned about the children's emotional needs (see Gerson, 1978).

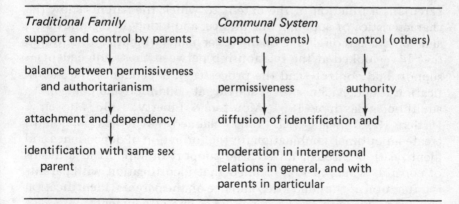

Figure 6.1

Communal and traditional child rearing—parental roles and resulting attachment and identification

Several objective factors reduce the sources of potential conflict among parents and children in the kibbutz. First, the lack of economic dependence of children. Second, the lack of authoritarianism in family relationships. Third, the opportunities for creating emotional ties to other objects. Since the family in the kibbutz is less central and the role of the parents as socializers less dominant, we can also expect less of a taboo against family "disloyalty" and more freedom for kibbutz children to criticize their parents.

The division of socialization tasks among several agents and the diffusion of the child's feelings over many figures in his social environment have a major influence on the identification of the kibbutz child with his parents. Comparing the communal situation with the traditional family situation shows that in the family situation the child identifies mainly with the roles and personalities of the parents. In the kibbutz, identification with teachers and nurses and with peers acts against an exclusive, or an intensive, identification with the parents (Talmon-Garber, 1970). Rabin (1965) referred to this process as "identification diffusion" and suggested that in the kibbutz the child experiences greater diffusion of identification over human objects. Findings in the Rabin (1965) study indicated that kibbutz children showed a lesser degree of identification with the same-sexed parent, when compared with the moshav group.

Most theoretical approaches to socialization in the family agree that the probability that a person would identify with his parents is a function of the extent to which the parents show the characteristics of support, nurturance, and liking on the one hand, and control and discipline on the other hand (Winch, 1962). Studies that have looked at the relationship between these antecedents— support and control—and the processes of dependence and identification found evidence for it starting at childhood and going on to adulthood (Bandura, 1961; Moulton & Liberty, 1966; Mussen & Distler, 1960). Sears et al. (1957) claimed that it was possible to create an optimal combination for the formation of dependence and identification through differential support or support as a means of control. Winch (1962) claimed that identification with parents is a function of the child's dependence on the parents. Identification will be greater with greater dependence and attachment.

Various characteristics of parent behavior should be related to both children's perceptions and identification. We should expect differences among parents in the degree of acceptance behavior (versus rejecting behavior) and in the degree of permissiveness (versus authoritarianism). These differences may in turn be related to the degree and quality of identification. The dimension of permissiveness versus authoritarianism seems most meaningful in differentiating parent behaviors in the traditional family setting from parent behaviors in the communal child-rearing setting. Because the parents in the communal child-rearing system are not the main socializers, we cannot expect them to be very authoritarian. Parents in the moshav families should be expected to be perceived as less permissive. One research question in this chapter concerns the relationship of differences in permissiveness on children's perceptions and children's identification with the parents, when both perception and identification are measured in these children as adults.

The ideology of communal child rearing included the idea that children may be protected from the effects of bad parenting through the involvement of nonfamilial caretakers. According to clinical reports (such as Kaffman, 1972; Nagler, 1963) this is not the case, which may reflect the crucial involvement of the parents in the system, despite all designs to the contrary. Kaffman (1972), on the basis of his clinical experiences with kibbutz families, stated that the importance and the content of parent–child relations in the kibbutz family equal those in the average Western nuclear family. In Minuchin (1974), the analysis of the kibbutz marital interaction shows a pattern that is quite common in Western society: the two partners report on the decisive influence of their respective parents on their personality development and, in turn, on their marital interaction. Each spouse discovers that the original opposite-sex parent is a "phantom partner" in the present marriage —a classical "oedipal" pattern, if there ever was one. The marriage of two kibbutz-raised adults is shown to be no different from that of family-raised Americans: the parents are "excess baggage" being carried over into a new relationship. Nagler (1963), who based his conclusions on clinical work with kibbutz children, claims that the apparent distance between parents and children in the kibbutz does not prevent the parents of disturbed children from remaining the primary objects for sexual and aggressive impulses and the primary objects for identification. Rosner, et al. (1978), in their study of the second generation in the kibbutz, report that members of the second generation rate their parents first in terms of the intensity of social contacts, compared to peers, friends at work, other kibbutz members, and other social groups.

One of the ways in which we have tried to assess the effects of different socialization environments is through the retrospective perceptions of adults. Our expectation was that the kibbutz adults would perceive their parents as more permissive, accepting, and allowing autonomy in their relations with their children, as compared to adults raised in the traditional family, who would perceive their parents as more authoritarian, strict, and restraining. At the same time, we expected that the kibbutz-raised adults would view their parents more positively when compared to the moshav-raised adults. We also expected the emotional ties of the kibbutz-raised adults to their parents to be less intense than is the case with the moshav-raised adults.

In the area of identification, we expected the kibbutz-raised adult to demonstrate a weaker identification with his parents. We expected members of the kibbutz group to see themselves as less similar to their parents than members of the moshav group. The latter would demonstrate a greater degree of identification, expressed in a higher level of perceived similarity. This expectation was related to the presumed diffusion of identification in the social environment of the kibbutz, compared to the focusing or identification on the parents in the traditional family.

Remembering Childhood Attachment

Early memories

In order to differentiate between perceptions of the relationship at the present and in childhood, the respondents were asked to describe their earliest memories with their mothers and fathers. This measure of early memories can be regarded as a projective technique (Ferguson, 1964), since early memories are necessarily selective and reflect a perception of a basic personal stand vis-à-vis significant others. Thus, the early memories were used as early relationships.

Three separate questions were asked to elicit early memories (see Personal Interview, Appendix I). They referred to "your earliest memory," "your earliest memory with mother," and "your earliest memory with father." Thus we could determine whether the parents (or other figures) were mentioned spontaneously and the nature of the memories mentioning each of them.

The earliest memory was claimed by a kibbutz male, who reported remembering his mother's breast, while being nursed by her!

The differences in the early social environments between the two groups were reflected in the other persons who were spontaneously included in the earliest memory. Table 6.1 reports on the distribution of other persons mentioned in the first memory. The kibbutz group reported more memories with no other persons, with both parents (during parental visits), and with peers. The moshav group reported more memories of "mixed" groups, including parents and siblings.

Early memories with the parents were rated by two judges on a 1-to-5 scale. A memory describing an unpleasant event received a score of 1, and a memory describing a pleasant event received a score of 5. A score of 3 was given to a neutral or ambivalent memory.

A three-dimensional analysis of variance was performed on the mean ratings of the two judges.

The difference between the two groups on early memories with the mother was significant at $p < .02$, and their difference on early memories with the father was significant at $p < .05$. In the

Table 6.1

Persons mentioned spontaneously in the earliest memory, for both groups

Group	Kibbutz	Moshav	Total
Self only	32	24	56
"Mixed" (more than one category)	8	14	22
Father	4	4	8
Mother	4	6	10
Both parents	7	0	7
Peers	14	4	18
Total	69	52	121

$x^2 = 14.731$

$df = 6$

$p < .05$

moshav group, more than half the early memories with the mother were rated as pleasant. In the kibbutz group there was an equal proportion of pleasant and unpleasant memories. Regarding early memories with the father, both groups show a tendency to relate mostly unpleasant memories. Still, the kibbutz group had a higher proportion of unpleasant memories and a lower proportion of pleasant memories.

Remembering Childhood

Semantic differential ratings of childhood

We asked our respondents to rate the concepts *MY CHILDHOOD* and *THE PLACE WHERE I GREW UP* as part of our Semantic Differential Schedule. This gave us an opportunity to check the global perception and valuation of childhood experiences and the child-rearing system. Figures 6.2 and 6.3 present the group profiles of the semantic differential ratings. The ratings of the kibbutz group for the two concepts are significantly more negative, which is consistent with the overall difference between the two groups in rating all concepts.

Parent preferences for siblings

The respondents were asked, as part of the Personal Interview, to indicate whether they remember any preferences on the part of either or both parents for one of the children in their family.

A positive parent preference was judged as any case of either a feeling or a clear memory, including any mention of preference except "I don't remember," "No," "Definitely not." Preference was recorded when the respondent reported that he himself was preferred or when other siblings were preferred. Both cases were judged reflecting tensions around parenting in childhood. There was no statistically significant difference between the two groups in the perception of childhood preferences for siblings in the family on the part of the parents. A similar proportion in both groups of more than half the respondents reported such preferences.

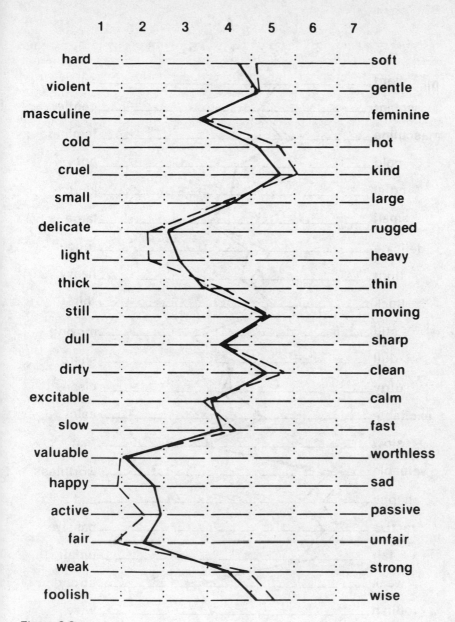

Figure 6.2

Mean profile of ratings for the concept MY CHILDHOOD on the semantic differential for the two groups

(kibbutz: solid line; moshav: dashed line)

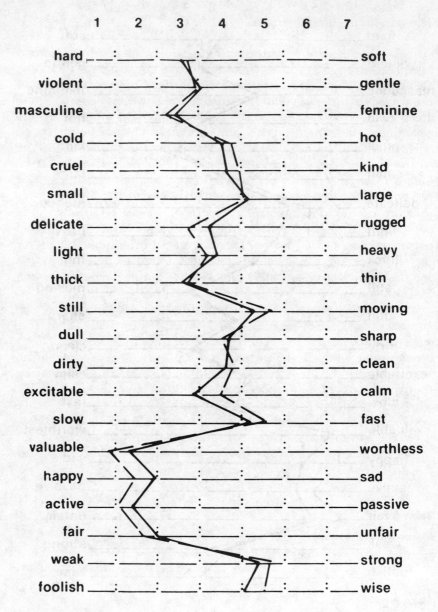

Figure 6.3
Mean profile of ratings for the concept THE PLACE WHERE I GREW UP
on the semantic differential for the two groups

(kibbutz: solid line; moshav: dashed line)

The parents as disciplinarians

Of all items dealing with the ways in which the respondents had been socialized, a Permissiveness Scale was constructed, including all areas in which the respondents reported their perceptions of the ways in which they had been disciplined by their parents. These areas included such things as the parents' emphasis on honesty and cleanliness, their methods of punishment, and their emphasis on performance in school. Replies to the items were rated according to the system suggested by Baumrind's (1971) classification. Two judges rated the replies on a five-point scale, where the parents' behavior was rated as authoritarian (a score of 1), authoritative (a score of 3), or permissive (a score of 5). To test the specific perceptions for each parent, two subscales were created: (1) father permissiveness and (2) mother permissiveness. Interjudge Reliability for the overall Permissiveness Scale was found to be $r = .93$, and for the Father Permissiveness and Mother Permissiveness, .88 and .84, respectively.

Means and standard deviations for each of the measures, in comparison between the two groups, are shown in Table 6.2, where higher scores reflect a higher level of permissiveness. Three-dimensional analysis of variance ($2 \times 3 \times 2$) done on the mean scores on all measures showed that kibbutz-raised adults perceived their parents as more permissive than did the moshav-raised adults, who perceived their parents as more authoritarian. This difference between the two groups was statistically significant at the $p < .0001$.

The differences in the Permissive–Authoritarian Scale for father and mother separated were statistically significant at the $p < .001$. (See Table 6.2.)

Table 6.2

Means and standard deviations on measures of permissiveness

Measure	Kibbutz (n = 75)		Moshav (n = 64)	
	M	SD	M	SD
P Scale	3.08	1.03	2.40	.85
Father P Scale	3.53	1.09	2.94	1.07
Mother P Scale	3.58	.89	2.78	.96

There was an overall sex difference, with women regarding their parents, especially their fathers, as more permissive. The permissiveness scale covered nine areas of parent behavior: punishment for refusal to obey, emphasis on cleanliness, emphasis on honesty, punishment for destructive acts, emphasis on grades in school, attitude to sex and sexual information, general strictness, type of punishment, and emphasis on achievement (based on items 110 and 111 in the Personal Interview, Appendix I). The difference between the two groups was consistent across seven of the nine items. The only areas in which differences were not uniform were sexual attitudes and sex information, where no difference was found in the case of mothers, but kibbutz fathers were more permissive, and emphasis on achievement, where there was no difference between the fathers in the two groups, but kibbutz mothers were more permissive. In no case were either moshav mothers or moshav fathers more permissive in any area.

PRESENT ATTACHMENT TO PARENTS

Present ties between respondents and their parents were measured in two ways:

1. on a scale reflecting an emotional dependence on the parents, referred to as the Attachment Scale;
2. on a global rating by judges of the emotional involvement of the respondent with his parents.

The Attachment Scale was constructed by using the Personal Interview items that dealt with the emotional closeness to the parents. The items included in the Scale deal with the extent to which the respondents turn to their parents to ask for advice or help in making decisions, the extent to which the parents are involved in the respondents' personal problems, and the extent to which the respondents view themselves as being close to the parents. The internal consistency coefficient for the scale was .86, after every item had been rated by two judges. A higher rating on this scale meant a closer tie to the parents. Global ratings by judges were given on the basis of the detailed replies to questions dealing with contact with parents. The ratings were based on the quality of the relationship, as described by the respondents:

whether the relationship is close and intimate, whether there is a real emotional involvement between the respondent and the parents, or whether the relationship seems shallow, without a real closeness. The ratings were on a 1-to-5 scale, from a description of a superficial relationship or no relationship (1) to a description of a close tie (5). Interrater reliability was .91. There was a correlation of .68 between the Attachment Scale and judges' ratings of attachment. A three-dimensional analysis of variance of the Attachment Scale data failed to show any significant statistical effects.

Looking at the judges' ratings for attachment, we found that the moshav group showed a higher level of attachment to the mother. This difference was significant ($p < .04$). There were no significant differences in ratings of attachment to the father. There was a clear sex difference, with women in both groups being more attached to their parents than men. This finding is similar to those obtained in other studies (Troll, 1971).

Valuation of Parents

The valuation of parents was measured by the way in which the respondents evaluated their parents' qualities in the Personal Interview (items 112, 113, Appendix I). Respondents' evaluations were scored in two ways:

1. by counting the number of positive and negative qualities assigned to each parent by the respondent; to control for verbal productivity, statistical analysis took account of the ratio of negative or positive qualities to the total number of qualities listed;
2. by using judges' ratings of the respondents' evaluations.

Judges' ratings were done on a one-to-five scale, from negative to positive (5 was the most positive). These ratings were based on the content of parent evaluations in the Personal Interview. To compare the valuations for the two groups, a three-dimensional analysis of variance was performed. There were no significant differences between the kibbutz and moshav groups on the relative number of positive and negative qualities in the description of the mother. In the case of the father there was a significant difference in the number of positive qualities only, with the kibbutz group listing more qualities than the moshav group ($p < .02$). In comparing the judges' ratings, based on the content of qualities listed by respondents in describing their parents, we found that the mother was evaluated more positively by the moshav group, compared to the kibbutz group ($p < .05$). There was no significant difference in evaluations of the father.

Parent Perception on the Sentence Completion Test (SC)

We looked at the concept of the family on the SC, which included three separate sets of sentence stems, dealing with father, mother, and the family atmosphere. Every set included four sentence stems, such as "Mother and me . . ." or "My family treats me like . . ." (See Appendix III). Responses to the sentence stems were classified as positive, neutral, or negative. Thus, when the stem is "My mother is . . .", the answer "My mother is wonderful" was judged positive, "My mother is 47" was judged neutral, and "My mother is cold" was judged negative. Two judges classified the responses, with the reliability coefficients being .81 for the Mother set, .87 for the Father set, and .63 for the Family set. Mean ratings were computed for each one of the three sets. No significant differences were obtained.

Semantic Differential Descriptions of Parents

Perception of parents was measured by comparing the respondents' ratings of their parents on all semantic differential scales. The ratings of the two groups were also compared on each semantic differential factor and across all scales. The ratings were on a 1-to-7 scale, with the higher scores reflecting more positive perceptions.

For each parent there was an overall mean score, across the 20 scales, and also a mean score for the factors of Evaluation, Potency, and Activity. Statistical analyses were done by a three-dimensional analysis of variance ($2 \times 3 \times 2$). The findings showed that on the concept of *FATHER*, the moshav group gave a more positive description than did the kibbutz group. The difference between the two groups was significant at the $p < .05$. Looking at the three factors, there was a significant difference, in the same direction, on the Evaluation factor and on the Activity factor. The difference on the Potency factor was not significant.

Findings for the concept of *MOTHER* were similar. The

mother was described more positively, across the 20 scales, by the moshav group than by the kibbutz group. This difference was significant at the $p < .02$. There was a similar finding on the Evaluation factor ($p < .01$). On the two other factors there was a similar trend, which was not statistically significant.

Figures 6.4 and 6.5 show the pattern of mean ratings on all 20 scales for the concepts *MOTHER* and *FATHER*. The figures show that the profiles are similar, and that in most cases the moshav group means were more positive.

Identification with Parents

Similarity in socialization

The Personal Interview includes a question on the way in which respondents treated their own children compared to the manner in which they were treated by their own parents (item 110, Appendix I). The similarity in socialization approaches was regarded as a measure of identification, since it is assumed to reflect internalized parental values. Those who describe themselves as similar to their parents in raising children reflect an acceptance of their parents as parents and as models for themselves. On this scale, based on Personal Interview items, there were no differences between the two groups. Members of both groups described themselves as being highly similar to their parents in the way in which they raised their own children.

Identification as Measured by the Semantic Differential

The degree of identification, as reflected in the semantic differential, is based on the difference between the respondent's ratings of self and his ratings for other figures, in this case the parents. Identification with the parents was measured by using the difference (D) between the ratings of the concept *SELF* and the ratings of the concept *MOTHER* and *FATHER* on the 20 scales. A lower D means a higher degree of similarity, and a greater degree of identification. A three-dimensional analysis of variance performed on the D scores showed no significant differences between the two groups. There was a clear sex difference, with women identifying with their mothers and men identifying more with their fathers.

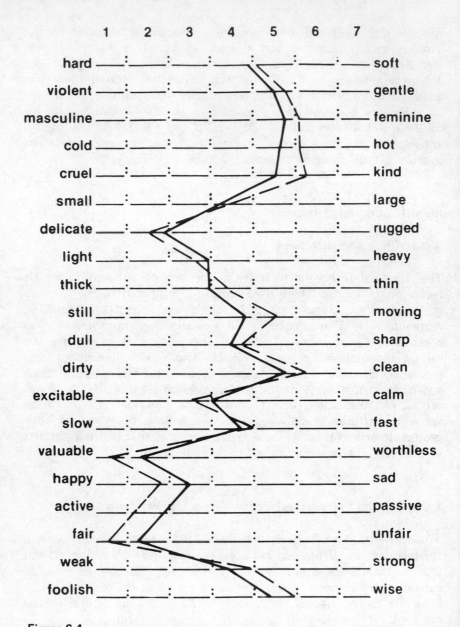

Figure 6.4

Mean profile of ratings for the concept MOTHER on the semantic differential for the two groups

(kibbutz: solid line; moshav: dashed line)

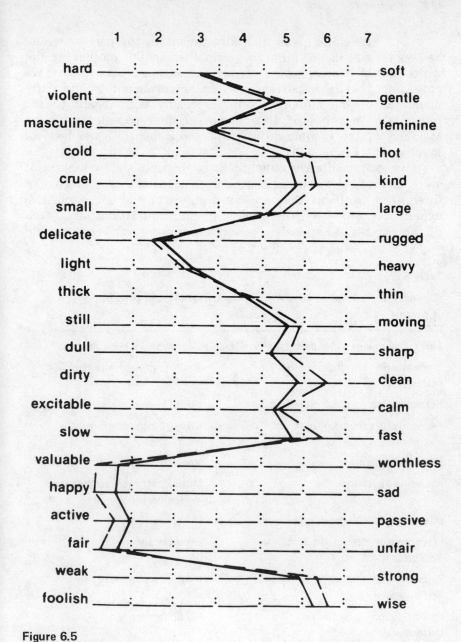

Figure 6.5

Mean profile of ratings for the concept FATHER on the semantic differential for the two groups

(kibbutz: solid line; moshav: dashed line)

Our expectation was that attachment to the parents would be less intense in the kibbutz group than in the moshav group, which would demonstrate a strong and intimate attachment. We have found more negative emotional involvement in the early memories of the kibbutz group, especially with regard to the father. On measures of attachment to their parents as adults, members of the kibbutz group indicated a slightly lower level of involvement. (Table 6.3.)

We examined early attachment retrospectively, by looking at early memories. These memories were from the ages of two or three, and in them the moshav group reported more positive experiences. Moreover, there was a distinctive relationship to each of the parents. The moshav group showed a positive perception

Table 6.3

Summary of findings on attachment, identification, and perception of parents

Early attachment – childhood memories	Moshav more positive
Remembering childhood on Semantic Differential	Kibbutz group more negative
Remembering parental preferences	No difference
Remembering the parents as disciplinarians	Kibbutz parents more permissive
Present Attachment Scale	No difference
Attachment Ratings	More attachment to mother in Moshav group
Evaluation of parents in interview	No difference
Perception of parents on Sentence Completion	No difference
Perception of parents on Semantic Differential	Moshav group more positive
Identification on Semantic Differential	No difference
Identification on parental style	No difference

of the mother, describing her in the memories in pleasant contexts. The kibbutz group reported more unpleasant memories with the mother, but there was also an equal proportion of pleasant ones. The early attachment to the father appears to be problematic in both groups, and most early memories of the father are rated as unpleasant and frustrating in both. It is important to remember that for many of our respondents the period of early childhood coincides with times of armed conflict, in 1947/48 and in 1956, when the fathers were away from home for long periods. Many of the memories included references to war situations. This may explain the negative references to the father, who was less involved in the family.

Our findings lend support to observations by earlier kibbutz researchers (Bettelheim, 1969; Golan, 1961; Rabin, 1965; Spiro, 1953) regarding the possible frustrating experiences of the kibbutz child. The frustrations resulting from child-rearing conditions in the kibbutz include the lack of continuity in a mother figure, frequent separations from the parents, and long periods away from them. The relationship with the parents is not the only one affecting attachment at an early age. The replacement of the metapelet after the first year, and periodical changes later on, once an attachment has been created, are a source of possible frustrations (Rabin, 1965). Those dissappointments and frustrations of the early years are reflected in the early memories of the kibbutz-raised adults. At the same time, we still have a significant number of positive early memories, especially in relation to the mother. This shows that the early contact with the parents is not characterized by frustration only, but also by positive events.

When we look at the findings on present attachment to the parents, we see that members of the moshav group report a slightly closer attachment to the mother. They describe their mothers in terms of expressing more personal involvement (such as caring and warm), and tend to ask for her advice and involve her in their personal problems. These findings were prominent especially in the case of moshav women. In members of the kibbutz group we found evidence for a lesser involvement with the mother, compared to the moshav group. More kibbutz-raised adults describe contacts with her as less intimate. They do not involve her in personal problems, and their descriptions are characterized by the mention of instrumental qualities (such as being a good housewife). At the same time, just as was the case regarding early memories, there is an equal proportion in the kibbutz group of those who describe close attachment to the mother, but there is an overall group difference. There were no differences between the two groups in present attachment to the father. Thus, while the moshav group on the whole reports emotional involvement with both parents, in the kibbutz group the attachment to the father seems stronger.

The finding of a lower level of attachment to the mother can be related to other observations on early experiences in the kibbutz. Spiro (1958) suggested that the early experiences of rejection in the kibbutz teach the child to avoid emotional attachments and reported a lower level of intimacy with parents among kibbutz adolescents. Gerson (1968) reported that kibbutz daughters demonstrated less intimacy in their relationships with their mothers than did moshav and city daughters. Bettleheim (1969) suggested that the kibbutz-raised fail to develop intimate relationships, not because of early frustrations and withdrawal, but because of the lack of opportunity to learn how to form such relationships. He defines an intimate relationship as one of dependence on a single figure, which makes the expression of both positive and negative feelings possible. Since such an experience is impossible in the kibbutz, the ability to form intimate relationships does not develop.

Earlier expectations regarding the supposedly weaker identification with the parents in the kibbutz were not supported in our findings. The fact that there were clear sex differences, with women identifying more with their mothers and men with their fathers, lends credence to our assumption that we have measured a central aspect of identification. The apparent contradiction between our results here and earlier findings in terms of identification with parents among the communally-raised may have to do with the age and the developmental stage of our respondents. While adolescence may be the time of the lowest level of identification with parents and the lowest level of perceived similarity to them, postadolescence and adulthood bring about a change. As people become older, they identify more with their parents and discover more similarities to them in themselves (Beit-Hallahmi, 1973, 1977). The similar level of identification in the two groups on the two measures can be interpreted to mean that kibbutz parents are indeed significant figures in the lives of their children, despite the presence of numerous significant others in early life. The significance of the parents attested to by the identification findings supports the notion of the importance of relations with the parents and their possible effects on other relations.

We have some evidence related to the importance of the parents among other socializers in the Personal Interview responses. The descriptions of the personalities and attributes of parents were equally detailed in the two groups. Kibbutz-raised interviewees made spontaneous references to "close" and "distant" relationships with parents, giving us proof, if we needed it, that this dimension was important to them and that such distinctions were often being made. The importance of parents in the kibbutz was most keenly felt by those who lost them in childhood. All kibbutz adults who lost their parents in childhood mentioned this as a major problem and a painful memory, something that affected them severely. Typical is the earliest memory produced by a kibbutz male: "I remember lying awake at night thinking why I don't have a mother." Similarly, cases of divorce affected kibbutz children severely, by their own testimony (see Gerson, 1978). The pain of loss was felt keenly by all those who lost a parent, and there seems to be no difference in subjective, spontaneous expressions of loss in the two groups.

We had expected that the kibbutz-raised group would regard their parents as more permissive, given the fact that in the kibbutz the parents were not the main disciplinarians. This expectation was specifically supported. The kibbutz parent was described as supportive and permissive and less punitive, compared to the moshav parent. The kibbutz parent was described as not using physical punishment, and putting less pressure on the child in the areas of school performance and responsibility. The moshav parent was described as more strict, using physical punishment, authoritarian, and valuing obedience for its own sake. This description was similar for both mothers and fathers.

Our findings show quite clearly that despite the realistic description of kibbutz parents as more permissive, they are nevertheless perceived by their children in more neutral, or even negative, terms, compared to the way members of the moshav group perceive their own parents. The semantic differential descriptions of the parents were consistently more positive in the moshav group. The kibbutz group produced more neutral or negative descriptions, especially of the mother. The differences between the two groups were significant on the Evaluation factor of the semantic differential, which signifies a good–bad continuum (Helm et al., 1971).

Thus, it can be claimed that members of the moshav group view their parents as more "good" than members of the kibbutz group. We can say that there was a consistent trend in parent perception, and that those perceptions were more positive in the moshav group.

One would expect that more permissive parents would be viewed more positively by their children, because permissiveness would lead to the reduction of ambivalence in parent–child relations. The explanations for this finding may lie in two factors tied to the nature of permissiveness. First, parent permissiveness is tied to a lower level of parental involvement in socialization, and to more psychological distance, or even a perception of neglect on the part of children. Second, if parents are more permissive, this also means that their children feel freer in criticizing them. In the kibbutz culture, the taboo against criticizing parents is minimal or nonexistent. This may contribute to a more balanced, ambivalent, or negative valuation of the parents as individuals. A relevant fact that should be mentioned here is that kibbutz parents are often addressed by their children, and referred to in speech, by their first names, rather than as "father" or "mother." This means that parents are viewed as individuals and not only through their parental roles.

Kagan & Moss (1962) found that children of authoritarian mothers did not criticize them after reaching adulthood. We can surmise that members of the moshav group are more reluctant to express negative feelings about their parents as a result of their more authoritarian upbringing, while kibbutz upbringing has the effect of making children more ready to express negative feelings and criticism.

One indication of feelings about one's parents and one's childhood is one's readiness to assume the role of parent. A problematic childhood may lead to turning away from parenthood; an unsatisfactory childhood may lead to a lack of involvement in intimate relations and to a lack of commitment in adult relationships. While we have some evidence that the generation of kibbutz founders was ambivalent about parenthood and also about its own parents, there is no evidence that the second generation is similarly affected. From our data it is clear that there is no difference between the two groups in their readiness to assume parenthood. If childhood for the kibbutz group was less satisfying, this is not reflected in the readiness of the kibbutz-raised to start their own families. A compensation hypothesis, which would state that those with unsatisfying childhoods would be more interested in parenthood in order to gain vicarious satisfaction through their own children is not supported. Both groups, as reported in Chapter 5, have the same rates of parenthood.

7

Patterns of Interpersonal Attachment: Sociability, Friendship, and Marriage

In this chapter we will attend to differences in styles of interpersonal interaction and involvement as we examine the respon-
tents' patterns of friendship, preferences for friendship, and marital
interaction in their current lives. Our assumption is that the
individual's habitual way of dealing with other people is related
to earlier instances in which he has experienced such interactions.
Since the group has distinctly different social environments as
children and distinctly different opportunities to learn ways of
dealing with interpersonal closeness, we should expect a different
mode of handling interpersonal contacts in members of the two
groups as adults. When studying patterns of interpersonal relations
in the two groups, we have looked at four levels of attachment
and involvement, from the most superficial to the most intimate.
The first level is that of feelings about humanity in general. How
does the individual see all other human beings? Are there any
humans he is attached to from a distance (such as admired leaders)?
The second level is that of sociability, which deals with general

Note: This chapter was prepared by Benjamin Beit-Hallahmi, Ruth Sharabany,
Noga Dana-Engelstein, Albert I. Rabin, and Eliyahu Regev. Based in part on
Dana-Engelstein (1978).

involvement in interpersonal contacts at the less intimate level. How interested is the individual in spending his time with others? How important to him are social occasions? How comfortable does he feel when first meeting strangers? All these have to do with the level of sociability. The third level is that of friendship. Does the individual have a close friend outside his family? How often do they see each other? What do they do together? What do they share? Does the individual confide in his friend? How close is the friendship? These questions have to do with the quality and nature of friendship, which may be very intimate and a very important attachment in the individual's life. The fourth level is that of relations with spouses. This is one relationship in which modern Western culture, which includes both the kibbutz and the moshav subcultures, expects a great deal of closeness and intimacy. The kibbutz marriage can actually serve as a prime example of a modern family, where the focus is on sexual and emotional gratification, after other family functions have been transfered to other groups in the community. What is the nature of closeness and support in the marriage relationship? This question deals with an attachment that is central in the individual's life and reflects his general capacity for interpersonal closeness.

THEORETICAL OVERVIEW

Considering that the kibbutz child-rearing system, starting with the multiple caretaking situation in infancy and continuing through the peer group experiences of childhood and adolescence, does not encourage one-to-one intimacy or make it likely, we should expect a style of cautious approaches to intimacy, limited invest-ment of feelings in one individual, and stronger attachments to groups and group values. If the peer group is the basis for emotional security (as suggested by Bettelheim, 1969), we can assume that it will become a major reference group for the individual member, and also a focus of emotional involvement. Conformity and an emotional involvement with the group do not encourage dyadic relationships, because dyadic relationships mean a commitment to an individual and not the group. The question is whether the two kinds of contacts can coexist. In addition to group pressure, there is another factor that may explain why continuous group contacts may lead to a reduction in intimate relations and that is the factor of fatigue. Middlebrook (1974) suggested that the reaction to excessive social contacts is a flight into aloneness. This may be explained as resulting from a tendency to maintain an optimal level of general stimulation. A person does not want to be alone all the time, but does not want people around him all the time. People may need some time to be alone. Laboratory studies of forced isolation provide support for this assumption. These studies show again and again a tendency for self-isolation and reduced openness (for example, Altman, Taylor, & Wheeler, 1971). It seems that the tactics used in coping with the psychological burden connected with intensive social contacts is that of avoiding emotional involvement with individuals in the group. When members of a group know that they are going to spend a long time together, they may utilize rituals to avoid confrontations and insist on conversation topics that are neutral and impersonal (Hagen, 1961). Thus, it seems that the constant physical presence of peers, which is a part of the kibbutz child-rearing system, may reinforce a tendency to avoid emotional involvement with individual group members. Literature dealing with the kibbutz situation reinforces our conclusions about possible effects of the group on dyadic relationships. The encouragement of cooperation and group ties coincides with the discouragement of close dyadic ties (Golan, 1961). The situational factor of close proximity to the peers may bring about psychological fatigue and the need for being alone (Nagler, 1963). What is implied is the basic contrast between intimacy and group ties, which fosters a tendency toward less intimate social relations.

Bettelheim (1969) states that the fact that the kibbutz child has not experienced the expression of both positive and negative feelings directed toward, and received from, a close, exclusive figure impairs his ability to maintain intimate contacts later on. The alleged tendency of the kibbutz-raised to develop numerous, but more casual, social contacts is explained by Bettelheim as related to the feeling of identity and value only in the company of other group members. The kibbutz-raised do not strive to develop a "personal ego," a separate personal identity, as they grow up, and the lack of "personal ego" leads to the need for the continuous presence of others in order to avoid a feeling of loneliness. This analysis implies an inverse relationship between the two levels of interpersonal relations—intimacy and sociability. Spiro (1958) described a process of "repressing" interpersonal feelings and explained it by the frequent changes in metaplot (nurses) at an early age, which presents the infant with frequent frustrations. In order to survive these frustrations, the infant learns not to become too attached to the metapelet, and then to people in general. Spiro refers to the resulting "syndrome" as the "introversion" of the kibbutz-raised.

Previous research on social responsiveness and sociability in the kibbutz indicated some differences in comparison to control groups. Rabin (1957b) compared kibbutz and moshav infants and found the kibbutz group to be less responsive to social stimuli. This was explained as resulting from the need to adapt to several caretakers and to frequent changes in caretakers. There were no such differences in older children, but the differences were found at the age considered (9–17 months) to be crucial to the development of social interest. Handel (1961) compared kibbutz and city adolescents, using the Q Sort technique to investigate self-concept. The findings showed that the kibbutz adolescents were more anxious in social situations and less expressive of their feelings. He describes the kibbutz adolescents as more sociable and less tolerant of loneliness, while being less open in any social contact. Since the instrument used by Handel was one of self-report, we might conclude that kibbutz adolescents *presented themselves* as less expressive of feelings in interpersonal contact. Jay and Birney (1973) who compared kibbutz and moshav adolescents, reported less anxiety among the kibbutz adolescents around social contacts, a reduced need for social approval, and no differences between the kibbutz and moshav groups in actual social contacts. Ziller (1973) reported that kibbutz children were lower on social interest compared to a matched group of city children. This was interpreted in relation to their tendency to avoid exclusive relationships.

Sharabany (1974) compared intimate friendships in 11- and 12-year-olds in the kibbutz and the city in Israel. The children were asked to give the names of six friends, and to respond to a list of questions about the nature of their relations with the first-named and the sixth-named friend. The results showed that kibbutz children reported a weaker tie with their best friends. In addition to Bettelheim's (1969) hypothesis regarding the emotional "shallowness" of the kibbutz-raised, Sharabany (1974) offered several alternative explanations for the lower level of intimacy in the kibbutz friendships. One is the effect of growing up in a relatively small community, where individuals know each other well, and many behaviors are common. The need to be explicit about feelings and thoughts may be reduced by the communality of experiences. The comparison of kibbutz children to moshav children, who have also been raised in a small community, gives us an opportunity to test this explanation. Another possible factor is that intimacy tends to be reduced in well-crystallized groups. Group cohesion has a reverse relationship to dyadic intimacy in the group (Thibaut & Kelly, 1959; Worthy, et al., 1969).

Sharabany (1974) also found a tendency for reduced exclusiveness in kibbutz friendships. There were more differences in the descriptions of "best friend" and "another friend" among city children, compared to kibbutz children, who showed more similarities in these two figures. It is possible that this finding is related to the diffusion of feelings among many significant others as a result of communal child rearing (Rabin, 1965; Regev, Beit-Hallahmi, & Sharabany, 1980).

VIEWING OTHERS

General View of Humanity

Members of both groups were asked, as part of the Personal Interview (item 69), to rate their views of humans in general. The item was worded as follows:

69. What is your personal philosophy about people in general? What would be your feeling as to the major defects of human nature (i.e., people too mean; too lazy; too sexy)? How should you rank the following items with respect to the degree to which they characterize most people?

    a. Tendency to be mean to others.
    b. Desire for power over others.
    c. Tendency to be lazy.
    d. Preoccupation with sex.

The respondents were required to place the numbers 1, 2, 3, 4 next to each of the options. When the two groups were compared, the order in which these options were ranked was found to be identical. It was b, d, c, a, for kibbutz men, kibbutz women, moshav men, and moshav women. Such a remarkable degree of agreement may reflect general cultural beliefs.

Admiring Others: Independence versus Identification

As part of the first section of the Personal Interview Schedule (item 17), each respondent was asked: "Everybody has some heroes he admires. Who are the three people you admire most?" Less than half our respondents named some admired person, and 80 out of 145 did not name anybody. Those who named admired persons included a variety of figures, from their spouses or members of their families to historical or literary figures. Two men named themselves as the only persons they admired. One was from the kibbutz group, and the other one from the moshav group. What they had in common was being career military officers.

The listing of admired figures gives us a measure of the conscious ego ideal of the respondents and shows a degree of healthy identification with immediate or distant models. Because of the great number of respondents who did not list anybody, this lack of response is of interest. What does the inclusion or the exclusion of admired figures mean, in this context? McClelland (1975) suggested that it is the dependent, "oral" person who is likely to draw strength from admired leaders. Thus, the existence of such figures in one's psychological world may be an indication of dependence, and the absence of such figures can also be regarded as a reflection of cynicism: "There is nobody to admire in this world." When we compared the two groups on the number of cases in which no admired figure was mentioned, no statistically significant difference emerged. The similarity between the two groups in their relative reluctance to name admired figures may reflect a general tendency, typical of Israeli culture, towards counterdependence and cynicism. While the average American can be readily expected to come up with his list of the "ten most admired personalities," usually inspired by the mass media, Israelis tend to be more critical and counterdependent.

SOCIABILITY IN THE TWO GROUPS

The definition of sociability in our study refers to the relative frequency of social contacts and the relative intensity of social activities. In sociability, the emphasis is on quantity and not quality of interaction. contrary to the emphasis in the definition of intimate friendship, and we may assume that the quantity is related to the more superficial nature of contacts. The low sociable respondent is the one who describes himself as having no friends, as not spending time with friends, as one who does not enjoy meeting new people and does not make new friends easily. High sociability is expressed in reporting on a large number of friends, ascribing importance to social contacts and readiness to contribute in social interactions.

Measuring Sociability with Interview Items

In order to measure sociability as a personality trait, a sociability scale was constructed, using items from the Personal Interview. The scale included items dealing with the quantity of social encounters rather than their intensity. The seven items in the final version were (numbers refer to items in the Personal Interview, Appendix I):

27. Do you have a lot of friends?
39. Do you look forward to meeting new people?
40. Do you enjoy having people over to your home?
41. Are you active in social groups?
49. Describe what you did last Saturday (all day).
44. Describe what you did in the past seven evenings.
82. Do you like having many friends?

Reliability of the Sociability Scale was measured by an internal consistency formula (Guilford, 1965) using the correlations between the single items and the scale score. The internal consistency score was .76. There were no significant effects in a three-way ANOVA on the Sociability Scale. Thus, our finding is that the two groups do not differ on this measure.

The Si Scale on the MMPI

The Si Scale of the MMPI, measuring social introversion, contains 70 items dealing with discomfort in social situations, lack of confidence and lack of social participation. There were no significant effects on the Si Scale of the MMPI in a three-way ANOVA, which again indicates no differences between the two groups in sociability.

Anxiety in Interactions with Strangers

Anxiety in interactions with strangers (or new acquaintances) was measured in two questions:

1. Answers to the Personal Interview item 43: "Can you give a detailed description of the last time you went to a gathering of strangers?" Such answers were rated by judges on a scale from 1 (low anxiety) to 5 (high anxiety).
2. Answers to the Personal Interview item 42: "Do you tend to be a bit tense when meeting new people?" These answers were similarly rated by judges, on a scale from 1 to 5.

As shown in Table 7.1, the kibbutz group showed a higher level of anxiety on the first item than the moshav group. This difference was statistically significant ($\chi^2 = 6.94$, $df = 2$, $p < .05$).

Table 7.1

Number of cases in each category on the continuum of "Anxiety in Meeting Strangers"

(Based on Judges' Ratings)

Group	Kibbutz	Moshav	Total
High Anxiety	17	3	20
Medium Anxiety	23	22	45
Low Anxiety	23	19	42
Total	63	44	107

$\chi^2 = 6.94$
$df = 2$
$p < .05$

Note: Only cases where the judges were able to reach a clear decision are included in this table.

There were no significant differences between the two groups on the second item. We might conclude that more members of the kibbutz group tend to show anxiety in interacting with strangers, when asked about it indirectly (in the first item), but when asked about it directly (in the second item), the difference that appeared before has now disappeared.

CLOSE FRIENDSHIP IN THE TWO GROUPS

We will differentiate between the two general levels of face-to-face relations outside the family of origin: one of deep, intimate relations as in close friendship or marriage, and the other of more superficial, more common, social relations. An intimate friendship is exclusive, with two people expressing their deepest feelings, while a sociable relationship is less intense and can be maintained simultaneously with many people, because the emotional involvement is much more limited. Close friendship does imply a readiness to share intimate experiences that would not be shared with nonfriends. The connection between friendship and intimate self-disclosure was demonstrated by Walker and Wright (1976). Also, a connection between feelings of intimacy and closeness and the sharing of secrets was described by Meares (1976), who suggested that some people may even produce false "secrets" to create intimacy. Knapp and Harwood (1977) also found that reciprocal candor was a critical ingredient in friendship, and that the absence of such candor would lead to acquaintanceship, as opposed to friendship.

Intimate friendship is meant to refer to the nature of a relationship with one other person, a best friend, and will be defined by three elements:

1. an emotional closeness reflected in self-disclosure of intimate concerns;
2. an expressed need for emotional closeness;
3. being emotionally involved in the relationship and being concerned about its continuation.

Thus, the definition of intimacy in friendship relies on the quality of the interaction. Lower levels were defined mainly through the lack of readiness for self-exposure in contacts with best friends. Readiness for intimate self-exposure would be expressed through talking about pressing personal problems and recognizing the need for such talks. Capability for intimacy would also be expressed through the intensity of emotional involvement and the concern about relationships. Involvement in intimate friendships was measured in six different ways.

1.   whether the respondent had a "best friend";
2.   scores on an Intimacy Scale measuring closeness with the best friend, based on the structured Personal Interview given all respondents;
3.   the quality of interaction with the best friend, as reported in the Personal Interview;
4.   the quality of interaction with the five closest friends, as reported in the Personal Interview;
5.   evaluations of friendship concepts;
6.   preferences for sociability versus close friendship.

1.   Relationship with Best Friend

Before analyzing the results of the Intimacy Scale scores, we checked to see whether there was a difference between the two groups in the number of those who reported having a best friend. The results are reported in Table 7.2. The difference between

Table 7.2

The number of respondents reporting having a best friend

	Kibbutz	Moshav	Total
No best friend	25	11	36
Having best friend	48	53	101
Total	73	64	137

$x^2 = 5.08$
$df = 1$
$p < .05$

the two groups was found to be statistically significant (below the .05 level). Thus, the moshav group is significantly higher in the number of respondents with best friends.

2. Differences on the Intimacy Scale

The Intimacy Scale was constructed from Personal Interview items dealing with intimate friendship. The ten items of the Intimacy Scale follow (numbers refer to items in the Personal Interview, Appendix I):

28. Who is your best friend (age, place of residence)? How frequent is the contact with the best friend?

29. How important is your best friend compared to members of your family?

30. Describe the contacts with your best friend. What do you do when you get together? What do you talk about? What are your common interests?

31. Every person has personal secrets and intimate experiences which he does not share with most people. Do you share these secrets with your best friend?

32. When you have a problem bothering you, do you share it with your friend?

33. Do you find it important to have a friend that you can open up to?

34. Are there sometimes conflicts between yourself and your best friend which then affect your general mood? (Describe specific examples)

35. Do you feel that you miss this relationship when your friend is away or the relationship stops temporarily?

36. In a list of five closest friends, how was the best friend ranked? (possible ranks: 1. superficial linking, with no mutual commitment. 2. fairly deep contacts, with mutual visits and help, but no intimate sharing; 3. intimate sharing and deep ties.)

38. There are people who find less deep friendships with a great

number of friends sufficient for them (1). On the other hand, there are those who strive for deep and intimate friendships with just a few friends or one close friend (2). Which one do you belong to?

The internal consistency score for the Intimacy Scale, based on the correlations between the individual items and the total scale score (Guilford, 1965), was .92.

Only those respondents who reported having a best friend were included in the analysis of the Intimacy Scale scores. A three-way analysis of variance, according to age group, sex, and kibbutz/moshav, showed a significant difference between the kibbutz and the moshav groups on the Intimacy Scale scores ($p < .005$). The moshav group showed a higher degree of intimacy in the relationship with the best friend compared to the kibbutz. There was also an overall sex difference, with women showing more intimacy than men. There were no age differences. We also checked for the possibility that marital status would affect the formation of intimate relations. No differences between married and nonmarried subjects were found.

3.   Instrumental versus Intimate Contacts with Best Friend

The contacts with the best friend were evaluated on a scale from instrumental contact (1) to intimate contact (5). Examples of responses to this item (item 30 in Personal Interview) are presented below, in an ascending order from more instrumental to more intimate.

Number 57, male, "kibbutz business, work issues";

Number 22, female, "work, my feelings about work, life in the kibbutz, raising our children, my satisfaction from work";

Number 76, male, "personal problems, family, kibbutz, memories of shared experiences";

Number 41, female, "We talk about everything, including the most intimate details of life."

A significant difference was found between the kibbutz and the moshav groups on a χ^2 test when this item was analyzed separately. The findings show that contacts with the best friend are more instrumental than intimate in the kibbutz group, as compared to the moshav group. There was also a significant sex difference, with women showing more intimate contact with their best friends than men.

4.   Perceptions of Best Friends and Friendship

General perception of friends and friendship were assessed in two ways:

1.   the ratings of *MY BEST FRIEND* concept on the semantic differential schedules;
2.   responses to items dealing with friendship on the Sentence Completion Blank.

Perceptions of the best friend were examined through the respondents' ratings of the concept *BY BEST FRIEND* on 20 semantic differential scales. The difference is in the expected direction: the perceptions in the moshav group are significantly more positive than in the kibbutz group. Figure 7.1 presents the two group profiles for the semantic differential ratings of the concept *MY BEST FRIEND*. There were no differences between the two groups on the items dealing with friendship in the Sentence Completion Blank.

5.   Intimacy versus Sociability in the Two Groups

On the last item of the Intimacy Scale, the respondent is asked for his preference between deep relationships with a few people and more superficial relationships with a greater number of people. In other words, he has to choose between what we have called "Intimacy" and what we have called "Sociability." A χ^2 test showed a statistically significant difference between the two groups in answers to this item. More members of the kibbutz group preferred numerous but superficial friendships compared to the moshav group, and more moshav members had "no preference." (Table 7.3.)

There was also a significant sex difference on the question of preference, with more men than women preferring superficial relationships. We can conclude that when given a choice (or when forced to make a choice) between social relationships that are less

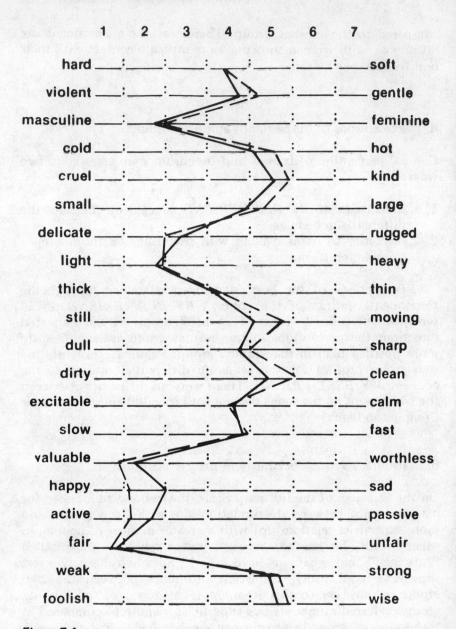

Figure 7.1

Mean profile of ratings for the concept MY BEST FRIEND on the semantic differential for the two groups

(kibbutz: solid line; moshav: dashed line)

Table 7.3

Preference for numerous friendships or for fewer deeper relationships in the two groups

Group	Kibbutz	Moshav	Total
No preference	2	10	12
Numerous, superficial	41	17	58
Few, deep	27	34	61
Total	70	61	131

$x^2 = 15.52$
$df = 2$
$p < .01$

intense but numerous, and social relationships that are deeper and fewer, kibbutz-raised adults prefer the first possibility (sociability). It should be noted, however, that this is a preference given in response to a direct question.

THE NATURE OF MARITAL INTERACTION AND SATISFACTION

The marriage relationship seems to be the most suitable social focus for examining the nature of intimate interactions. Members of both groups belong to a culture that views the family and the married couple as the social unit within which intimacy is not only allowed but encouraged and expected. The moshav subculture preserved the structure and the functions of the traditional family. When the kibbutz family lost its functions in production, in consumption, and in the socialization of children, the intimacy function became even more central and salient. We may assume that members of both groups grew up within subcultures that socialized them to view the marriage relationship as the expected and sanctioned setting for intimacy and mutual emotional support. At the same time, we have observed earlier in this chapter that there are forces in the early experiences of the kibbutz-raised that would act against socialization into exclusive intimacy. We have also observed the presumed effects of these forces in adult behavior, namely in the differences in intimate friendship. This may lead to the expectation that the same forces that led to the creation of different norms of intimate friendship in the kibbutz-raised would lead to a different style of marital interaction, or at least to a difference between the two groups in styles of marital interaction. The marital relationship seems to be an appropriate place to look for the answer to the question of the generality of what we have found above. In other words, is the different style of same-sex friendship that we have found so far in the kibbutz group part of a general interpersonal style? Looking at the marital interactions of both groups seems to be an appropriate way of modifying, or generalizing, our earlier findings.

We have included several measures of marital interaction and feelings about marriage in our various research instruments. Following Gilford and Bengston (1979), we will divide our findings according to two dimensions: *interaction*, namely, the reported behaviors of the marital partners; and *sentiments*, namely the feelings expressed by the partners about each other or the institution of marriage in general.

As we reported above (Chapter 5), the two groups were almost identical with respect to rates of marriage. About two-thirds of the members in both groups were married at the time of the follow-up. Almost all those who were married were also parents, and the average number of children for the parents was quite similar. This indicates that at least in terms of the readiness to enter marriage and to maintain the marital relationship there were no differences between the two groups. The fact that partners remain married and marriages survive, is, of course, no indication of real happiness or marital satisfaction. We have tried to assess the quality of the marital interaction and marital satisfaction in several ways.

Sexual Relations between Spouses

Two Personal Interview questions dealt with the frequency of sexual relations during the first year of marriage and during the current year. The mean number of years since marriage was highly similar for the two groups: 11.21 years for the moshav and 10.81 for the kibbutz. As could be expected, there was a decline in the frequency of sexual intercourse per week from the first year of marriage to the current year. The reported means were as follows: for the first year of marriage, the kibbutz group mean was 3.27 and the moshav group mean was 3.60. Female members of the moshav group reported a mean of 3.90 per week, while moshav males reported a mean of 3.35. Kibbutz females reported a mean of 2.86, and kibbutz males had a mean of 3.48. It is important to remember that no respondents were married to other respondents, so the discrepancies are not unreasonable. The differences between the groups were not statistically significant. With regard to current frequencies of marital sexual intercourse, the picture was quite similar. Again the moshav group reported a higher mean (2.34 vs 2.06 in the kibbutz group), and the moshav females reported the highest frequency, with a mean of 2.76, while moshav males reported a mean of 1.94. In the kibbutz the mean for females was 2.00 and for males 2.09. The differences between the two groups did not reach statistical significance.

Dependency and Sharing in Marriage

To assess the extent of dependency and sharing in the marital pair, we used a group of Personal Interview items dealing with dependency–nurturance items, phrased as follows:

76. When you are stumped by some decision you have to make, what do you usually do? Can you recall the last time such a situation occurred?

77. To whom do you usually go when you want to talk over a problem?

78. How often do you talk over personal things with your parents, love objects, peers, other authority people?

79. What do you do under these conditions:

    a.   Not sure of a certain purchase?

    b.   Don't feel well?

    c.   You are thinking about changing jobs?

The responses to these items were compared in terms of the frequency with which the spouse was mentioned as someone to turn to in times of problems of difficulties. There were no differences between the two groups on any of the items, and the proportions of the respondents turning to their spouses for support in the two groups were identical. Spouses were mentioned more often than anybody else in response to items 77 and 78, which refer to personal difficulties. Respondents in both groups emphasized with the same frequency that the spouse was the person to turn to first with all personal problems and difficulties and the person with whom intimate experiences were shared. The differences between the description of sharing with the best friend and sharing with spouses were rather striking. The two groups showed the same tendency to share difficulties and intimate experiences with their spouses, while sharing with the best friend in the kibbutz group was clearly less intimate.

Sentiments about Marriage

First, on the Sentence Completion Blank, item 22 ("I think that married life is . . .") drew 57% positive responses from the moshav group, but only 39% positive responses from the kibbutz group. This item reflected feelings about marriage in general. On the Personal Interview, two items asked the respondents to list the present strengths and weaknesses of their spouses. Responses to these two items were divided on the basis of the number of personal characteristics mentioned as strengths or weaknesses, as follows: Rank of 5 to replies mentioning only weaknesses, rank of 4 to replies including more weaknesses than strengths, rank of 3 to replies including an equal number of strengths and weaknesses, rank of 2 to replies mentioning more strengths, and rank of 1 to replies mentioning only strengths and no weaknesses. The two groups differed on this measure, with mean ranks of 2.48 for the kibbutz group and 2.11 for the moshav group. A MANOVA test by sex and group showed a significant main effect for group ($F = 5.295$, $df = 1/92$, $p = .024$), showing that the kibbutz group was more critical of spouses.

Expectations from the marital relationship were measured on a special addendum to the interview, which was given to each named respondent to fill out. It included the following instructions:

Individuals have many expectations of their spouses. In your own married life, what is the order of your expectations from your spouse (please rank order the following)? (1 = high.)

sexual satisfaction
affection
emotional security
sharing parenthood
sharing in the economic sphere
maintaining family prestige
respectable and likeable appearance in the community

This addendum was filled out by 42 respondents in the moshav group and 48 in the kibbutz group. The ratings given by members of both groups to each area of the marriage relationship were compared and presented in Table 7.4.

There were sex differences in two areas. Emotional security was ranked higher by women (significant at the .001 level), as was also economic sharing (significant at the .024 level). The first area may represent a cultural difference between men and women. The area of economic sharing does not have the same meaning for members of the two groups. Most respondents from the kibbutz

Table 7.4

Mean ranks expectations from spouse in seven areas of married life, by group

Area	Kibbutz		Moshav		Significance of difference
	M	SD	M	SD	
Sexual satisfaction	2.54	1.66	2.85	1.35	N.S.
Affection	2.39	1.62	2.58	1.26	N.S.
Emotional security	2.91	1.57	2.23	1.42	$^*F = 4.48$
Sharing in parenthood	2.85	1.16	2.85	1.49	N.S.
Economic sharing	5.60	1.55	4.85	1.55	$^*F = 4.33$
Family prestige	5.50	1.21	5.65	1.30	N.S.
Appearance	5.41	1.33	5.62	1.15	N.S.

$^*p < .05$

group still live in kibbutzim, where the family is not an economic unit. For members of the moshav group, the family is definitely an economic unit, and the moshav women are quite active in work on the family farm. This explains both the difference between the groups and the difference between the sexes, because moshav women ranked this area higher than any other group ($M = 4.42$; for kibbutz women $M = 5.07$). The other significant group difference, in rank for emotional security, may reflect a real difference in the way the marriage relationship is thought of. This area represents the largest gap between the two groups. The fact that members of the kibbutz group indicated lower expectations in the area of emotional security may be interpreted as related to their friendship and intimacy styles, described earlier in this chapter.

In summary, we can say that there were no differences between the two groups in terms of the quality of marital interaction, but there were differences in the area of marital sentiments, with the kibbutz group expressing less positive sentiments toward marriage in general and toward their spouses. There is also an indication that their conceptions of interaction in marriage are different, as reflected in some of their expectations.

DISCUSSION

Sociability in the Kibbutz-Raised

In our conceptualization we introduced the differentiation between the level of superficial interpersonal relations with many persons ("Sociability") and the level of close relations with a few persons ("Intimacy"). This differentiation has been made, before the present study, on a theoretical level. Rabin (1965) discussed the moderation of emotional contacts with significant others and the diffusion of these contacts over a large number of figures. Bettelheim (1969) differentiated between the "easy social exchange" that is very common in the kibbutz and intimate contacts, which are not encouraged. We differentiated between "intimacy," defined on the basis of *quality* of interpersonal interaction, and "sociability," defined on the basis of *quantity* of interpersonal interaction. Our expectations were that the kibbutz-raised would demonstrate more sociability, but less intimacy.

What we found at the level of sociability was that the two groups were quite similar in regard to social activities and interest in such activities.

Intimate Friendship in the Kibbutz-Raised

The kibbutz-raised expressed fewer intimate feelings in their contacts with their friends and were rated as less emotionally involved.

All the analyses showed consistently a significant and clear difference between the two groups in terms of intimacy, as defined in this chapter. Kibbutz-raised adults show significantly less emotional closeness to their best friends, as compared to moshav-raised adults, and they prefer more superficial relationships over those in which intimate sharing is central. There were clear differences between the sexes on the intimacy measures, with males showing less readiness to express intimate feelings. The sex differences found on our measures indirectly support their validity and are in agreement with previous findings about the greater involvement of females in friendships (see Strommen, 1977). The question that still remains has to do with the psychological mechanism underlying this interpersonal style.

What is common to theoretical views mentioned so far (Spiro, 1958; Bettelheim, 1969) is the assumption that interpersonal affect, as expressed by the family-raised, is "natural" and "obvious," existing potentially in every individual, and if it does not reach full expression among the kibbutz-raised, it must mean that the original affect is "repressed" or prevented from being expressed in some other way. This assumption may be the result of an "anthropological bias," according to which the behavioral norms of the observer's own culture are obvious and not in need of being explained, and any case of different behavior in another observed culture is a distortion or variation of the original phenomenon, which is then in need of an explanation.

Another possible explanation presented now attempts to respond to the challenge of this possible bias. This explanation is based on an alternative assumption, according to which natural human potential makes possible a moderate affective reaction, closer to what is observed among the communally-raised. Environmental conditions in childhood may intensify this initial moderate affective reaction, causing what is observed among the family-raised. According to this explanation, the communally-raised are not "repressing" their feelings and are not consciously suppressing them, because repression or suppression are possible only for feelings that are already in existence. According to this view, it is the affective intensity of the family-raised that should be explained.

What, then, is the reason for the intensity in interpersonal affect among the family-raised? This explanation sees emotional ambivalence directed to the parents in childhood as the factor that forms a personality with intensive interpersonal affect. Regev, Beit-Hallahmi, and Sharabany (1980) found that family-raised children direct more negative and positive feelings toward members of their family, than do communally-raised children, whose feelings about family members are mostly positive. Devereaux et al. (1974) reported similar results, which contain an allusion to our explanation: family-raised children regard their parents as supportive and disciplining simultaneously, while the communally-raised regard their parents as mainly supportive. The metapelet in the kibbutz is regarded by the children as the disciplinarian, as she takes over most of the disciplinary duties of the parents in the nuclear family. This point is not in dispute: the metapelet in communal education is the frustrating disciplinarian, while the parents are nurturant and supportive (see Gerson, 1978). In the nuclear family, the parents are both frustrating and supportive. We assume that children growing up under both systems are endowed initially with the same potential for negative and positive feelings. Communally-raised children direct most of their negative feelings to the metapelet, who is one of several significant figures, while family-raised children direct both negative and positive feelings toward the most significant figures in their lives—their parents. Negative hostile feelings directed toward supportive figures create guilt feelings, which in turn threaten the emotional integrity of the child. To keep his emotional integrity, the child develops a mechanism of positive, compensatory affect.

Another explanation for the reduced importance or exclusive friendship in the kibbutz has been offered by Spiro (1958), when he suggested that the whole kibbutz community can be regarded as an extended family, because of the decline of the nuclear family in the kibbutz and the transfer of functions to the whole community. This "family" atmosphere may reduce the need for dyadic relations and may increase the overall feelings of security for the individual. This picture is somewhat idealized in emphasizing the positive nature of communal life-sharing. It is still possible, and likely, that the extended family spirit of the kibbutz community will leave room for intimate friendships. We may want to consider another factor that is not as extensive, in terms of the community, as the one mentioned by Spiro, but may be quite significant. This is the security of the small-group situation that is enjoyed by the kibbutz child and in which several peers may be experienced as "good friends," even though no single one is "best friend." The peer group provides a stable environment, directed and protected by attentive adults, which fulfills the child's social needs. In such an environment, the need for an exclusive, intimate friendship may be reduced.

The Quality of Marital Relations in the Kibbutz-Raised

Our findings regarding the quality of interaction in marriage and sentiments about marriage in the two groups indicate that the kibbutz-raised may have a different style of relating in marriage, and that their expectations may be different. It is possible that the "functionless" nuclear family in the kibbutz (Talmon-Garber, 1970) creates different expectations for emotional support. The individual was seen as the problem for a collective, and the satisfaction of individual psychological needs could not be eliminated the way family functions were. Spiro (1956) suggested that the main functions of the marital unit in the kibbutz (since it had lost most of its traditional functions) was to satisfy the need for intimacy. If this is the case, we may hypothesize that kibbutz children were socialized not to expect it in other contexts. The need for intimacy and psychological security was the last function saved for the family and centered in it. One cannot fail but notice that this is the main remaining function for families and marital unions in most modern societies, and in this respect the kibbutz family is a very modern form of the family (see Davis, 1937; Beit-Hallahmi, 1979). This may explain one of the sources of socialization for friendships in the kibbutz and the form of friendship that is typical of the kibbutz-raised. If all intimacy is reserved for the marital couple, then there is not much left for same-sex friends.

A Theoretical Recapitulation —
Socialization for Friendship and Intimacy in the Kibbutz

In our questions about "your best friend" we have tapped a psychological realm of experience dating back to middle childhood, when patterns of friendship are first developed. Our respondents, with few exceptions, responded to the questions about best friends with information about their relationships with persons of the same sex and about the same age as themselves. The Hebrew term we used (*Ha-Haver Ha-tov*) has a clear connotation of a relationship with a peer and is first used in childhood. Theoretically, the formation of friendship in childhood, as a model for later intimacy, was developed by Sullivan (1953), who coined the term "chumship" to describe that early relationship. We have little doubt that we have tapped a psychological process, and a psychological style, which parallels Sullivan's ideas. The concept of *best friend*, for our respondents and for us, brings back experiences of the pre-adolescent stage, as defined by Sullivan (1953). It is during the preadolescent phase of childhood that a chumship, an intimate friendship with a same-sex peer, develops. The chum is a confidant with whom we can share our secrets and whom we can ask for help. The chum, unlike others in the environment, responds to us with support and acceptance. The chumship becomes the prototype of later intimate relationships and is a crucial step in personality development. As Sullivan (1953) describes it (p. 246),

Intimacy ... means ... closeness ... intimacy is that type of situation involving two people which permits validation of all components of personal worth. Validation of personal worth requires a type of relationship which I call collaboration, by which I mean clearly formulated adjustments of one's behavior to the needs of the other person in the pursuit of increasingly identical—that is, more and more nearly mutual—satisfactions. . . . In preadolescence not only do people occupy themselves in moving towards a common, more or less interpersonal objective, such as the success of 'our team,' or the discomfiture of 'our teacher' as they might have done in the juvenile era, but they also specifically and increasingly move toward supplying each other with satisfactions and taking on each other's successes in the maintenance of prestige, status, and all the things which represent freedom from anxiety, or the diminution of anxiety.

Thus, the experience of intimate friendship in preadolescence is a necessary milestone in developing adult interpersonal attachments. Maas (1968) demonstrated the connection between preadolescent chumship experiences and adult intimacy styles. Adults were classified as "warm" or "aloof" in terms of capacities for intimate relationships. It was found that the "warm" group had more enduring chumship relationships during preadolescence (see Mannarino, 1976, 1978a, 1978b).

It is evident that the chumship experience during preadolescence in the kibbutz is different from the chumship experience in the moshav, in two main ways. First, the kibbutz child is already a member of unique and powerful small group of peers with whom he had lived closely for years and with whom he has shared some of the things normally shared with the chum. The most crucial learning in preparation for adult friendship may occur in the peer-group, in the relationship with members of the group, with whom the kibbutz child shares so many of his experiences. We may hypothesize that in a nuclear family the relations with siblings play a role in preparing the individual for close friendship in adulthood, serving as models for close peer relations. In the kibbutz, the peer group experience may set the stage for learning the social role of close friends. The importance of the peer group in the lives of kibbutz children cannot be underestimated. This group can be compared to natural preadolescent groups, but the latter are normally one-sex groups whose activities are independent of the adult world or in opposition to it. The kibbutz peer group is different from the natural preadolescent groupings in that it is made up of both boys and girls and in the amount of control exercised over it by adults. These adults do have definite opinions about the kind of, and the extent of, friendship in these peer groups. The official ideology of friendship in peer groups is part of the general ideology of kibbutz child rearing. As described by Golan (1961), it is ambivalent about exclusive dyadic relationships within the peer group. Such relationships were seen as undermining the feelings of community and cooperation that kibbutz child rearing has adopted among its goals.

Adult styles of friendship and intimacy are developed through these formative stages: infancy, when the first interpersonal attachments are formed; childhood, when same-sex intimate friendship appear for the first time; and adolescence, when heterosexual intimacy appears on the scene.

There are two levels of antecedents that determine the adult style of affiliation: first, the social level of community life and community norms and, second, the level of the individual personality that experiences the concrete results of community norms. In the case of the kibbutz we have a community emphasis on commitment to the group and the discouragement of strong dyadic ties. This explicit ideology creates a structure of socialization that reduces the role of parents in the early experiences of their children, and creates a primacy of the peer group in the child's life. At the individual personality level, what is created is the capacity for sociability, reduced attachment to same-sex friends, and expectations of intimacy from marriage. Our interpretation of the findings in the area of friendship and intimacy is informed by the notion of a socialization into adult friendship style and an ideology of friendship, which is conveyed to members of any culture in the process of growing up. It is also informed by the psychodynamic and interpersonal approach to early interpersonal experiences. Our findings on interpersonal relations in the kibbutz-raised are generally consistent with the psychoanalytic approach, which regards intimate relations in adult life as a generalization of early intimate contacts with the mother. The special pattern of early experiences with the parents and with other significant figures in the communally-raised has created a special adult pattern of intimacy and friendships. These findings are the first obtained with adults who have been communally raised. Previous studies (Regev, 1977; Sharabany, 1974) have obtained similar findings with children of different ages. Thus, we have a consistent picture of continuity from childhood to adulthood in the area of interpersonal relations.

8

Self-presentation, Psychological Distress, and Affective Expressiveness

In the preceding chapters we gave an account of the general adaptation of the two groups, their attachments and interpersonal relations, as well as their attitudes toward significant figures in their lives. Some of the results reported reflect, to a degree, upon personality style as it becomes expressed in the business of everyday living. In contrast, the present chapter concerns more the intrapsychic processes and characteristics of the two groups. We want to go beyond what is immediately visible and overtly noticeable, to enter into the phenomenological world of the respondents and assess their view of themselves and their own capacities. We further assess signs of possible internal stress and strain, which may be characterologically present as indices of conflict. Thus, we are interested in processes underlying the visible external "phenotype."

Specifically, the areas we are looking at are:

1. the valuation of psychological self;
2. the expression of psychological distress in conscious self-presentation;

Note: This chapter was prepared by Benjamin Beit-Hallahmi, Albert I. Rabin, Ruth Sharabany, Noga Dana-Engelstein, and Baruch Nevo.

3.   consistent, unconscious styles of behaving across situations and responses.

To assess these three areas, we are using data from our various research instruments: the semantic differential, the sentence completion blank, the MMPI, the personal interview, and the biographical questionnaire. Several measures based on different instruments are combined to form conclusions in each area.

VIEWING AND VALUING THE SELF

We have asked our respondents to express in various ways, directly and indirectly, their views of themselves in terms of adequacy, their personal past, present, and future. Results for the two groups on measures of self-esteem and self-perception are presented here.

1.   Self-esteem: rating self-adequacy

On the Personal Interview (item 75), respondents were asked specifically to rate themselves on several traits: responsibility, sexual attractiveness, intelligence, and athletic ability. There were no differences on the first three traits between the two groups. On athletic ability the difference was statistically significant, with the kibbutz respondents rating themselves better ($p = .01$).

2.   Self-esteem: satisfactions and dissatisfactions

In another measure of self-esteem the interviewee was asked the following: (items 72, 73, 74, Personal Interview, Appendix I):

72.   What are some of the things about yourself that you are most dissatisfied with?

73.   What are some of the things you are satisfied with?

74.   What would you like to improve in your personality?

This is another measure of how adequate the respondent feels in regard to various areas of personal functioning.

Examples of answers to these items follow, taken from the report on participant 70, a kibbutz woman:

72. "Getting upset too easily, lacking mental balance, does not know how to assert herself, giving up too easily."

73. "Healthy, and keeping her figure after 4 pregnancies, making progress in the area of education, and that gives her a lot of confidence; happy about the opportunity to prove herself."

74. "Achieving a more balanced mental attitude."

The answers to these three items were classified in five content categories. Responses were scored in terms of concerns in any of the categories: social behavior, character, competence and productivity, psychological resilience, and family role. A comparison of the two groups showed that significantly more members of the kibbutz group mentioned being dissatisfied with the area of competence and productivity, as Table 8.1 shows. Members of the kibbutz groups were also significantly less likely to mention their character as an area with which they were satisfied, on item 73. There were no significant differences in any of the other areas listed above. There were no differences on item 74.

3. Semantic differential: self/ideal self discrepancy

On the semantic differential schedule we included the concepts of *SELF* and *IDEAL SELF*. Measuring the gap between self and ideal self concepts has been common in psychological research

Table 8.1

Dissatisfaction in the area of competence and productivity for the groups

Group	Kibbutz	Moshav	Total
Mentioned	44	22	66
Not mentioned	33	46	79
Total	77	68	145

Corrected $\chi^2 = 7.976$
$df = 1$
$p < .01$

as an index of self-esteem and adjustment. There were no differences between the two groups on the self/ideal self discrepancy, as measured by the semantic differential.

4.   Feelings about sex roles

All respondents were asked for their views on the advantages and the disadvantages of the roles of both sexes. These questions were seen as reflecting the individual's basic attitude toward his or her gender, the degree of acceptance of one's biological sex. A negative attitude toward the role of one's own sex may reflect a personal dissatisfaction and not just a general view (items 18, 19, 55, 60, 61 in the Personal Interview; item 74 on the MPPI). Female respondents were asked to express their feelings about childbirth, menstruation, and their memories of the menarche. These items were chosen as reflecting general attitudes toward the feminine role and femininity (items 62, 63 in the Personal Interview).

Overall, there were no major differences between the two groups as the overwhelming majority in both groups accepted their sex and sex roles.

5.   Semantic differential ratings of concept related to the self

Comparing the semantic differential ratings of the two groups over eight concepts gave us a way of assessing their general view of others and themselves. When the two groups were compared on all 8 concepts using a repeated measures design (BALANOVA) a significant effect was found ($F = 13.462$, $df = 1$, $p < .005$). This indicated that there are group differences in the evaluation of the set of eight concepts, with the moshav group providing more positive evaluations of all concepts consistently. Moreover, a planned a priori contrast test showed a highly significant group effect for every single concept (F values for the concepts were: 10.147, 5.399, 5.773, 6.161, 8.276, 6.737, 7.889; $df = 1$; 396; $p < .001$). This means that the general difference between the two groups was also expressed on each one of the concepts. (Figures 8.1, 8.2, and 8.3.)

We have reported earlier on the differences between the two groups in the perceptions of their parents (Chapter 6), their friends (Chapter 7), and their childhood experiences (Chapter 6). In this section we are presenting the group profiles for the concepts *ME, ME AS I WOULD LIKE TO BE* (ideal-self), and *THE FUTURE*.

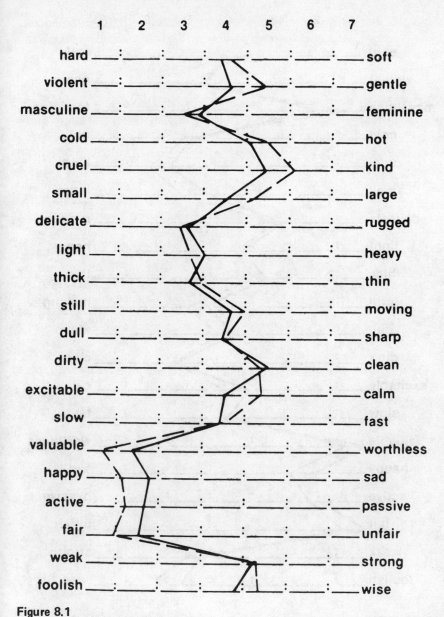

Figure 8.1

Mean profiles of semantic differential ratings on the concept ME for the two groups

(kibbutz: solid line; moshav: dashed line)

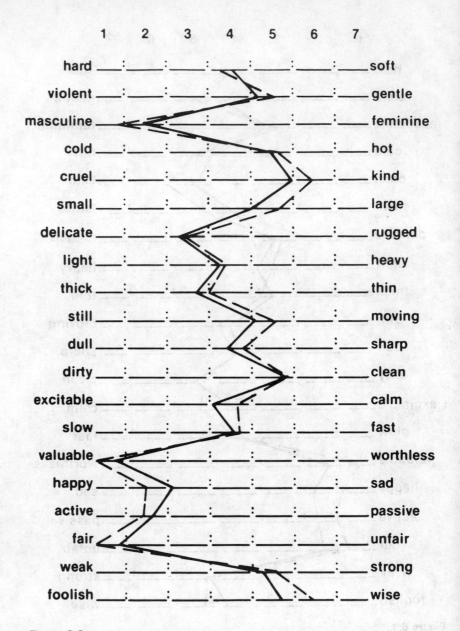

Figure 8.2

Mean profiles of semantic differential ratings on the concept THE WAY I WOULD LIKE TO BE for the two groups

(kibbutz: solid line; moshav: dashed line)

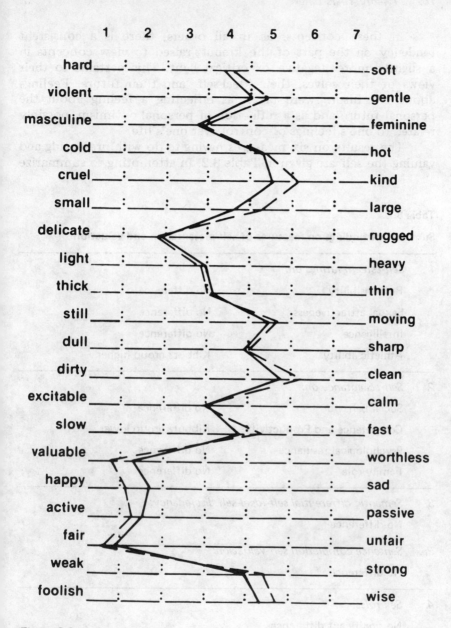

Figure 8.3

Mean profiles of semantic differential ratings on the concept THE FUTURE for the two groups

(kibbutz: solid line; moshav: dashed line)

In these concepts, as in all others, there is a consistent tendency on the part of the kibbutz-raised to view concepts in a slightly more negative or critical light. This pertains to their views of their selves, their ideal-self, and their future. Feelings about the future were taken as reflecting a feeling about the personal future and as a reflection of personal optimism, possibly related to one's feelings of control over one's life.

The results on six measures having to do with presenting and valuing the self are given in Table 8.2. In attempting to summarize

Table 8.2

Summary of findings on measures of self-presentation and valuation

1.	*Self-esteem ratings on:*	
	Responsibility	No difference
	Sexual attractiveness	No difference
	Intelligence	No difference
	Athletic ability	Kibbutz group higher
2	*Self-acceptance on:*	
	Social behavior	No difference
	Competence and Productivity	Kibbutz group lower
	Psychological resilience	No difference
	Family role	No difference
3.	*Semantic differential self-ideal-self discrepancy:*	
	No difference	
3a.	*Sentence completion self-valuation:*	
	No difference	
4.	*Sex roles:*	
	No significant differences	
5.	*Semantic differential ratings of concepts related to the self (ME, ME AS I WOULD LIKE TO BE, THE FUTURE):*	
	Kibbutz group more negative	

the findings presented in Table 8.2, we can say that the kibbutz-raised group is very similar, or even higher, on some aspects of self-esteem, as measured by Personal Interview and Sentence Completion. This group is also significantly more negative on self-ratings on the Semantic Differential concepts.

SELF-REPORTED PSYCHOLOGICAL DISTRESS

Several measures of self-reported psychological distress were used to assess the presence of personal concerns, symptoms, and other indications of difficulties in personal adjustment. Findings from these methods are reported below.

1. MMPI

The proportion of subjects in the two groups that filled out the MMPI was similar. MMPI answer sheets were filled out by 61 (39 male and 22 female) members of the kibbutz group and 59 (36 male and 23 female) members of the moshav group; the answer sheets were scored for the standard clinical and validity scales.

Following the suggestions by Butcher and Tellegen (1978), two sets of mean scores were used for the standard scales: non-K-corrected T scores based on Israeli norms (Butcher & Gur, 1976), and raw scores. Group profiles are presented in Figures 8.4 (males) and 8.5 (females).

What is clear from the figures is that the kibbutz groups score consistently higher on all clinical scales and on Scale F. They score lower on L. Statistical tests (ANOVA) on the mean raw scores found significantly main group effects below the .05 level for scales Pa, Sc, and Ma.

Statistical tests (MANOVA) on the mean T scores showed group effects, significant below the .05 level, for scales F, Pa, Sc, and Ma. When the mean scores for the two groups on all clinical scales were compared to those of the standardization sample used by Butcher & Gur (1976), we found that both groups in our study were lower than the standardization group, made up mostly of city-raised Israeli students in their twenties.

Several analyses of the MMPI were performed:

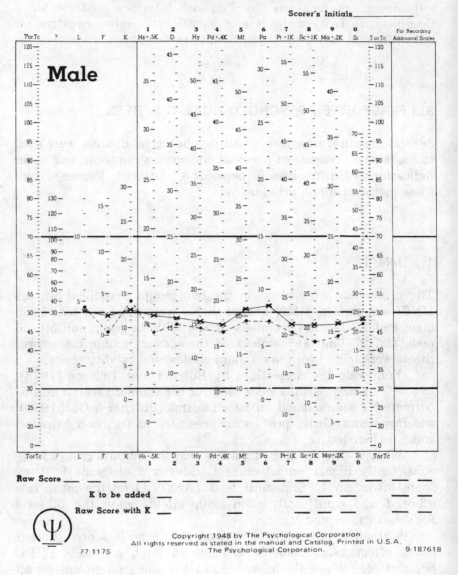

Figure 8.4

Mean MMPI profiles for males in the two groups, using Israeli norms

(kibbutz: solid line; moshav: dashed line)

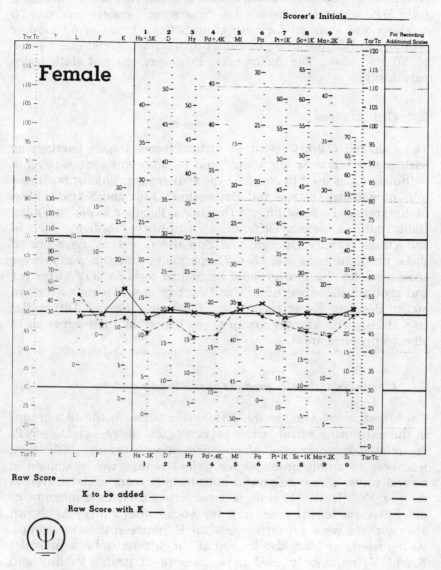

The Minnesota Multiphasic Personality Inventory

Starke R. Hathaway and J. Charnley McKinley

Female

Figure 8.5

Mean MMPI profiles for females in the two groups, using Israeli norms

(kibbutz: solid line; moshav: dashed line)

1.   Scores of 70 and above

A number of profiles in which at least one clinical scale T (excluding scale MF, which is considered a "character" scale) score was 70 or above was counted for both groups. Only 5 out of 59 moshav profiles, and 12 out of 61 kibbutz profiles had at least one T score of 70 or above. The differences, however, are not statistically significant.

2.   Critical items

The Caldwell (1969) list of 69 critical items, largely overlapping with scales F and Sc and considered to represent serious psychopathology, was used to compare the two groups. The list is divided into nine areas: Distress and Depression, Guilt and Suicide, Ideas of Reference, Persecution and Delusions, Peculiar Experiences and Hallucinations, Sexual Difficulties, Authority Problems, Alcohol and Drugs, Family Discord, and Somatic Concerns. Each one of these problem areas was scored separately, and the results were compared for the two groups. Statistical tests (ANOVA) for sex and group differences found significant group differences for two areas: Peculiar Experiences ($p < .044$) and Sexual Difficulties ($p < .016$). The kibbutz group's was higher in these areas, as in all nine problem areas.

3.   Openness and defensiveness as related to distress

The question of whether the differences between the two groups in the expression of subjective psychological distress on the MMPI are related to their level of openness about personal difficulties, readiness to admit problems, or defensiveness, was examined in several ways. There are several built-in indicators of defensiveness on the MMPI. The K scale is most often used as a measure of defensiveness or the tendency for social desirability. As shown above, there were no differences on K between the two groups. As reported, we have also looked at the difference between scales F and K, commonly used as a measure of profile validity and defensiveness (Graham, 1977).

It was decided to estimate the degree of defensiveness in test-taking of both groups. This was done by counting the number of profiles with F-K scores of at least −8. It was found that the proportion of defensive profiles, as defined by this measure, was highly similar in both groups for both sexes. The totals were 68% defensive profiles in the kibbutz group and 65% in the moshav group.

We decided to go one step further and compute the mean F-K scores for both groups. The results showed that the mean F-K score was higher for the moshav group (M = −9.01, SD = 7.65) than for the kibbutz group (M = −5.73, SD = 10.73), which would indicate a higher level of defensiveness in the moshav group, but this difference achieved only marginal statistical significance in a MANOVA Test ($p < .06$). As an additional measure of defensiveness, we scored the MMPI answer sheets for the Denial Scale developed by Haan (1965). There were no significant differences between the two groups, which came very close to the means reported for the original standardization sample reported by Haan.

2.   Symptoms and Psychosomatic Inventory

There were two specific lists of psychosomatic symptoms that the respondents had to check, one in the Personal Interview and one in the Biographical Questionnaire. The psychosomatic inventory in the Personal Interview was taken from Kagan and Moss (1962). It included 27 symptoms (see Appendix 1) such as nightmares, diarrhea, backaches, and stomachaches. This list was read aloud by the interviewer, and the respondent was asked to indicate whether he had had any of the symptoms during the past year. Members of the kibbutz group reported a significantly higher ($M = 3.14$) number of symptoms than members of the moshav group ($M = 2.33$). The difference was statistically significant at $p < .05$. When we looked at specific symptoms on the list, the following picture emerged: the most frequent symptoms in both groups were headaches and backaches, with less than half and more than one third in both groups (29 and 22 out of 66 in the moshav group; 35 and 25 out of 77 in the kibbutz group) reporting headaches and backaches, respectively. The two symptoms that showed the two groups to differ were diarrhea and chest and heart pains; 23 out of 77 kibbutz respondents and 8 out of 66 moshav respondents reported suffering from diarrhea $\chi^2 = 5.589$, $df = 1$, $p < .05$), and 18 out of 77 kibbutz respondents and 4 out of 66 moshav respondents reported chest and heart pains ($\chi^2 = 6.909$, $df = 1, p < .01$).

3.   Anxiety Symptom Checklist

On the Biographical Questionnaire, the respondents were asked to check on a list of fifteen symptoms, taken from checklists used to assess anxiety. They included insomnia, headaches, muscle tremors, fainting spells, and so forth.

When responding to the anxiety symptom checklist, 21 out of 78 kibbutz respondents did not check any symptoms, compared to 26 out of 68 moshav respondents. Among those in both groups who had checked at least one symptom, members of the kibbutz group had a significantly higher mean compared to the moshav group, with a t of 1.99, significant at the .05 level (two-tailed). The range was between 1 and 10 in the kibbutz group, and between 1 and 8 in the moshav group. Table 8.3 presents the means for both groups in the symptom checklists.

The means for both groups on the two lists of psychosomatic symptoms are low, but the differences between them are significant. When these averages are compared to the findings of large-scale surveys of psychiatric symptoms (Srole et al., 1962), it becomes clear that the higher average for the kibbutz group does not reflect a debilitating degree of symptomatology. Rather, it could be interpreted as reflecting a higher anxiety level or a greater readiness to admit to problems, or both.

Table 8.3

Scores on the Symptoms and Psychosomatic Inventory, and on the Anxiety Symptom Checklist, by group

Measure	Kibbutz			Moshav			
	N	Mean	S.D.	N	Mean	S.D.	Difference
Inventory	77	3.14	2.71	66	2.33	1.99	$F = 4.004$ $p < .05$
Checklist	57	2.86	2.42	42	1.90	1.39	$t = 1.99$ $p < .05$

4. Self-reported Psychological Treatment

On the Biographical Questionnaire, respondents were asked whether they had had any kind of psychological treatment or counseling. There was a significant difference between the two groups on this item. More kibbutz respondents reported having had some kind of psychological treatment (27 out of 78, versus 7 out of 68). The greater utilization of psychological services by the kibbutz group may be related to the higher level of anxiety and the higher number of symptoms in that group, or it may be explained on the basis of the greater availability of such services, which are paid for or provided by the community. The population of kibbutz members and the kibbutz-born can be described as being more sensitized to psychological problems and more ready to seek professional help than most other social groups in Israel.

IS THERE A KIBBUTZ PERSONALITY STYLE OF "AFFECTIVE MODERATION" OR "EMOTIONAL INHIBITION"?

Is there a general tendency on the part of the kibbutz-raised to be unemotional, unfeeling, or at least unexpressive? Are there any such specific tendencies toward expressing one kind of feeling and not another? The "emotional inhibition," "repression," or moderations hypotheses assumed a generalization from early experience with a significant other to all later relationships. The early experiences of the kibbutz infant, which are characterized by the lesser availability of one significant, continuous relationship, are assumed to hamper the ability to express feelings. The less consistent relationship with a mother figure means *suppressing* those personal feelings that are a part of all intimate ties. This suppression is generalized to other situations where intimate ties can be expected to develop. It might be suggested that the experience of group living at close quarters would encourage holding strong feelings at bay, for the benefit of adjustment to the group. This later experience would reinforce the tendency toward moderation that was first acquired in childhood.

It has been hypothesized, in connection with the notions of emotional moderation discussed above, that the kibbutz child-rearing system, with its strong group emphasis and group living conditions, strengthens in the kibbutz-born the tendency to avoid free expression of personal feelings, especially if they are likely to create problems for the group; the group experience, which starts very early in life, is central. The group environment encourages a measure of frustration toleration and control over needs that is unusual for young children. It will not encourage an open expression of anxieties and frustrations. At the same time, there are also permissive elements in the kibbutz environment that may moderate the pressure toward repression.

The allegedly inhibited emotional style of the kibbutz-raised may be said to be a reflection of a "response style" or a result of basic emotional "flatness." In the case of a response style, the conception is of feelings being kept suppressed, below the surface. In the case of emotional flatness, the conception is of a general lack of strong feelings.

There have been different theoretical conceptions of the tendency of the kibbutz-raised toward emotional moderation or inhibition. Rabin (1965) pointed to the number of significant others in the child's life as a possible source of affective moderation. Rabin also found a greater degree of instinctual repression and less emotional involvement with family members in the kibbutz group of respondents, when studied as children and adolescents. Another researcher, who dealt with the consequences of frequent changes in caretakers during infancy and suggested the idea of suppression of any deep interpersonal affect, was Spiro (1958). He suggested that the repeated frustrations that are the lot of the kibbutz infant when his metaplot are changed teach him not to become attached to the caretaker and, later on, to other people. He learns to approach any new interpersonal contact with caution, because each such contact contains in it the seeds of repeated disappointment. This, according to Spiro, is the source of what he named the "kibbutz introversion" syndrome that has negative consequences for interpersonal adjustment in the form of avoiding relationships and affective expressions. Another relevant hypothesis is that suggested by Bettelheim (1969), who followed Erikson's (1963) conception of developmental stages. Bettelheim claims that the kibbutz infant experiences fewer frustrations around "mistrust" during his furst year of life, being independent of just one caretaker, and at the same time enjoys a smaller number of "trust" experiences because of the lack of a continuous mother figure. The resulting personality is one that is, on the one hand, less frustrated and therefore less in need of expressing bitterness and frustration and, on the other hand, tending to *avoid* positive and intense emotional attachment. The lack of experience in attachment to one significant figure in infancy is the basis for what Bettelheim calls the "flatness" of the kibbutz personality.

Two studies using the 16PF test found differences between kibbutz and nonkibbutz groups that seem to support the notion of a more reserved emotional tone in the kibbutz population. Zak (1976) compared 73 kibbutz teachers to 129 city teachers, and found that kibbutz-born teachers appeared to be more "introverted." Tal (1978), in a study comparing kibbutz high-school students to city high-school students, found similar indications of introversion and reservedness.

Findings bearing on possible differences between our two research groups in *style* of affective expression are reported in this section. We have tried to pull together all findings drawn from our various instruments that may have some implications in regard to this question.

1. The Repression–Sensitization (R–S) scale of the MMPI

The variable of Repression–Sensitization (Byrne et al., 1963) is a continuum of readiness for emotional expression or the way in which a person handles his own emotionality. At the operational level, repression is defined as follows:

1. Repression is the tendency to avoid the expression of personal feelings.
2. If personal feelings are expressed, they will usually be "positive," since there is a tendency to avoid the expression of anxiety and threat and the mention of weaknesses and past traumas.

Sensitization is the opposite of repression and can be defined as follows:

1. Sensitization is the tendency to express feelings about personal matters to an exaggerated degree.
2. Feelings expressed around personal topics are mainly negative, and there is a tendency to *exaggerate in expressing anxiety, tension, and in relating weaknesses and past traumas.*

There was no significant difference between the two research groups on the Repression–Sensitization scale of the MMPI.

2.   Self-presentation on the Personal Interview Schedule.

Judges' ratings were obtained for the positive and negative qualities included in the respondents' self-descriptions on the self-esteem items on the Personal Interview Schedule (see Appendix 1). Qualities mentioned were rated as instrumental if they were external and neutral, such as "a good housewife," or demonstrated professional competence. A quality was considered personal if it referred to a character trait such as instability, sensitivity, and so forth. A χ^2 showed a significant difference between the two groups on the judges' ratings of instrumental versus personal traits in self-presentation. The moshav group showed more personal traits in their self-presentation than did the kibbutz group ($\chi^2 = 5.48$; $df = 2, p = .024$). (Table 8.4.)

3.   Defensiveness in self-presentation on the Personal Interview Schedule

The presentation of self in the Personal Interview was also rated

Table 8.4

Instrumental versus personal traits in self-presentation in the two groups

Group	Kibbutz	Moshav	Total
More instrumental (ratings 1 + 2)	32	16	48
Equally instrumental and personal	7	15	22
More personal (ratings 4 + 5)	35	31	66
Total	74	62	136

$\chi^2 = 7.48$
$df = 2$
$p < .05$

by judges in terms of overall defensiveness. There were no significant differences on this measure.

4. *Ways of handling hostility in the two groups*

We might hypothesize that if the kibbutz group shares an inter-personal style of "avoidance," that would lead it away from direct expressions of interpersonal hostility. If an "affective moderation" style exists, it should work against the direct expression of hostility, especially if we follow Byrne et al. (1963).

The interview items dealing with hostility and included in our analysis were the following (numbers refer to the item numbers in the Personal Interview, Appendix I):

64. People differ in the situations that make them irritated or angry. What situations tend to anger you? What do you do?

66. Can you recall the last time you were mad or irritated? Why? What did you do?

67. How do you respond to the following situations?

  a. Husband or wife is irritable and nags you.

  b. Child pesters you.

  c. Child won't obey you.

  d. Something you did was a flop.

  e. Friend doesn't invite you to a party.

  g. You're in an argument with someone and the person implies you are stupid.

  h. Competing with someone and you lose.

68. a. Do you ever find yourself suddenly thinking of people you are angry with?

  b. If so, do you think of retaliation?

  c. How do you feel when these thoughts occur?

The answers to the above items were rated by two judges from 0 to 4 on the basis of the level of expression of direct hostility. Reliability was checked by computing Pearson correlation coefficients between the two sets of ratings. The average reliability coefficient for the 12 items was .694. MANOVA tests were performed on the scores for the 12 Hostility items, checking for effects of group (kibbutz versus moshav) and sex. Statistically significant group effects are found only in the case of item 67.c (child won't obey you), with the moshav group having a higher score. Members of the moshav group reported more direct hostility, which may be directly related to their experiences, as both children and parents.

5.   *Findings on friendship styles*

The findings regarding intimate friendship style in the kibbutz group can be viewed as related to the kibbutz "repression" hypothesis. The findings regarding intimate friendship show clearly that members of the kibbutz group report a lesser degree of intimacy with their best friends, as compared to members of the moshav group. One possible explanation for that finding is emotional repression or suppression. The kibbutz-raised adult suppresses feelings in intimate relationships, since he has learned to do that beginning in infancy. The extended presentation and discussion in Chapter 7 can be viewed as reflecting one aspect of kibbutz personality style, where some tendency toward emotional inhibition is evident.

6.   *Findings on the valuation of self and the world*

Findings in this area tend to show the kibbutz group tending slightly more in the direction of Sensitization rather than Repression, to use the terms employed by Byrne (1963). The overall difference on the rating of all concepts on the Semantic Differential Schedule can only be interpreted as reflecting a more negative view of the self and of the other objects. Members of the kibbutz group rated all concepts less positively, including *SELF, IDEAL-SELF, MY CHILDHOOD, MY FUTURE, MY FATHER, MY MOTHER, MY BEST FRIEND*, and *THE PLACE WHERE I GREW UP*.

7.   *Findings on psychological distress in self-presentation*

The findings, presented above, of group differences and similarities on the MMPI seem to go directly against any conception of the kibbutz-raised as "repressors." There are no differences between the two groups on the MMPI measures of defensiveness that could be expected to be a reflection of repressive tendencies. On the other hand, the kibbutz group is higher on all the clinical scales, and members of the kibbutz group show a clear tendency toward "sensitization," in the way they report their psychological distress. The higher scores of the kibbutz group on scale F and on the critical items list also go against any conception of kibbutz "repression" and show them to be quite sensitized, according to the definition, that is, expressing more negative affect.

Similarly, the findings on the two symptom lists can only be interpreted as pointing away from a view of the kibbutz-raised adult as a "sensitizer" when it comes to negative experiences. The fact that the kibbutz-raised are more likely to have had some form of psychological treatment would also place them in the direction of "sensitization." The findings that have a bearing on the question of a "repressive" personality style are summarized in Table 8.5 below.

The mixed results obtained in a comparison of the two groups on measures of Repression–Sensitization as a personality trait may be the outcome of a definition of this trait, which was too broad

Table 8.5

Summary of findings related to possible "affective moderation" as a personality style

1.	R–S scale on the MMPI	No difference
2.	Repression rating in early memories	Kibbutz group more "repressing"
3.	Repression ratings on self-esteem items	Kibbutz group more "repressing"
4.	Ratings of defensiveness on self-esteem items	No difference
5.	Handling hostility	No difference
6.	Intimate friendship style	Kibbutz group less expressive
7.	Valuation of self and others	Kibbutz group more "sensitized"
8.	Psychological distress measures	Kibbutz group more "sensitized"

and unspecific. It is possible that members of the kibbutz group have a tendency toward affective moderation as a consistent trait in specific situations or areas of behavior. The tendency toward affective moderation may be reflected in the style of friendship developed by the kibbutz group and reported above (Chapter 7). It is also possible that the experience of kibbutz child rearing creates only a partial trend toward repression as a personality style.

In terms of the findings presented here, we must reach the following three conclusions:

1. The kibbutz-raised cannot be characterized as "repressors," in the sense suggested by Byrne (1963).
2. There are specific areas, especially having to do with inter-personal relationship, where the kibbutz-raised are less emotionally expressive.
3. The kibbutz-raised do not hesitate to express negative affect and have a tendency to report more personal difficulties. In this sense, they are "sensitiziers" (Byrne et al., 1963).

Overall, the personality differences between the kibbutz and moshav participants are not very striking. There are no major differences in self-esteem, self-evaluation, or sex roles. Although the responses of both groups to the MMPI are well within normal limits, the kibbutz respondents tend to score higher on this test, indicating, perhaps, greater experience of stress. Three scales only showed greater evaluation in the kibbutz group; the Pa scale (greater sensitivity), the Sc scale (interpersonal anxiety), and the Ma scale (higher energy level for life's tasks). The symptom check-lists also pointed to a significantly larger average number of symptoms checked by the kibbutz group. Both groups, however, checked relatively few symptoms. One investigator (Murphy, 1978) found that higher scores on symptom checklists are not so much a reflection of life stress or ego weakness, but of concern with self-actualization, of self-awareness, and of less concern with immediate needs and economic security. This is consistent with the findings concerning self-actualization reported in chapter 5.

9

Our Findings: Summary, Analysis, and Integration

In this chapter our aim is to pull together all the diverse findings concerning our kibbutz and moshav subjects, based on the many hours of testing and interviews to which they were exposed. The conscientious reader who has waded through the data-based reports and theoretical discussions in the previous chapters will, hopefully, find some closure in the present summary. Some readers may have set for themselves the less arduous task of skipping from the first few stage-setting chapters to this one: the outcome of the plot. In addition, the authors themselves found this undertaking useful. It helped us to pull things together and find out what it all means—to try and make sense of it all. Having concluded our own journey through this research project, we are ready to summarize here briefly what we have done, for our own benefit and for that of others. We will go again, step by step, over our research procedure, our findings, and our conclusions.

SUMMARY OF FINDINGS

It may be recalled that the main reason for our embarking on this investigative journey was to assess the long-term effects of communal child-rearing system, as practiced in the Israeli kibbutzim in the 1950s, upon the adult persons who have experienced it in their formative years. The adults we have studied were investigated in 1955 (Rabin, 1965) when they were infants, children, and adolescents. As in the original study, the present one is a comparative one in which persons reared under conditions of communal child rearing (kibbutz) were compared with those reared in the nuclear family setting (moshav). The question arose—if early childhood experience is as important to later personality development as most psychological theories assert, then what would the effects be of the particular variation on Western child-rearing practices represented by the communal (kibbutz) system? Would this system in which infants were cared for mostly by several nonfamilial agents and were constantly surrounded by numbers of peers and significant others produce a unique sort of person? Communal child rearing attracted much attention because of the allegedly limited and discontinuous contact between the infant and young child with his biological mother or her surrogate. However, pointing out the lacunae in the system does not tell the whole story, nor does it provide a full understanding of it. There are aspects of the system, especially the constant effect of the peer group, that are essential for its more complete understanding. We find that it is an articulated system of multiple "mothering" (caretaking) designed to socialize the child into membership in his community through early involvement with, and attachment to, the group. A major task of the infant and young child in the kibbutz setting, then, are the demands for early adaptation to several caretaking figures as well as to the immediate peer group, of which he becomes a member shortly after birth.

Of the original 181 individuals who comprised the "experimental" (kibbutz) and "control" (moshav) groups, 155 were located, and 146 participated in our follow-up project twenty years later.

A multidimensional and multiple instrument approach was employed in the study. We used five research instruments, listed below:

1. the Personal Interview (Appendix I), a structured schedule for a face-to-face interview with each member of the research groups, conducted with 145 participants and taking between 2 and 4 hours;
2. Biographical Questionnaire, including 80 items, filled out by 146 participants on their own and taking up to 45 minutes;

3. a Hebrew version of the MMPI, filled out by 120 subjects on their own, and taking between 2 and 3 hours;
4. a Semantic Differential Schedule, including 8 concepts and 20 rating scales, filled out by 120 participants on their own and taking about 20 minutes;
5. Sentence Completion Blank, including 51 sentence stems, filled out by 126 participants on their own, and taking less than 20 minutes (Appendix II).

The last four instruments were left with the participants following the Personal Interview and mailed by them to the researchers.

The five research instruments provided us with a wealth of data, which were then analyzed not by instrument but by areas of functioning. Thus, for example, information on the participants' relationships with their parents was gleaned from the Personal Interview, the Semantic Differential, and the Sentence Completion Blank.

The findings can be placed under three general rubrics in which differences and similarities between the two groups studied can be conveniently presented. First we will consider the overall life situation of the two groups, their social roles, and their adaptation to them. Secondly, we will summarize the findings in the interpersonal and intrafamilial sphere of social relations. Third, and finally, the "deeper" psychological and intrapsychic characteristics that are relevant to the personality development of our respondents will be considered and discussed.

Overall Adaptation

1. A majority of individuals in both groups, kibbutz and moshav, live in the same type of community in which they had grown up as children.
2. The rates of marriage and parenthood are nearly identical for both groups.
3. As far as educational level is concerned, the levels achieved were quite similar for both groups. A somewhat higher percentage of the university-educated from the moshav reflects some of the earlier restrictions on higher education in the kibbutz movement.

4. Slight differences between the groups with respect to occupational satisfaction were noted. Occupational aspiration differed, due to the traditional kibbutz policy of encouraging "generalists" rather than specialists.
5. Consonant with previous reports, we found that kibbutz members were represented in significantly larger proportions in the officer ranks and in volunteering for combat duty in the Israeli Defense Forces.
6. Although there were some individual differences in the degree of productivity and performance in both groups, the general conclusion would be that the vast majority of both groups are fully-functioning and well-adjusted members of their communities.
7. Within the kibbutz-raised group itself, the 19 members who no longer lived in the type of community in which they had grown up did not differ markedly from those remaining with respect to general adaptation. They seemed to cope well in other social settings.

The Interpersonal Realm

Considering the early differences in the patterns of intrafamilial relationships, we were interested in investigating possible parallel differences between the groups once they had reached adult status. In addition to the attitudes and relationships to parental figures, the research led us naturally to the exploration of interactions and relationships with others beyond the family of origin.

Some of the relevant findings are summarized in the following statements:

1. Moshav-raised adults more often evaluate their childhood in positive terms than do their kibbutz counterparts. Furthermore, the moshav-raised tend to respond with more positive early memories of their parents than do the kibbutz respondents.
2. The latter point is quite interesting in view of the fact that the kibbutz group's memories clearly indicate greater permissiveness on the part of their parents, as compared with the moshav controls.

3. As adults, the moshav-raised also seem to view their parents in more positive terms than does the kibbutz group (who tend to be more critical); moreover, they also indicate a greater degree of attachment to their parents. This, of course, is not at all surprising in view of the early encouragement and later cultivation of independence of the children in the communal child-rearing system.

4. Interestingly enough, despite the findings discussed above, there are no differences between the kibbutz and moshav-raised adults in the extent of identification with the parents. The young parents in both groups report parenting practices very similar to those they themselves experienced as children.

5. Outside the family setting there are differences that are worthy of note in the formation of friendship. A somewhat smaller proportion of kibbutz respondents have a "best friend" with whom they have a close relationship and emotional attachment. More kibbutz respondents, as compared with those from the moshav, are interested in more instrumentally oriented and casual friendships. Conversely, more moshav respondents profess deeper and greater emotional involvements in friendships.

6. In many areas there are no differences in the marital adjustment and relationships between the two groups. There is some evidence, however, that kibbutz members tend to be more critical of their spouses and, generally, more critical of the institution of marriage.

Some Personality Variables

Finally, a summary of a number of characteristics generally placed under the rubric of "personality" is in order. We were particularly interested in comparing the groups with respect to their "internal adaptation" as contrasted with evidence of "external" and interpersonal adaptation considered in the previous sections. Brief concluding statements about those dimensions appear below.

1. On standardized measures of overall mental health (or pathology), the indications are that both groups are well and show up better than Israelis in general.

2.　There does not seem to be any marked difference between the groups with respect to self-esteem.

3.　Kibbutz respondents tend to describe themselves as more anxious than those of moshav. Moreover, they report greater frequencies of physical symptoms and illness.

4.　There seems to be a general difference in evaluative style. Kibbutz respondents tend to view themselves and others in less positive terms than do the moshav-raised participants.

Overall, both groups appear to be psychologically healthy, with the kibbutz group exhibiting a somewhat less positive and optimistic style in most response situations.

Table 9.1 summarizes the findings, presenting comparisons between the two groups on 66 specific measures. Of those, we have found statistically significant differences on 28 measures. This means that on more than half the measures we had no differences. In most cases the two groups were more similar than dissimilar. In those cases where differences were found, the question is that of their direction and meaning. Is there any consistency in all the differences found? Are the kibbutz-raised consistently different, or are the differences unsystematic and haphazard?

The results show that despite an overall similarity between the two groups, there are also subtle psychological differences, which may reflect the long-term effects of early experiences. Members of the kibbutz-raised group differ in their relationships with others and in the ways in which they present themselves to the world.

There are few differences between the two groups in overall social adaptation, but more differences in close relationships with parents, friends, and spouses. The communally-raised also report a higher level of psychological distress. What do the findings mean in terms of previous hypotheses regarding the possible effects of communal child rearing?

Table 9.2 presents a list of common hypotheses, taken from the literature, regarding the effects of communal child rearing as it was reflected in communally-raised adults and the support given to these hypotheses by our findings.

Table 9.1

Summary of comparisons between the two groups

Psychosocial adaptation

Present community of resisdence, compared to 1955	No difference
Marital status	No difference
Parenthood rates	No difference
Number of children	No difference
Education level	No difference
Occupational satisfaction	Similar
Choice of ideal occupation	Different
Self-actualization as a life-goal	Kibbutz group higher
Family role as a life goal	No difference
Economic success as a life goal	Moshav group higher
Contribution to society and community as a life goal	No difference
Military rank	Kibbutz group higher

Relations with parents

Early memories with parents	Moshav group more positive
Remembering parental preferences for siblings	No difference
Remembering parents as disciplinarians	Kibbutz parents more permissive
Rating CHILDHOOD on semantic differential	Moshav group more positive
Evaluating parents in Personal Interview	No difference
Evaluating parents on Sentence Completion	No difference
Rating parents on semantic differential	Moshav group more positive
Identification with parents on semantic differential	No difference

(continued)

Table 9.1 (continued)

Identification with parents on parental style	No difference
Present attachment scale	No difference
Present attachment ratings	More attachment to mother in Moshav group

Interpersonal attachments

Views on humanity in general	No difference
Self-report on admired figures	No difference
Sociability scale	No difference
Si scale of the MMPI	No difference
Ratings of anxiety in interaction with strangers	Kibbutz group higher
Self-report of anxiety in interaction with strangers	No difference
Having a best friend	Moshav group higher
Intimacy (in friendship) scale	Moshav group higher
Emotional contact with best friend	Moshav group higher
Closeness of contacts with five friends	Moshav group higher
Ratings of best friend on semantic differential	Moshav group more positive
Preference for close friendship	Moshav group higher
Dependency in marriage	No difference
Evaluation of marriage	Moshav group more positive
Evaluation of spouses	Moshav group more positive

Self-Esteem

Self esteem ratings on:

Responsibility	No difference
Sexual attractiveness	No difference
Intelligence	No difference
Athletic ability	Kibbutz group higher

Self-acceptance on:

Social behavior	No difference
Character	Kibbutz group higher
Competence and Productivity	Kibbutz group lower
Psychological resilience	No difference
Family role	No difference
Semantic differential self-ideal-self discrepancy	No difference
Sentence completion self-valuation	No difference
Sex roles	No significant differences
Semantic differential ratings of concepts related to the self: (Me, Me as I would like to be, The future)	Kibbutz group more negative

Psychological distress

MMPI clinical scales	Kibbutz group higher
Symptoms and Psychosomatic Inventory	Kibbutz group higher
Anxiety symptom checklist	Kibbutz group higher

Affective expressiveness

R–S scale on the MMPI	No difference
Repression scale in early memories	Kibbutz group more "repressing"
Repression rating in early memories	No difference
Repression ratings on self-esteem	Kibbutz group more "repressing"
Ratings of defensiveness on self-esteem items	No difference
Handling hostility	No difference
Intimate friendship style	Kibbutz group less expressive
Valuation of self and others	Kibbutz group more "sensitized"
Psychological distress measures	Kibbutz group more "sensitized"

Table 9.2

Summary of findings in relation to several hypotheses regarding the effects of communal child rearing

---

Maladjustment hypothesis:

communally raised adults will be lacking in
psychosocial competence, due to childhood
deprivation.   Rejected

Internal distress hypothesis:

communally raised adults will experience
more anxiety and symptoms, as a result
of early deprivation.   Minimally Supported

Parental attachment hypothesis:

communally raised adults will be less
attached to their parents.   Minimally supported

Uniformity hypothesis:

communally raised adults will show a
great deal of homogeneity as a group   Rejected

Low sex differentiation:

communally raised adults will show fewer
and less pronounced psychological
differences between the sexes.   Rejected

Intimacy hypothesis:

communally raised adults will be less
capable of forming close, intimate
relationships.   Partially supported

APPROACHES TO INTERPRETATION AND INTEGRATION

The context of our research includes all relevant other studies on
the kibbutz, and we will not be able to offer a coherent interpretation without considering them. So, our task in this chapter
is to review relevant psychological studies of communal child-

rearing and to glean from them conclusions and questions, to be discussed in the light of our own findings.

The most serious problem in obtaining a coherent picture of findings from psychological studies on communal child rearing is that of comparing and combining studies from different historical periods. A general survey of psychological research on the kibbutz would include studies from the 1950s together with studies from the 1970s. Both kinds of studies claim to be, and justifiably so, about the kibbutz. The problem is that they do not deal with the same kibbutz environment. The kibbutz of the 1970s is not the kibbutz of the 1950s, nor is child rearing in the kibbutz of the 1950s child rearing in the kibbutz of the 1970s (see Beit-Hallahmi & Rabin, 1977). The problem of combining findings from different periods can be solved only if we can specify the variables involved in the studies and the changes in them. Studies from different periods in the history of the kibbutz child-rearing system can be compared, provided that they deal with aspects of the system that have not changed over the years.

Some comments on methodology in kibbutz studies are in order. Research on child rearing in the kibbutz has been of several kinds: clinical–observational (Bettelheim, 1969; Caplan, 1954), anthropological (Spiro, 1958), and psychological–systematic (for example, Kohen-Raz, 1968; Rabin, 1965). The number of systematic studies is surprisingly low, compared to the attention given to kibbutz child rearing in the literature. Some of the most quoted publications on the kibbutz (for example, Bettelheim, 1969) are based on extremely limited observations, and when it comes to studies of the kibbutz system, there seems to be an almost inverse relationship between the frequency of citation and methodological rigor. Since the body of reliable findings is limited, one should proceed with caution toward inferences and conclusions. Speculations and inferences from observations and clinical data have their value, but they should be recognized as such. It should also be noted that the better-controlled studies (for example, Nevo, 1977) have found few differences between kibbutz and nonkibbutz groups.

The most important distinction we have made when going over previous psychological studies of the communal child-rearing system is that between observational and comparative studies. While observational studies are based on direct study of the communal system alone, comparative studies use a quasi-experimental design based on a control group (or a contrast group), thus avoiding as far as possible observer bias.

The observational studies of communal child rearing are usually based on work by one observer, who enters one kibbutz community and interacts with it in the natural setting. Such studies follow the anthropological tradition and may be described as "clinical," "episodic," or "impressionistic." The main source of data for analysis are the vivid participant observers' direct impressions of life in the community, and individual community members. Observational studies of this kind are important sources for ideas and hypotheses. Descriptive data and hypotheses derived from observational studies provide us with guidelines for comparative and experimental research studies. While observational studies may provide us with useful hypotheses, comparative and experimental studies provide us with a specification of system variables and their effects. Experimental studies, which are based on manipulations of variables within the communal system (Fox, 1977; Maccoby & Feldman, 1972) are quite useful in elucidating the consequences of the system in individual behavior.

The comparative design is clearly the best one for any research on the effects of child rearing. We have decided to use the observational, noncomparative studies as sources for hypotheses and ideas. Despite the fact that these studies may be said to lack in methodological rigor and sometimes in knowledge of the culture and historical understanding, the observers (such as Spiro, 1958; Bettelheim, 1969) proved themselves to be both astute and theoretically sophisticated. The observational studies of the kibbutz won attention and acclaim despite their methodological limitations, thanks to the ability of the observers to crystallize important issues and ask significant questions. Thus, we have not accepted their conclusions as such, but as hypotheses, and valuable ones, to be tested. We have taken only findings of comparative studies as reference points, checking our own conclusions against theirs. Our own study is, of course, a comparative study. Its advantage is that we do not make any statements regarding findings that are not based on comparisons with another group.

There are several "classical" questions that have often been raised in studies of the kibbutz and are often presented as hypotheses, or conclusions, in observational studies. The questions that psychologists have asked about the kibbutz child-rearing system were both of a theoretical nature (for example, will changes in mother–child relationships support psychoanalytic predictions?) and of an "applied" nature (for example, what can be learned from the kibbutz experience to improve other child-rearing systems?) Findings on the kibbutz from the literature of psychological research are presented below, together with our own findings, as they relate to several areas of functioning. These findings constitute tentative answers to some of the frequent questions regarding the effects of communal child rearing.

Overall Development in Children—
Overall Competence in Adults

The evidence from studies trying to assess the general developmental level of communally-raised children is not always clear-cut. Some studies show retarded development in infancy (Caplan, 1954; Rabin, 1961, 1965), but the majority of studies dealing with kibbutz infants have shown no developmental retardation (Fried, 1960; Gerwirtz, 1965a; Kohen-Raz, 1968). Handel (1961) found lower self-reported maturity among kibbutz adolescents, but Rabin (1965) found more maturity among 10-year-old children and among adolescents in the kibbutz. Goldstein and Borus (1976) found that kibbutz children at the ages of 36 to 54 months showed higher receptive and expressive language ability, compared to a matched group of city children. Kaffman (1972), in a study of enuresis in the kibbutz, found that the incidence of enuresis in the kibbutz for ages 6 to 7 was much higher than that for family-raised children, and for children over age 10 the rate was much lower for kibbutz children. Regressive enuresis in response to situational stress was found to be quite uncommon in kibbutz children. Kaffman's interpretation of the findings, however, is not in terms of developmental problems or psychopathology. In his view, the higher rate of early enuresis in the kibbutz can be explained as reflecting more permissive attitudes and practices with regard to toilet training.

Some symptoms of pathology reported for younger age levels seem to disappear later on (Jarus et al., 1970; Kaffman, 1965a, 1967). Some of the disagreement in findings may also be due to different sampling during various periods, while the kibbutz child-rearing system was undergoing significant changes. The more recent studies show no developmental deficits, a fact that can be explained as the result of more individualized and relaxed caretaking in infancy. Findings of developmental lag and retardation in kibbutz children were common in the 1950s, but not since then. Later studies show either no differences between the kibbutz group and the control groups, or a superiority in the kibbutz group. We can safely assume that there have been changes in the child-rearing system since the 1950s, in the direction of a lower infant/caretaker ratio and more flexible parent contacts, and these are reflected in the improved developmental picture at an early age.

Only a few studies before this one have looked at kibbutz-born adults. Their findings show the kibbutz-born young adult to be effective, productive, and well-adjusted in his overall functioning (Amir, 1969; Nevo, 1977; Rabin, 1965). Preale, Amir, and Sharon (1970) found a high level of perceptual articulation and differentiation in the kibbutz-born (compared to members of other subcultures in Israel), which, in turn leads to higher effectiveness. This higher level of differentiation was explained on the basis of the differentiation among various socialization agents experienced by the kibbutz-born at an early age. Pirojnikoff, Hadar, and Hadar (1971) found that kibbutz-raised adults were lower on the Rokeach Dogmatism scale than a matched group of urban Israelis.

Nevo (1977), comparing two matched groups of city-raised and commune-raised adults, found no meaningful differences on a Hebrew version of the California Personality Inventory. This was interpreted to mean that kibbutz child rearing does not produce a clearly defined difference in personality traits.

As we have shown in Chapter 5 above, there were no significant differences between the two groups in fulfilling their adult roles in their respective communities. Both groups are made up of well-functioning adults, able to carry out culturally defined tasks with ease and success. In the areas of social role performance, work, and achievement, the two groups seem to function quite well, following the respective paths set by their communities in terms of self-expression and self-actualization in the public world of work and vocation. We have found differences in the desire for personal success. Ambitions seem to be less self-centered in the kibbutz-raised. The lower level of personal ambition among the kibbutz-raised was noted with regard to the seventeen-year-olds in the original study (Rabin, 1965).

Relations with Parents

The evidence so far shows quite clearly that identification of kibbutz children with their parents is more diffuse (Luria, Goldwasser, & Goldwasser, 1963; Rabin, 1957b, 1965; Rabin & Goldman, 1966; Spiro, 1953) but nevertheless positive. Since childhood experiences in the kibbutz are expected to reduce ambivalence toward parents, attitudes toward them are expected to be more positive. This is indeed the finding (Devereux, et al., 1974; Rabin, 1965; Spiro, 1958). There is support for the claim that the father in the kibbutz is more nurturant and less authoritarian than is the father in the traditional family. Rabin (1965) reported that members of our own research group as adolescents were "less intensely involved affectively with members of their family" (p. 179). The important psychohistorical fact is that the generation of kibbutz founders was made up of individuals who had rebelled against their own parents and who had either negative or ambivalent feelings about the family and about being parents. What we see in the second generation, the children of the kibbutz founders, is the outcome of ambivalent parenting. Both the general functioning of the kibbutz-raised adults and their specific, unique characteristics are a result of that ambivalence.

Our findings in Chapter 6 above show that kibbutz parents were perceived by their children—who were now adults—as more permissive and less authoritarian, but this did not bring about an overall more positive evaluation. Members of the moshav group perceived their parents more positively than did the kibbutz group. Present attachment to the parents in the kibbutz group was less intense, and early memories of childhood in which the parents are mentioned were more negative in tone in the kibbutz group. There were no differences in identification with parents between the two groups. The kibbutz parents were a part of a socializing system that extended through the community, part of a system of socializing agents. There was a continuity between the parents and the community in terms of values and social roles—one level of functioning. There was a discontinuity in terms of individual personalities and their effects on children— another level of functioning. The parents in the kibbutz affect the second generation as a group, that is, as models, through their involvement in child rearing as a group, through their design for child rearing, and as individual parents. In addition to general problems of differences between parents and their children, there are special intergenerational problems in the kibbutz that are unique to it. The first generation of kibbutz founders has the image (and the self-image) of being pioneers and achievers, and in creating their communities in a struggle against considerable odds. This collective image has been presented to the children as a model that they should emulate and follow, but they could never equal or surpass. The second generation has grown up in the shadow of the first generation of heroes and giants. Intergenerational comparisons are quite common in the internal kibbutz literature, and in most comparisons members of the second generation find themselves lacking both in personal qualities and in external opportunities. These comparisons between the generations, which may be initiated by both the founders and their children, often express resentment or lead to it.

Capacity for Interpersonal Attachment

The diffusion of identification and the reduced attachment to a few objects at an early age would lead to a reduced capacity for (or the need for) intimacy (Bettelheim, 1969; Spiro, 1958). Support for this hypothesis was found by Handel (1961), who used self-reports, and by Sharabany (1974), who compared friendships among 11- and 12-year-olds in the kibbutz and in the city. Regev, Beit-Hallahmi, and Sharabany (1980), in the first study comparing kibbutz children raised under family-based sleeping arrangements to communally-raised kibbutz children and to city children, found differences in the level of emotional expressiveness. The study found that communally-raised kibbutz children differed from family-raised kibbutz children, and from city children, in their expressive style. The results showed that communally-raised children were lower on both positive and negative affective expression toward other people, thus supporting the "moderation" (Rabin, 1965) hypothesis. Compared with the less intense parental identifications in the kibbutz, the peer group becomes very significant psychologically, and strong feelings of solidarity and group identity are formed (Etzioni, 1957; Golan, 1961; Rettig, 1966). Devereux et al. (1974) reported that peers in the kibbutz were perceived as secondary to the parents, and there was no difference from city children in this respect, but the kibbutz peers were seen as exerting more control. Communally-raised children were found to behave less competitively with their peers as compared to city children in several studies (such as Shapira, 1976; Madsen & Shapira, 1977). Nahir and Yussen (1977) reported better social skills in kibbutz children, as compared to city children.

Our findings show that there are indeed specific areas in which affective moderation and diffusion are prominent in the kibbutz-raised. In trying to evaluate the quality of interpersonal attachment in the communally-raised, we have to consider findings on differing kinds of interpersonal involvement. Our major findings are in the areas of friendship and the relations with parents. In both cases, members of the kibbutz group show a lower level of closeness and attachment.

It is possible that there is indeed a different interpersonal style that is typical of communally-raised adults. The conditions of communal child rearing, not only in early infancy but later on in childhood and adolescence, leave their mark in the form of a different need for attachments and a different style of intimacy and friendship. In intense, exclusive relationships typical of the nuclear family, strong emotions are likely to develop in both positive and negative directions. This creates the ambivalence that is accepted as natural in close one-to-one ties. The communal experience may reduce both positive and negative feelings in the relationship and thus bring about reduced ambivalence.

Anxiety and Psychological Distress

Since the kibbutz caretaking situation was perceived as lying somewhere between maternal deprivation on the one side and normal maternal contacts in the traditional family on the other, it has often been assumed that the relative deprivation would have its effects in the form of a greater prevalence of psychopathology. Some of the first observations on the kibbutz attempted to estimate the prevalence of pathological symptoms. Caplan (1954) found more symptoms only for young ages (up to the age of 7), but Kaffman (1965a) found no particular prevalence of psychopathology in kibbutz children. Kaplan De-Nour et al. (1970) reviewed the literature on psychopathology in kibbutz children and concluded that there was no clear evidence for a higher level of psychopathology in the kibbutz-raised. Nevo (1977) found no differences between kibbutz-born and city-born adults on the California Psychological Inventory.

Our findings on the measures of psychological distress (or "psychopathology") can be summarized as follows:

1. The levels of distress displayed by members of both groups on these measures were far from "pathological." The MMPI scores reflected a level of distress that was for *most scales below the mean for Israeli respondents*, and the scores on the symptom checklists did not reflect any impairment in normal adjustment. One interpretation of the findings in the area of self-reported concerns and psychological distress is that the kibbutz group is reporting psychological concerns more openly as a result of a kibbutz norm of openness and directness. It is possible that such a norm, if it exists, is related to the experience of group living.
2. Members of the kibbutz group were higher on all the measures of distress, that is, the MMPI clinical scales, the Psychosomatic Symptoms Inventory, and the Anxiety Symptom Checklist.

The overall level of functioning in the two groups was quite similar and quite adequate, as was shown in Chapter 5. Cases of extreme maladjustment were rare. There was one psychiatric hospitalization in the kibbutz group with a diagnostic of schizophrenia and one psychiatric hospitalization in the moshav group with a diagnosis of manic-depressive psychosis.

If our findings on the higher level of distress in the kibbutz group represent the presence of real difficulties, we have to suggest explanations for the sources of such difficulties. One possible source is the experience of group living in early and later life, which is likely to result in many pressures.

IS THERE A "KIBBUTZ PERSONALITY"?

The question regarding the "kibbutz personality" can be put in very concrete terms. Can the communally-raised be easily identified? Can they be picked out of a crowd? Are there psychological "fingerprints" that would give away a kibbutz "product"? Many people claim that they can splot a kibbutz-raised person, not just by physical appearance (there is still a physical stereotype of the "kibbutz member" in Israeli society), but through his behavior. Is this possible, and what would be the telltale signs of communal upbringing? From what we have been able to determine, the psychological and behavioral differences between the communally-raised and the family-raised in Israel are subtle, rather than striking. Beyond the general expectation that the personality of the kibbutz-raised would be different from that of individuals raised in the nuclear family, there are two more specific hypotheses that have been stated time and again in the literature in various forms. One suggests that the personality of the kibbutz-raised would be marked by a higher level of psychopathology, because the communal child-rearing setting is one of deprivation and trauma to the developing child. The other suggested that a "kibbutz personality" could be defined on the basis of a combination of personality traits that would appear together. This combination of traits, and each of those, would be related to specific antecedents in early experience. Thus, for example, the "kibbutz personality" would show more moderation and diffusion in interpersonal affect.

On the basis of the findings presented so far, we may conclude that the personality of the kibbutz-born is nonpathological, effective, and shows moderate but positive attachment to others. As noted above, the most striking general finding is that the majority of studies, and especially those complying with more rigorous methodological standards, found few differences between kibbutz and nonkibbutz groups. It has been suggested, with some supporting data, that Israeli culture as a whole is more collectivistic than most Western cultures today (Crandall & Gozali, 1969), and thus it becomes more difficult to separate the effects of kibbutz child rearing from the general effects of the culture. From a theoretical viewpoint, one may want to conclude that the case for the kibbutz as a separate culture producing a separate "personality" still has to be proven. From an "applied" viewpoint, one can point to the absence of pathology and to the presence of effectiveness and productiveness despite multiple mothering.

A Note on Kibbutz "Uniformity"

As mentioned above, several observers of the kibbutz child-rearing system (such as Bettelheim, 1969; Caplan, 1954) have suggested that one of its effects may be a tendency toward a greater uniformity in personality structure and personality traits. The primacy of the peer group, the less personal caretaking in childhood, and the emphasis on collective goals and collective responsibilities would, according to this hypothesis, act to reduce individual differences in personality traits. We decided to test this "uniformity hypothesis" by looking at our various statistical tables, which have been based on a great number of separate measures. While looking at the statistical variance on the different measures and scales, it became clear, as it should become clear to the reader, that no such tendency for uniformity can be observed. We should reiterate again what has been said by Rabin (1965, p. 207):

The incorrect assumption is that the early (and later) environment of the Kibbutz child is so uniform and stereotyped that the product does not vary greatly. In reality, the early interaction of the infant with his peers in the nursery and toddlers house, with his parents and metapelet and, subsequently, with biological siblings, during the daily visits to the parental quarters, provide a great degree of variability in the interpersonal and physical environment. Later, the child is open to a broader range of influences extending to the friendly, and frequently doting, Kibbutz membership . . ..

To be sure, we do not possess a quantitative index of originality and variability, but mere inspection of the range and distribution of the responses and of the various indices based upon them points to tremendous variability in content as well as in personality structure of the Kibbutz youngsters. This observation does not in any way invalidate our conclusions about some congruity in character and its structure. We are talking about group trends and central tendencies that have high probabilities of occurrence in the Kibbutz. The inference from similarities between members of a group, along a limited number of dimensions, is not equivalent to saying that the individuals are devoid of uniqueness. The nomothetic approach does not imply a denial of the ideographic pattern.

With regard to sex differences, the picture is very similar. There is no indication that psychological differences between the sexes have been blurred or obliterated in the kibbutz. When sex differences were found for the moshav contrast group, they were also found for the kibbutz group. We found a number of sex differences, in such areas as friendship and psychosomatic complaints, that are quite consistent with sex differences found elsewhere. Thus we may conclude that there is no evidence in our data to support the notion that there is more uniformity or homogeneity among the kibbutz-raised. We have found sex differences on a variety of measures, and in all cases the differences were in the direction expected from previous research. Thus, for example, women were found to identify more with their mothers, and men were found to identify more with their fathers; women were found to prefer intimate friendship more than men, and so forth. These sex differences were consistent across the two groups, that is, they appeared in both the kibbutz-raised and the moshav-raised. The meaning of these sex differences is twofold. First, they tell us that our instruments are valid, since our results are consistent with those of other studies. Second, they indicate that the sex differences were not mitigated by the communal child-rearing system. Despite many impressions to the contrary, there are rather clear boundaries in terms of role definitions for the two sexes and in terms of psychological functioning for the kibbutz-raised.

IMPLICATIONS

Child Rearing and Personality Development

While we have employed all the proper scientific caveats when discussing our findings so far, our caution is even greater when we approach the question of the general implications of the study. How can we best apply the lessons of our specific findings to more general areas of interest? How far can we generalize in making statements about child-rearing practices? We are well aware of the fact that many readers will regard even tentative statements as authoritative recommendations, despite our many reservations and qualifications.

Lessons to be learned from the kibbutz experience are sought by a variety of audiences, both lay and professional. The interest in the kibbutz does often appear in the context of alternative community planning and alternative family styles. Lessons from the kibbutz experience are also sought by experts and laymen concerned about child care in single-parent families, day care centers, and communes. In other cases, the kibbutz is mentioned as an example of social experiments in general, and lessons from it are used to understand—or predict—other experiments. The many historical changes in the kibbutz itself, in addition to our scholarly caution, makes us reluctant to generalize about the lessons to be learned from this unique experiment. At the same time, we know that our readers are clamoring for implications beyond the boundaries of the phenomenon under study. We cannot hide behind our scientific disclaimers. If the communal child-rearing system was an experiment, what are the results? If we regard the kibbutz as an experimental laboratory, the question is then how much can we generalize from the "laboratory" to the "real world."

Our major theoretical question, and the question that has been addressed by many students of the communal child-rearing system, is that of the development of attachment. How does the child growing up in the communal system differ from other children in developing the basic capability for human attachment? This general capability for attachment will then be expressed in many ways, in attachments to family members, peers, friends, and spouses. Our findings here are relevant to this general question. Psychodynamic theory, in its most orthodox forms, claimed that without the family environment the developing personality will not experience intimacy and attachment and will not be able to experience them in later life. This is a strong hypothesis, and in its weaker form it merely suggests that any deviance from the basic nuclear family experience will lead to deficiencies in the ability to experience attachment and intimacy. The preoccupation with the separation from the mother in the literature on the kibbutz may be regarded as the negative side of the "kibbutz mystique." It may reflect the effects of psychodynamic theory as well as cultural anxieties about the decline of the nuclear family. Early experiences in the area of attachment certainly have consequences, but the consequences are specific and modified by other structures in the child's environment, and by later experiences.

The specific outcome of multiple caretakers in early childhood may depend on the total community context in which the multiple caretaking is being done. Attachment to parents is formed and remains significant even when the parents are only a part of a multiple caretaker group. These attachments remain significant throughout life. Kibbutz-raised adults expressed the importance of their parents in their lives no less than did adults in the contrast group. The number of alternative attachments does not abolish parental centrality and importance. Dyadic attachment, especially in the form of friendship, is reduced in importance, an effect that can be specifically related to the peer-group experience.

We need to stress both negative and positive aspects of early kibbutz environment. Absence of a constant motherly figure and of family interaction may be compensated for by close peer relations and attendant security. Another central emphasis in psychodynamic literature is that on early childhood experiences as crucial for further development. Is the traditional emphasis on early childhood just a matter of cultural and theoretical bias? Our findings here definitely seem to support this theoretical emphasis. Many of the differences between the groups can be tied to the experience of the early years of life, though these cannot easily be separated from later conditions. We are looking not only at the outcome of childhood experiences, but at the outcome of a whole system, with a great deal of continuity among the different parts of the system. The effects of culture occur not only in early childhood, but also later, as a result of ideology and social norms; these have to be included in a theory of personality development in adulthood. We do not assume that all formative experiences take place in early infancy, but the combined effects of infancy and childhood seem to have an effect, and there is some stability in personality structure by the time the child reaches the age of 10 (Kagan & Moss, 1962).

What our study of the kibbutz has taught us is that, in addition to the many experiences of discontinuity in childhood, discontinuity in relationships and in caretakers, there is also a great deal of continuity in terms of the whole child-rearing system. There may be many crises around separation and discontinuity, but there are also compensations in terms of the overall structure. The conception of kibbutz child rearing as being nonfamilial or extrafamilial cannot be maintained. It is clear from our findings that socialization is both familial and extrafamilial. Experiences outside the family, with nonfamilial caretakers and with the peer group, are important, but not exclusive. The parents are still very important figures in the life of kibbutz children and leave their marks in terms of personality development.

What makes a difference is not just the existence of several significant others, but the kind of relationship that develops between the child and the caretakers. Is this a relationship of trust and support, or one of neglect and deprivation? Kaffman (1972b) suggested the hypothesis that involvement with multiple caretakers would increase feelings of security, because it would decrease ambivalence and dependence and allow more independent development. Similarly, Shouval et al. (1975) suggested that multiple caretaking reduces conformity.

Group Care versus Family Care of Young Children

The care of young children in most cultures is based on multiple caretaking. The mother–child exclusive bond is an idealized picture or a myth, portrayed in great works of art but out of step with reality. The theme of the Madonna and her child is so powerful in art because it expresses a powerful yearning rather than familiar realities. One problem in theoretical comparisons between the nuclear family and other forms of child rearing is that an idealized form of the nuclear family is often used as a point of reference.

The reality of the contemporary nuclear family is that children are likely to interact less with their parents and more with non-familial agents. The number of children in day care centers in the United States is constantly growing. In 1977, there were more than a million children in a variety of day care centers. There is an increasing number of single-parent families (formerly called "broken homes"), more families with two working parents, and increasing number of women in the work force. All this leads to an increased need for group care for children. While we may find faults with the various forms of group care and their products, we do not need an unusual knowledge of human history to observe that not all products of family child rearing are uniformly perfect. Defenders of the family, those who want to preserve it as the only locus of socialization, are really putting an impossible burden on it. The family is called upon to solve all of the community's and society's problems (see Lasch, 1977).

The applicability of the kibbutz child-rearing experience to the day care situation in the United States is limited; the situations are essentially quite different, despite the similarity in multiple caretaking. The crucial difference seems to be in the role of the mother and in the limited involvement of other nonfamilial care-takers, as compared to the kibbutz situation. In reality, all children are socialized by multiple caretakers. The question is not one of either family or group caretaking, or of the family versus the community; it is one of continuity between the family and the community and support for both.

The difference between day care systems in the United States and the kibbutz system is, in most cases, in their connections with the surrounding community. Generally, day care is a system for substitute care and not a part of interlocking community systems. The caretakers may not have any relationship to the child and his family outside the day care center. The differences between the communal child-rearing situation and the day-care situation are more important than the similarities. It is true that in both situations there is a significant involvement of nonfamilial agents in early socialization, but the crucial difference is in the setting within the community. The evaluation of any child-rearing situation has to be done in the context of the total community, which includes other support systems and determines the general conditions of life for children and their caretakers.

10

The Kibbutz Child-Rearing System: Past, Present, and Future

We cannot emphasize often enough and strongly enough the *historicity* of our findings. Our findings do not deal with "the kibbutz" in general, but at one particular historical period in its development. The kibbutz is changing, and the kibbutz child-rearing system is changing and has been changing dramatically over the past twenty years. These historical changes are likely to lead to generational changes. Children growing up in the kibbutz of the 1970s are likely to become somewhat different adults than the ones who grew up there during the 1950s. These historical changes are of interest not only because of their implications for our findings but also because they involve such radical changes in the child-rearing system itself, leading to what may be the complete disappearance of communal child rearing in the kibbutz. The abolition of a social institution may often be interpreted as a consequence of the institution itself. In the case of communal child rearing, many observers may regard the changes as reflecting on the psychological consequences of communal child rearing, or resulting from them. Put very simply, this view states: "The system didn't work, so it was changed." The historical picture of change in the kibbutz, and in the kibbutz child-rearing system, is, of course, more complex, and deserves closer attention.

Any social organization as complex and as lively as the kibbutz, which has been in existence for over 70 years, must be expected to undergo significant changes in order to survive in a changing environment. In any area of kibbutz life we can expect changes, together with continuities. In the area of the family, historical changes occur within the framework of long-term historical and cultural continuities. Variations and vicissitudes are united by the same basic theme. Recent observers have suggested that the family in the kibbutz has been revived and is now appearing as a strong component of the community, if not as a challenge to the whole kibbutz system. This development is viewed against the background of antifamilistic ideology and practice (Talmon, 1974) that has been for many years one of the main characteristics of the kibbutz movement. It may be interpreted in several ways, either as a revolution (or counterrevolution), a sharp departure from the earlier tradition, or a continuation of existing tendencies that have never disappeared from the kibbutz scene. In order to appreciate the nature of the revival or survival of the kibbutz family, we have to take a long historical look at the forces that have worked for and against the family at the ideological and practical levels.

RECENT CHANGES IN KIBBUTZ CHILD-REARING PRACTICES

Over the past 15 years, there has been a major trend toward closer parent–child contacts and toward more individual caretaking patterns in the communal child-rearing system. The changes have taken three major forms: (1) family sleeping arrangements for infants until a certain age (in some cases until adolescence), (2) provision of more metaplot (caretakers) for the infants' house and (3) greater involvement of parents in communal child rearing. Until 1950, family-based sleeping arrangements were in effect in only four kibbutzim. Since then, the new arrangement has spread over many more kibbutzim in the rightist federation and to some kibbutzim in the moderate federation; the debate over sleeping arrangements has spread to all three kibbutz federations (Shepher, 1971). Changes from the communal sleeping arrangement to the family sleeping arrangement have been noted for some years now (Shepher, 1969).

In the family-based sleeping arrangement, the children return to their parents in the afternoon and then stay there until the next morning, when they go back to the children's house. This arrangement may begin at different ages. At some kibbutzim it starts at age 6; at others it starts at birth and extends until age 12. In this latter group, most of the crucial elements in traditional kibbutz child rearing disappear. Under the family-based sleeping arrangement, the mother becomes the most significant figure, the parents become the main socializers, and the metapelet and the peer group recede in importance. The children's house may be compared to a day care center, the influence of which may be significant in some respects but cannot be compared to the influence of the "classical" children's house.

Family-based sleeping arrangements abolish the most unique aspect of kibbutz child rearing—multiple mothering at an early age. The children are transferred to communal children's houses later on, but the bond with the mother is formed at an early age. The parents no longer see the children only during recreation periods, when parents and children play together, but they now have to discipline their children and train them in all areas of social behavior. Peer-group influence is reduced but not altogether abolished; the collectivist orientation in child rearing remains very much in existence, and the peer group remains very stable. Unlike city children, for whom it is rare to spend their time with the same peer group from kindergarten through high school, kibbutz children spend most of their time, until the age of 18, with a limited number of peers. As a result, they are exposed to fewer social stimuli, their environment is more uniform, and they identify strongly with their peer group.

The return to traditional, nonkibbutz child-rearing patterns also involves a change in relationships between siblings, who assume a more significant role in early childhood. In those kibbutzim where the infants are still in the infant's house, better caretaking in infancy can prevent whatever initial deprivation kibbutz infants may have suffered from in the past. It may also create greater attachment to the metapelet (nurse) at this stage. Something else that is changing and will continue to change is child-rearing attitudes. Studies of first-generation and second-generation kibbutz mothers indicate a change in terms of putting more emphasis on individual attention to children, encouraging more affectional ties with parents, and considering motherhood as an important role for every woman (Rabin, 1964, 1970). We have reason to believe that historical changes in the kibbutz child-rearing system have included not only changes in formal procedures and role definitions, but also many changes in attitudes and informal norms (Gerson, 1978). The historiography of kibbutz child rearing and the kibbutz family is still in its infancy. We still have much to find out about the actual behavior of kibbutz caretakers and kibbutz mothers in the past.

The tension between the kibbutz community and the individual family has been noticed for a long time. Irvine (1952) observed already in 1950 that "the whole balance between group and family life gradually shifts in favour of the family" (p. 256). The family was regaining some of its functions even then, and the interaction between parents and children in any given family presented a challenge to communal child rearing. Diamond (1957) was able to state that the family in the kibbutz was recrystalizing and reasserting itself, and he considered the antifamilistic stage in the kibbutz as temporary. In 1963, thirteen years after her first visit, Irvine (1966) was able to discern many indications of the growing importance of the family and the regaining of more socialization roles. Mother–child interaction during infancy was encouraged, including an on-demand feeding schedule, with mothers not only breastfeeding but also bottlefeeding their children. Irvine also recorded the growing campaign in favor of family-based sleeping arrangements.

The "revival" of the kibbutz family can be determined by looking at the functions it is regaining today. In most kibbutzim, the family is regaining functions in the area of consumption and socialization. The dining hall is no longer the only place where meals are prepared and consumed. Families eat together, away from the rest of the commune. The family is also likely to own more appliances, such as TV sets and refrigerators, which are likely to create a further separation in consumption patterns between it and the kibbutz.

The main fact of life in the kibbutz today and in the kibbutz future is the existence of strong nuclear families, who have regained many functions in consumption and leisure-time activities. Informal socializing is done within the nuclear family, around a private TV set, with food from a private refrigerator. This is going to have concomitant effects on child rearing. The dining room used to be the social center of the old kibbutz, and what made it into a center was in part economic necessity and consumption arrangements. It was the only place where meals were served, the only warm place in winter, and the only place where a cold drink was available in the summer. It was also the place where the public radio set was available, and around it members would congregate to listen and react to what they were hearing. With the growth of the family and the rise in living standards, food, drink, radio, and television are now available in the family apartment, together with all the amenities of modern life. The family apartment, as a place where the extended family congregates, has become the social center. The place where the married couple lived used to be referred to as a "room." Now it is known as an apartment, since it is bigger and has more conveniences. Breakfast and lunch are still eaten in the dining room, but dinner is often eaten in the privacy of the apartment.

Because the typical kibbutz family may include more than two generations, it has developed into an extended family, with several generations and several separate household units, which in some kibbutzim is a significant social unit. We can differentiate between the nuclear family, which has regained some of its functions in the kibbutz today, and the extended family, which has also become an important component of the kibbutz community. The phenomenon of the extended family is new, and its functions go beyond those of the nuclear family. It provides a competing subidentity to its members, who remain, nevertheless, committed to the kibbutz community.

Talmon-Garber (1974) found that the "functionless" family was only transitional. There were two factors that led to the renewed emergence of the family unit. One was the growing economic and social differentiation in the kibbutz structure. The kibbutz economy demanded more specialization and organization and less spontaneity. The social structure was also changing, with additional groups of members joining and making the original founders into a minority, in some cases. A second factor was the appearance in force of the second generation. The arrival of children contributed to the enhanced status of the family, since the parental role, despite its earlier marginality, gradually became more central. This is because children are the focus of family life in the kibbutz. Marriage itself did not entail a redefinition of roles, but the appearance of the second generation changed the emphasis from rebellion to continuity. The family could no longer be an enemy. The kibbutz had grown and developed physically and economically; it was no longer the intimate community of the first generation. There was much less sharing and much more alienation. In this situation the extended family, or the nuclear family, has become the group to which members can relate and with which they can identify. Communal child rearing was a part of communal living. When life in the kibbutz became no longer communal, or less communal than it had been, the communal child-rearing system declined.

PSYCHOHISTORICAL SOURCES OF COMMUNAL CHILD REARING

The vision of creating a new way of life in the kibbutz led to the creation of new role definitions. Every person was going to have a chance to develop his full potential within the collective. New role definitions for men and women, based on equality and cooperation, were developed. There was a rejection of what had been regarded as traditional family life. The founders of the kibbutz were in open rebellion against their own parents, a rebellion sometimes taking the form of a total rejection of the institution of the family. The rebellion against traditional family patterns included a move toward equality between the sexes and the abolition of traditional sex roles, especially in the area of work. Thus, the emphasis was put on the dismantling of the traditional bourgeois family, with its close mother–child bonds, which could be perceived as promoting selfishness and individualism. Communal child rearing was seen since the earliest days of the kibbutz movement as a major task for the whole commune.

What image of parents did the generation of kibbutz founders have? What image were they trying to avoid? What image were they trying to transmit to their own children? Rapaport (1958) mentions "the rebellion against the patriarchal authority of the East European Jewish Father" (p. 590). The kibbutz founders, having experienced this patriarchal authority themselves, were determined not to let their children undergo the same experience. By centralizing and professionalizing child-rearing functions, the influence of parental disturbances and idiosyncrasies could be avoided. It was the central concern over children, in what Rapaport described as a child-centered society, that served as another argument against the family. The traditional family was regarded as harmful in carrying out its basic task of child rearing. Other arguments against the traditional family included the subordinate position of the mother, the "hypocritical morality fostered by the conventions and economics of the marriage bond" (p. 590), and its narrow loyalties and emotional life.

Spiro (1956) emphasizes the rebellion of the kibbutz founders against traditional Jewish culture and against bourgeois European culture as a source of the changes in the nuclear family in the early kibbutz. The rebellion against the parents included two basic ideological oppositions, the secularism of the children against the religiosity of the parents, and the socialism of the children against the bourgeois way of life of the parents. Many religious parents objected to Zionist secularism, which refused to wait until the coming of the Messiah for wordly salvation, and to their children's readiness to neglect the customary ways of making a living in favor of a precarious adventure in an underdeveloped land. Diamond (1957) suggested that life in the *Shtetl*, the Jewish small town in eastern Europe, was the antithesis against which kibbutz founders reacted when they created the patterns of kibbutz life. "Original sin, the sin of life in the Shtetl, is opposed to redemption, the perfection achieved by living . . . within the Kevutza" (p. 83). The profound rejection of the tradition of Shtetl life included a determined effort to eliminate all traces of the Shtetl family. Diamond describes the Shtetl father as authoritarian, symbolizing tradition in his actions and role, and the mother as nurturant and over-protective. Eliminating the old, declining family would create the new person, free of the burdens of Jewish tradition and history. The founders of the kibbutz did not trust themselves to do the job of child rearing, since they were bound to recreate their own rejected self-image. The kibbutz family thus no longer served as a mediator between society and the child. Rather, society had become the main socializing agency.

Irvine (1952) suggested that the creation of the communal child-rearing system was related to the internal conflict of the kibbutz founders when they had to assume the role of parents. "It is apt to be difficult for the rebellious child . . . to assume the responsibilities of parenthood, since this involves identification with the rejected parents; so the relegation of parental function is a natural and welcome solution of a dilemma" (p. 250). By relegating child rearing to supposedly professional authorities, the parents did not have to assert authority themselves. This is a psycho-historical analysis, which deemphasized the practical and social reasons that created the kibbutz child-rearing system. Its practical advantages cannot be denied, of course; it freed women to assume full-time work roles, and lent itself to more efficient management in allocating community resources.

The demographic structure of the population of devoted pioneers, who came to Palestine from Europe ready to settle on the land, was unique. It included mostly young males in their late teens and early twenties and a minority of females. Most of them were unmarried, so that the family for them did not exist, or existed only as something they had left or rejected. Talmon (1959) observed that in the early stages of the kibbutz movement there was "a certain basic incompatibility between intense collective identification and family solidarity" (p. 469). There is an inherent contradiction between the values of equality and communal sharing, which are universalistic in emphasis, and the particularistic values of the family, which would disrupt a communal system based on equality by introducing further distinctions among members. Any kind of family attachment can be regarded as the potential beginning of inherited preferences, if not privileges. Any commitment to the family is a commitment to a group other than the community. This contradiction was noted in the earliest days of the kibbutz.

Zvi Schatz, one of the legendary originators of communal ideals in Palestine, wrote in 1918: "The family is being destroyed, and religion is dying. But the eternal values of human life will survive, only changing their outward forms, because the need for a familial environment is deep and natural. . . . Thus, a family based on religion, a new religion created by the working people in their own land. Based on mental relations and not on blood relations, the family will be revived, in the form of small, communal, modest work groups" (quoted by Hurvitz, 1960). Another member of the founders' generation expressed the tension between the family and the kibbutz in the following way: "Life in the kibbutz was hard on the family, and the family was hard on the kibbutz. Even today there are kibbutzim who are fighting against the family as a dire enemy. . . . Persons with a purely collective ideal regress and are bound by privacy. Love in general, the love of two persons is a most private choice, and it separates two people from the rest of the group and locks them into an 'island of happiness' around which the waves of collective life are breaking" (quoted by Hurvitz, 1960). Therefore, the obligation to the collective and to collective tasks took precedence over kinship obligations. The formation of families at this stage introduced a new source of conflict, since the families were regarded as a competing focus of commitment.

The redefinition of family functions was aimed at counteracting this basic conflict. Transfer of function from the family to the kibbutz was the most important aspect of the "collectivization" of the family. There was also, according to Talmon, a strong "anti-familistic bias" in patterns of informal social relations and leisure-time activities. Husband and wife were discouraged from spending their free time together and encouraged to take part in group activities. Nevertheless, Talmon emphasizes that the family was not abolished, and it existed as a special unit within the collective. The family still provided physical and emotional intimacy and an exclusive subunit, psychologically separate from the larger group.

Spiro's observations about the loss of function in the kibbutz family (1954) have led to one of the best-known misunderstandings in modern social science. He concluded that the family in the kibbutz does not exist, and thus the kibbutz is different from all other known human societies. Spiro (1954) followed Murdock's (1949) definition of the family, which "is a social group characterized by common residence, economic cooperation, and reproduction. It includes adults of both sexes, at least two of whom maintain a socially approved sexual relationship, and one or more children, own or adopted, of sexually cohabiting adults" (Murdock, 1949, p. 1). As Spiro pointed out, the kibbutz family did not include economic cooperation, a common residence (the children do not reside with the parents), or the function of socializing children. Nevertheless, Spiro (1956) concluded that the family in the kibbutz did exist in a psychological sense, though it does not exist in a structural-functional sense. He mentioned two kinds of evidence for psychological significance of the family in the kibbutz: one was the mutual attachment of parents and children; the other was the social recognition given to this group by the community as a whole. The lack of a common residence for the whole family is still the case today in most kibbutzim, but it is far from being the rule in every kibbutz. Irvine (1952) observed that the kibbutz has not abolished the role of the parent, but only modified it. The tasks related to child rearing have been reallocated.

The history of the early kibbutz movement in Palestine is by no means well known or well understood. Historical scholarship has only recently started to examine critically the evidence and to separate established fact from hearsay and speculation. We may now be entering the era of the revisionist history of the kibbutz. More and more evidence is being unearthed, showing that even in the early days of the kibbutzim what seemed like a radical departure was not so radical in reality. True equality between the sexes might have never existed, and traditional division of labor in the economic sphere was maintained. Women were assigned to service jobs from the beginning, and when it came to production, women were always in the minority. Part of the early descriptions of the kibbutz community as without any marriage formalities and without the emphasis on sexual morality can be understood today as projections on the part of more conservative observers. Changes in the status and function of the family were not sudden and radical. Rather, they were gradual, with transitional rather than revolutionary changes taking place.

Findings that showed that the traditional sex role pattern within the family has not been abolished came from psychological studies and observations. The consequences of family structure and role definitions can be observed in the products of socialization— the children. Thus, looking at the psychological data based on observations of kibbutz children, we can learn about structure and function in the kibbutz family. Evidence shows quite clearly that kibbutz children experience no problems with sex role differentiation (Rabin, 1965). Kugelmass & Breznitz (1966) showed that the perception of parents by kibbutz adolescents was no different from the perception of parents by city adolescents. In both cases the father was perceived as the instrumental leader in the family, while the mother was perceived as the expressive leader. This differentiated perception was another indication that the traditional division of labor between the sexes in the family had survived in the kibbutz.

One useful way of viewing the kibbutz family is by looking at the transfer of functions from the family to other institutions. The modern nuclear family has been regarded by sociologists as losing functions to other institutions (Davis, 1937). The "loss of function" theory nevertheless suggested that the modern family was losing its traditional functions as a production unit, was giving up some of its socialization functions after the appearance of modern universal education, but was keeping a major function in providing for the emotional and sexual satisfaction of the husband–wife pair and in providing some socialization and much emotional support for the children. The emotional support function was regarded as ensuring the survival of the family and proving its value to society. The kibbutz family has given up its economic production functions, its economic consumption function, most of its socialization functions, but not its emotional support and sexual union function. Thus, the kibbutz family can be regarded as another variation of the modern nuclear family.

Explaining the Change

The explanations for recent changes in child-rearing practices in the kibbutz may be sought in several areas. There might have been changes in the ideology of child rearing, based on the experiences over the years. There might have been wider structural changes within the kibbutz, and there might have been wider changes in the surrounding Israeli society that have influenced the kibbutz movement. We will try to examine all relevant factors, starting with possible changes in educational philosophy. Was it self-criticism by kibbutz educators and parents that led them to "mend their ways" in the more conservative direction? Has it been the development of greater psychological-mindedness and sensitivity to the shortcomings of "orthodox" methods? Has feedback from psychological studies affected the kibbutz community?

The relationship between the kibbutz movements and social science research has not always been an easy one. Initially, social scientists were critical and kibbutz members were defensive. Psychoanalysts' preliminary interest in the kibbutz as a deviant or potentially pathological pattern of life, especially in the area of child rearing, has not endeared the researcher to the kibbutz community. Moreover, a utopian, struggling movement tends to view outside observers not sharing its ideology as potential critics and enemies. One should bear in mind that the kibbutz has always been a minority subculture, fighting against the destructive influences of the wider society that would reduce it to a smaller minority or abolish it altogether. We should remember that because of tensions with the wider society, very few utopian communes have survived as long as the kibbutz. In this context, it is easy to see why studies by outside researchers were regarded as hostile incursions, aimed at tarnishing the image of an idealistic enterprise. At the same time, there were other factors that led kibbutz movements to assume a different and more positive attitude toward social science research. The first factor was the special psychological-mindedness of the kibbutz leaders, especially in the area of education. Communal education in the kibbutz was based on theoretical foundations that included psychodynamic theory (Golan, 1961; Rabin

& Hazan, 1973). Kibbutz educators have regarded themselves as an educational avant-garde, conscious of the psychological consequences of what they are planning. Psychoanalytic concepts have been in usage in the kibbutz movement since its beginning, and this prepared the ground for acceptance of psychological research as an ally (Katz & Lewin, 1973). The second factor was the feeling within the kibbutz that the results of psychological studies vindicated kibbutz child-rearing methods. Indeed, the "kibbutz personality" as it emerges from psychological studies is quite positive, and so there was little need to modify the child-rearing system that brought it about.

We chose to look at the changes in child-rearing practices in a wider context. We decided to ask whether these changes had been unique and isolated or whether there had been changes in other aspects of the kibbutz system that may have been observed, and they are all in the same direction of increased privatism and "familism." The changes have been economic, political, ideological, and psychological. Changes in the kibbutz child-rearing system since 1955 parallel general historical changes in the kibbutz as a community, and in the kibbutz within Israeli society (Beit-Hallahmi & Rabin, 1977).

A growing conservatism is being manifested in all areas, and the changes in child rearing are just one part of the general trend. In terms of the relationship between the original kibbutz ideology and later historical developments, we might say that the trend is from ideological purity to ideological compromise. Many of these changes are too recent to have been studied systematically, but they are easy to observe (Rabin, 1971) and have been noted by all students of kibbutz life in recent years. Considerable evidence regarding the changes and the often heated discussions that accompanied them is available in the periodical literature of the kibbutz movement. There is general agreement on two points: the comprehensive nature of the changes, covering almost every aspect of kibbutz life, and the unified direction characterizing all of these changes.

One of the main aims of the kibbutzim has been settling the land, and the kibbutzim started as agricultural collectives. The past 25 years have seen a growing industrialization so successful as to turn many kibbutzim into holding companies for a variety of enterprises. The ideological change away from socialism has been correlated with the actual change in patterns of production and consumption. What was started as a deliberate attempt to create a working class is now a comfortable bourgeoisie. Economic success and the use of hired labor, either directly or indirectly, have changed both the reality and the image of the kibbutz. The indirect use of hired labor is done through regional industrial plants, which are held in partnership by several kibbutzim and are physically separated from them. The profits from these regional plants are divided among the partners, and members of the partner kibbutzim serve as managers, while many of the workers are hired nonmembers.

Eisenstadt, Weintraub, and Toren (1967) describe two sources of change—internal and external—in the kibbutz. The main internal changes have been the numerical growth, related to economic development and growing division of labor, in each separate kibbutz. A second internal change was the maturation and aging of individual members, accompanied by the establishment of families and the rearing of children. The development of a multigenerational community has entailed the routinization and differentiation of social roles within the kibbutz and the development of subsystems, such as the family.

Talmon-Garber (1959b) first suggested that changes in the status and function of the family within the kibbutz social structure were the main indicators of general changes in kibbutz society. Every developmental change in the social organization of the kibbutz was reflected in a change in the function of the family. The small groups of young kibbutz founders, where group solidarity was paramount, viewed the family as a problem, a possible competitor for solidarity. Thus the family became narrowly limited in function. It was mainly the unit of sexual cohabitation and reproduction; its socialization function was secondary or minimal; it had no economic function in production or consumption. This form of a family with very few functions was only temporary. Two factors contributed to the reemergence of the family as central in the social structure of the kibbutz. One was the appearance of children in great numbers. The second was the growing differentiation and specialization in the kibbutz economy, which led to a greater differentiation in the social structure. Gradually the family acquired more functions, both in economic consumption and in socialization. The change that is of most interest to us, of course, involves the reemergence of the family as a major socializer.

Rosner et al. (1978) found that members of the kibbutz second generation were more familistic than members of the first generation, and that women were more familistic than men. This was measured through attitudes toward family-based sleeping arrangements. When comparing their findings to those of earlier studies by Talmon-Garber (1954) and Shepher (1967), they note the increase in familistic attitudes over time, which will increase the likelihood of the practice of family-based sleeping arrangements. The fact that members of the kibbutz second generation, who are themselves the products of communal child-rearing, want to move away from it and establish familial child rearing, raised many questions. The most natural interpretation to this fact is that members of the second generation are reacting to the deficiencies of the system, which they have experienced directly. Other interpretations are possible. The tendency of kibbutz-raised adults (and especially women) to support the change from communal child rearing to family-based child rearing can be viewed as a rebellion against their own parents, which continues the innovative tradition of the first generation, and as a reflection of a belief that the "other system," which is not too well known, must be better ("the grass is greener"). It is also, of course, a result of real dissatisfaction and frustration with the state of women in the kibbutz. The frustration with the communal child-rearing system is not usually expressed in terms of the children's needs but in terms of the needs of their mothers.

A case may be made for the connection between the recent changes in child-care patterns and the development of sex-role specialization in the kibbutz. Women in the kibbutz have been regarded as the carriers and proponents of familistic tendencies, as a result of their frustrations in the traditional kibbutz system. The basic problem with kibbutz sex roles has been euphemistically referred to as "the problem of women" (Rabin, 1970; Gerson, 1971).

Complete sexual equality and sharing of work responsibility has been one of the ideals of the kibbutz movement. The needs of the kibbutz in its earlier years were for more manpower for physical, mainly agricultural work, and women were regarded as equal partners in sharing the burden. Communal child rearing contributed to the freeing of women from the traditional tasks of mothering, so that they were available as workers. The ideal of sexual equality has been far from reality even in the earlier days of the kibbutz (Rabin, 1970; Tiger and Shepher, 1975), but the present situation is similar to those found in other areas of kibbutz life. Recent developments in the kibbutz show a pattern of consistent movement toward a more traditional pattern of sex roles, marriage, and family life and a clear revival of the traditional division of labor between the sexes. As Tiger and Shepher (1975) show, there is a clear polarization of work between men and women, with men in the productive branches of the kibbutz economy and women predominantly in communal services. Women are involved in the same types of jobs that fit the traditional female role, except that most of these jobs serve the whole community and not just the family. Thus, women have concentrated on communal service jobs, including kitchen, the laundry, the infants' and the children's houses, and so forth. Women are almost excluded from agricultural field work or industrial jobs (Tiger and Shepher, 1975). Historically, Shepher's (1969) observation seems to hold true: "In contrast to most modern societies, the kibbutz community is moving from more egalitarian to more polarized division of labor" (p. 573).

Talmon-Garber (1974) indicates that women in the kibbutz have been in favor of greater family autonomy and a greater role for the family in child rearing. Her explanation for the apparently greater familism of women is based on the change in women's roles in the kibbutz over time. In the early days of the kibbutz movement women were equal partners in the labor system since the birth rate was low and the members were all young. Gradually, women's reproductive role became predominant, limiting their involvement in hard physical labor. Men dominated the productive work role in the kibbutz, since work was becoming more specialized and demanded permanent work assignments. In 1950, Irvine (1952) observed that "frustrated maternal feeling" was a factor in the change to more familistic patterns of child rearing in the kibbutz. She reported several changes in traditional customs, which could be attributed, according to her, to a joint effort on the part of frustrated mothers and psychologists. She was already able to report the first move toward family-based sleeping arrangements. She also mentioned the objections of ideological leaders to changes in the child-rearing system.

Schlesinger (1970) regarded the dissatisfaction of women as one of the major forces behind what he termed the kibbutz crisis. He suggested specifically that women have not accepted the communal child-rearing system and would like to see an end to the "separation from their children."

The economic success of the kibbutz and the rise in living standards made the participation of women in heavy physical labor unnecessary. Manpower in the kibbutz became less of a problem, and one of the practical reasons for communal child care was thus removed. The service jobs in which women have specialized are for the most part routine, thankless jobs. Investing more in the family is one major way in which kibbutz women can find more personal satisfaction, as opposed to the frustrations and impersonality of the communal service jobs. Rabin (1970) presents data on the discontent of kibbutz women with their service jobs, and their support for familism. The growing return to family-based sleeping arrangements has been correlated with the return to the traditional division of labor among the sexes (Shepher, 1969). It is possible to conceive of the kibbutz now as a collective of families and no longer as a collective of individuals. Within this collective women are returning to their traditional roles as family caretakers and withdrawing from the roles of collective caretakers. Since these new roles are more satisfying to women, it is understandable why they become the main supporters of familism (Talmon-Garber, 1974). Men in the kibbutz continue to derive their satisfactions and status from their productive work jobs (Tiger & Shepher, 1975).

Generational differences are clearly central in the historical changes within the kibbutz. Only the first generation of the kibbutz could be genuinely revolutionary and unconventional. Following generations cannot be revolutionary if they carry on the kibbutz tradition. In this sense, they must be conservative. The second generation of the kibbutz, which is the first to be born and raised there, is now the dominant group in many kibbutzim. For this generation, and for succeeding ones, the kibbutz is not a new venture into utopia but the reality into which they were born. They were not selected, much less self-selected, like their parents. They are more pragmatic and less idealistic. Recent trends in the kibbutz include a "consumerist" life-style that consists of (1) aiming for higher living standards to match the life-style of the Israeli middle class, (2) greater freedom in making career choices, and (3) an emphasis on specialized higher education and individual success. All of these represent departures from the early kibbutz ideology. The importance of outside pressures on the kibbutz cannot be minimized. The kibbutz, as a minority avant-garde movement, has treated the wider society with ambivalence. One of the aims of kibbutz education was to immunize and isolate youngsters from the influences of the nonkibbutz world, but the growing economic and political involvement of the kibbutz in the larger society has made isolationism impossible.

Historical changes in the wider context—the State of Israel—have brought about a different atmosphere in the kibbutz movement, which has entailed many changes in social relationships and patterns of family life. Some of the important general changes in Israeli society that the kibbutz community could not escape were the rise in living standards, the decline of socialist ideals, and the general political and ideological trends in Israel, which, in the last 25 years, has changed in the direction of a growing alliance with capitalism and the United States and a decline in adherence to socialist ideas and movements. One of the major ideological changes in a majority of the kibbutzim in the 1950s was the change in attitude toward the Soviet Union and toward socialism in general. The events of the late Stalinist period in the USSR, the changes in the Soviet Union after the death of Stalin, and the 20th Congress of the Communist Party of the USSR caused a great deal of soul-searching and criticism among socialists and Marxists all over the world. For left-Zionist kibbutzim the period of the 1950s was a time of severe ideological crisis, which most of them resolved by dissociating themselves gradually from the Soviet way to socialism; there was an increased level of doubts and criticism about the USSR. In the 1960s and 1970s, and very clearly since the 1967 War, the Zionist component of kibbutz ideology has become dominant and the socialist component has become marginal. This was directly related to the shifting role of political Zionism on the world scene. The kibbutzim had been very important tools of the Zionist movement before the founding of the state. As patterns of idealistic and militant behavior became institutionalized, the tradition of kibbutz life was seen as dysfunctional.

The kibbutz movement has been for many years the elite of political Zionism, serving as an ideal for those Zionists who were less committed than kibbutz members. Changes in political Zionism itself, its crises and problems, together with its high points, are reflected in kibbutz history. The relationship between the kibbutz movement and Zionism is often paradoxical. The founding of the State of Israel in 1948, which was a great achievement for Zionism, created a crisis for the kibbutz movement. The voluntarist tradition of the kibbutz movement became less important with the appearance of a centralized state bureaucracy and a centralized military. The waves of new immigration that followed the founding of the state brought in a population that was culturally different from that of the kibbutz and contributed to making the kibbutz more of a minority in Israel.

The feeling of mission and struggle, the stand of opposition to traditional culture, and the support of social renewal can no longer be maintained. Being the elite of Zionism meant not only a feeling of mission, but also a certain burden to be carried, not always voluntarily. It must have created resentment on the part of some kibbutz members, especially in the second generation. The feelings of a common mission used to be an important source of support in the kibbutz community, and a source of psychological compensation for many physical hardships. This feeling of mission is no longer part of the kibbutz spirit. The turning point has been the change in the self-image of the kibbutz movement vis-à-vis the society around it. Once the kibbutz had changed its view of its mission from the vanguard of the change to socialism to a socialist enclave coexisting with capitalism, a basic transformation was underway. The image of the kibbutz in the eyes of most kibbutz members today, especially in the second generation (Rosner et al., 1978), is not that of a social vanguard but of an end in itself. The kibbutz is regarded as a good suitable way of life for individuals, but not as an organization that is going to change the world around it.

The connection between overall ideology and child-rearing patterns becomes clear once we look at changes within the three kibbutz federations (leftist, moderate, and rightist) with regard to child rearing and to other aspects of kibbutz ideology. We would predict that the more orthodox (that is, leftist) kibbutzim would keep the communal pattern of child rearing, while reforms in the direction of the traditional (nonkibbutz) family should appear in the less orthodox (that is, rightist) kibbutzim. This is indeed the case, with clear connections between ideological orthodoxy in child rearing and in other areas: changes in child-rearing patterns first appeared in the rightist kibbutzim and are now becoming more prevalent in the moderate kibbutz movement. The change in each individual kibbutz is decided upon by majority vote, following a decision in principle by the particular kibbutz federation.

Our suggestion here is that changes in child-rearing patterns in the more traditional direction are positively related to changes in the economic structure of the kibbutz in a more conservative direction. Those kibbutzim that are more "orthodox" in child-rearing issues are likely to be more "orthodox" in other areas.

Today, family-based sleeping arrangements are most common in the rightist kibbutz federation and almost unknown in the leftist federation. Shepher (1969) reported a correlation between family sleeping arrangements and a greater degree of ideological indifference on the part of kibbutz members. Within the same kibbutz federation it was found that members of kibbutzim where communal sleeping arrangements were in effect showed a greater degree of ideological involvement and readiness for public-service roles than did members from kibbutzim where the family-based sleeping arrangement was in effect.

The Future of Kibbutz Child-Rearing

Given recent changes in the kibbutz, it is possible to predict that the trend from kibbutz child rearing back to the traditional family will continue in the near future. Since, as we have shown, changes in economic, social, and ideological factors have brought about changes in child rearing, the continuation of those background trends in the "bourgeoisation" of the kibbutz will lead inevitably to a reduction in the differences between kibbutz and city child-rearing patterns. One can conceivably picture a point at which communal child rearing will be limited to only a few orthodox kibbutzim.

Psychologists should now write about the "classical" or "historical" kibbutz, as opposed to the present one, which is certainly a paradox for a movement that seemed to embody a breakdown of some basic human traditions and a rebellion against all of history. One can no longer speak of the "kibbutz" in general but must be more specific. If the kibbutz is to continue as a child-rearing laboratory, experimental conditions have to be specified and monitored. The kibbutz is no longer a single child-rearing laboratory, but it includes several different laboratories (or experimental conditions). What we observe is a general pattern of departures from the original kibbutz ideology, a pattern that encompasses all areas of life in the kibbutz. The changes in child-rearing patterns make up one component in this wider historical trend.

Given these general conditions, some writers feel the resurgence of the family may be the most serious threat the kibbutz has ever faced. Schlesinger (1970) predicted that "within the next 25 years, we may see a complete change in the kibbutz family system, to a way of life which approximates our own type of family" (p. 271). Talmon-Garber (1974) predicted that the family would become a competitor to the whole kibbutz system, if familistic tendencies were not integrated within the collective way of life. It seems easy to predict that present trends in the kibbutz will continue and become stronger in the future, and it will become more familistic and more individualistic than ever before. Whether these trends will have the effect of eventually abolishing the kibbutz as we know it today is doubtful, but it is clear that it is becoming drastically different from the "classical" kibbutz of the period between 1920 and 1950.

Predicting future trends in the development of any human system is a risky business, but we feel that several predictions can be made about the directions of future changes in the kibbutz. In the future, the kibbutz will develop into a community of families, very much like the moshav, with the only difference being the community ownership of the means of production. The kibbutz family will be the unit of consumption and will become more important in socialization, though the group caretaking system will still play an important role in child rearing. Even in the future, we cannot expect kibbutz child rearing to be completely family-based. There is still going to be an emphasis on group child rearing and on non-familial caretakers, and there is going to be an emphasis on community and collectivisim in education.

It seems safe to predict that in the future the family in the kibbutz will assume more and more functions and that communal child rearing will become a minority phenomenon. But the importance of the peer-group will decline, and the kibbutz infant will experience interaction with fewer significant others. This will eliminate the crucial variable that was supposed to bring about the uniqueness in the personality of the kibbutz-raised person. If we go back to our theoretical overview of Chapter 1, in which we point to the interaction between social structure, child rearing, and personality structure, then we can predict now that following the social structure changes and the changes in the child rearing system, there will be changes on the individual level. If a specific child-rearing pattern is assumed to lead to a certain personality pattern, then a change in child-rearing methods in any direction should lead to differences in the previously established pattern. The historical changes should lead to differences between the "baseline" personality and the present one that are important both factually and theoretically. Generalizations about the "kibbutz personality" should be kept close to empirical findings. Moreover, the changes in child-rearing practices give us an opportunity to test again our theoretical notions. Historical changes have set up a natural experimental design. Children growing up now under the communal sleeping arrangements can be compared to children growing up under the family-based sleeping arrangement in a neighboring kibbutz.

The internal developments in the kibbutz community seem to move along two continua, one psychological and the other structural. The structural continuum poses the family and the community at its two ends, and it seems that the rise of the family leads to a decline of the community and vice versa. The psychological continuum, paralleling the structural one, is that of solidarity versus intimacy. The family is tied to intimacy, the community to solidarity. Shorter (1975) proposed a reverse relationship between community involvement and intimacy, which parallels the historical decline of the local community and the rise of the nuclear family. If this is the case, then the minimal nuclear family was typical of the kibbutz in its early stages of high communal involvement (see Talmon-Garber, 1970a), while the late kibbutz is characterized by a decreased communal spirit (and practice) and a much stronger family.

The kibbutz was moving in accordance with trends in modern Western society when it minimized the functions of the family in the past. Today it seems to be moving against the dominant trend in reestablishing family functions. Paradoxically, the kibbutz is again out of step with much of its environment in these recent developments. While the family outside the kibbutz seems to be in crisis, losing most of its functions, the kibbutz family is now gaining functions and becoming a vital social unit in the community.

As the kibbutz child-rearing system moves closer to the traditional family pattern, any differences between kibbutz children and controls found in the future are likely to be the result of ideological education, not early childhood experiences. But as we have seen, the decline in the distinctiveness of the child-rearing system is directly related to the decline in ideological distinctions, so that all differences are likely to be minimal. This outcome of the historical process of kibbutz child-rearing development is likely to disappoint readers who have expected the kibbutz to provide neat answers to complicated pyschological questions. We have to remind those readers again that the kibbutz was not designed as a psychological laboratory. Its value to psychologists was and is in its being an experiment of nature, which, being also historical, did not promise to provide laboratory results.

Appendix I

Personal Interview Schedule

I.   Explanation of purpose of interview and assessment schedule

1. Name.

2. Permanent address.

3. Marital status.

4. Place of original (1955) contact.

5. Where else have you been since 1955? Places and duration.

6. Your educational history.

7. Occupational history as adult.

8. Present occupation.

9. What do you like about your present occupation?

10. Are you satisfied with your present occupation? If not, why?

11. Reasons for choosing this occupation.

12. How did your spouse feel about your choice?

13. How did your parents feel about your choice?

14. How important was the security of the occupation you chose?

15. For some people, the prestige of a job influences their choice; in choosing this job did you think about its prestige?

16. What do you think is the ideal job for you?

17. Everybody has some heroes he admires; who are the three people you admire most?

18. What are the most enjoyable aspects of being a wife/mother?

20. What changes would you make to make your job more pleasant?

21.-26. For working subjects

21. Could you describe the positive and negative aspects of your present boss? What do you like and dislike about him?

22. Same as 21 for *past* bosses?

23. Are there any feelings of tenseness when you are talking with authority (boss, professor)?

24. How do you react and feel when boss criticizes you? When boss tells you to do something in a hurry? What do you do in these situations?

25. Do you tend to talk much with the boss about problems in the job?

26. *Detailed description of last* interaction with boss.

27. Do you have many friends?

28. Who is your best friend? Age? Place of residence? Frequency of contact?

29. How important is this friend compared to members of your family?

30. Describe the nature of contact with your best friend. What do you do when you get together? What do you talk about? What are your common interests?

31. Everybody has personal secrets and intimate experiences that he does not share with most people. Do you share these secrets with your best friend?

32. When you have a problem bothering you, do you share it with your friend?

33. Do you find it important to have a friend that you can open up to?

34. Are there sometimes conflicts between you and your best friend, which then affect your general mood? (Describe specific examples.)

35. Do you feel that you miss this relationship when your friend is away or the relationship stops temporarily?

36. Do you have other good friends in addition to the best friend? List age, sex, and location of up to 5 close friends, and rate your degree of closeness to them. (Possible ratings: 1. superficial liking, with no mutual commitment; 2. Fairly deep contacts, with mutual visits and help, but no intimate sharing; 3. Intimate sharing and deep ties.)

37. If you don't have a best friend, do you miss having such a relationship? Would you want to have a best friend? If you do, why don't you have one?

38. There are people who find less-than-deep friendship ties with a great number of people sufficient for them. On the other hand, there are those who strive for deep and intimate friendship with just a few friends or one close friend. Which group do you belong to?

39. Do you look forward to meeting new people?

40. Do you enjoy having people over to your house?

41. Are you active in social groups?

42. Do you tend to be a bit tense when meeting new people?

43. Can you give a *detailed description* of last time you went to a gathering of strangers?

44. Describe what you did *last Sunday* (*all day*). Describe what you did for the *past seven evenings.*

45. What are the organizations you belong to? How do you feel about their ideas?

46. Any leadership roles?

47. Some people like to be leaders and some don't . . . What about you?

48. What are the important goals in your life?

49. What are some of the things you want to do or to obtain in the next year?

50. What are your hobbies and interests? Reading? Sports? Carpentry? Music?

51. What are some of the things you are very "good" in? Cooking? Golf? Gardening? Photography?

52. What do you do in your spare time?

53. Is it important for you to feel a sense of accomplishment? Do you feel bad about *not doing more* with your life?

54. Some people tend to keep a great many things in order. Do you tend to keep your personal things in order? Which things are kept orderly and which are not?

55. Are you usually on time for appointments?

56. Describe in detail the *first hour of activity after waking up this morning.*

57. Do you find yourself saving papers, nails, letters, etc.?

58. Do you decide things quickly or *mull over* your decisions? Give detailed description of last few decisions you have made.

59. What do you think are *advantages* of male role? Female role?

60. What do you think are *disadvantages* of male role? Female role?

61. Have you ever thought of being of opposite sex?

62. Do you think childbirth is gratifying? Painful?

63. Attitude to menarch? Menstruation?

64. People differ in the situations that make them irritated or angry. What situations tend to anger you? What do you do?

65. What kinds of people do you tend to take a dislike to (i.e., talkative, conceited, stupid, homely, authoritarian)?

66. Can you recall the last time you were mad or irritated? Why? What did you do?

67. What is your reaction to the following situations?

    a.   Husband or wife is irritable and nags you or is sharp tongued with you.

    b.   Child pesters you.

    c.   Child won't obey you.

    d.   Something you did is a flop (i.e., cake falls, lose a goal).

    e.   Friend doesn't invite you to a party.

    f.   Involved in a tedious task that requires patience.

    g.   You're in an argument with someone and person implies you are stupid.

    h.   Competing with someone and you lose.

68. Do you ever find yourself suddenly thinking of people you are angry with or mad at? Think of retaliation? How do you feel when these thoughts occur?

69. What is your personal philosophy about people in general? What would be your feeling as to the *major defects* of human nature (i.e., people too mean; too lazy; too sexy)? How would you rank the following items with respect to the degree to which they characterize most people?

    a.   Tendency to be mean to others.

    b.   Desire for power over others.

c.   Tendency to be lazy.

d.   Preoccupied with sex.

70. Do you get *involved* and become eager to win when you're playing any games (i.e., tennis, cards), involved in an argument? Do you feel badly if you lose?

71. Did you try hard to get good grades in school? Why?

72. What are some of the things about yourself you are most dissatisfied with?

73. What are some of the things you are satisfied with?

74. What would you like most to *improve* in your personality?

75. Self-ratings on intelligence, attractiveness to opposite sex, responsibility, athletics, etc.

76. When you are *stumped* by some decision you have to make, what do you usually do? Can you recall the last time such a situation occurred?

77. To whom do you usually go when you want to talk over a problem?

78. How often do you talk over personal things with your parents, love objects, peers, other authority people?

79. What would you do under these conditions:

a.   Not sure of a certain purchase; not sure whether to buy it for yourself; not sure if it's worth the money?

b.   Don't feel well?

c.   You are thinking of changing jobs?

d.   Thinking of what college to go to?

e.   Thinking of what kind of a car to buy?

80. How are the finances handled in your family? Who writes the checks, fills out tax forms, etc.

81. Some people don't like going for help or advice; does this apply to you?

82. Do you like to have a lot of friends?

83. If a friend asked you to go with him and you didn't want to go, would you go?

84. Do you feel bad if you are snubbed by someone; or not invited to a party that some of your friends are going to?

85. Do you feel bad if a (girl, boy) doesn't go out with you after a date or two?

86. Would you like to be able to make friends more easily?

87. Do you tend to disagree with the opinions of your friends in cases where you think you are in the right?

88. Do you tend to worry if you feel you have insulted a friend by accident?

89. Do you sometimes feel left out of things?

90. Do you keep in contact with your parents (write, call, visit)?

91. Do you sometimes discuss your problems with your mother or father?

92. When you're away from home, do you tend to be lonely for the family?

93. Would you like your husband (or wife) to assume more responsibility? Would you like to assume more responsibility?

94. Would you say that you are close to your parents? To both of them? To either one?

95. Do you have brothers or sisters? Age and place of residence (list).

96. How often do you get together with them?

97. Are any of your siblings closer to your parents than you are?

98. When did you start dating? Brief history of dating?

99. Did you go steady or not?

100. How frequently did you go out in beginning? At present?

101. Did you neck a lot? Pet? Intercourse?

102. What are the things you *look* for in a love object?

103. What are the things you *dislike* in a love object?

104. What are the strengths and weaknesses of present love object?

For married subjects: 98–101 same as above and then:

105. When did you meet present mate? How long before married?

106. What were the things about present mate that attracted you?

107. What *were* his or her weaknesses?

108. What *are* his or her strengths?

109. How frequently do you have intercourse? At present? Frequently during first year of marriage?

110. Many parents tend to raise their children somewhat differently than they were raised. Can you remember similarities and differences between what you did and your father (or mother) did on:
    a.   Punishment for disobedience?
    b.   Emphasis on being clean? On being honest?
    c.   Punishment for hitting or destruction?
    d.   Emphasis on good grades?
    e.   Emphasis on religion? What is your attitude toward religion?
    f.   Sex information?

111. As you grow older you get a better picture of your childhood and your parents. How would you describe each parent with respect to:
    a.   Strictness.
    b.   Kind of punishment.
    c.   Acceleration to achieve in school.

112. What would you say were your mother's strengths? Weaknesses?

113. What would you say were your father's strengths? Weaknesses?

114. What is your earliest memory?

115. What is your earliest memory with your mother? Your father?

116. Most children feel that each parent had specific preferences for them or their sibs. Do you recall such preferences?

117. Do you remember any childhood fears?

118. Did you complete your compulsory military service? Branch of service?

119. How long did you serve? Rank?

120. Combat experience?

121. Military decorations.

122. War injuries, if any.

123. Any difficulties during military service?

124. Any psychological problems during military service?

125. Symptoms and psychosomatic inventory. Which of the following have you had in the last year? How intense or frequent?

    1. Fears
    2. Nightmares
    3. Insomnia
    4. Sleepwalking
    5. Acid stomach
    6. Vomiting
    7. Constipation
    8. Loose bowels
    9. Nausea
    10. Hives
    11. Rashes

12. Acne
13. Pains in heart or chest
14. Obesity
15. Headaches
16. Asthma
17. Hayfever
18. Heart pounding
19. Breathing irregularity
20. Twitches
21. Hot–cold spells
22. Faintness
23. Nervous habits
24. Stuttering
25. Back pain
26. Muscle pain
27. Chronic illnesses

Appendix II

Sentence Completion Blank

1. I think that father only sometimes

2. When I have no hope to succeed

3. I always wanted

4. The future appears to me

5. My leaders

6. I know it is silly but I am afraid

7. In my opinion, a good friend should

8. When I was a small child

9. When I see a man and a woman together

10. In comparison with most families, mine

11. At work I get along best

12. My mother

13. If only I could forget the moment that I

14. If only my father were

15. I think that I have the capacity to

16. I would be definitely satisfied if

17. I hope

18. In school my teachers

19. Most of my friends do not know that I am afraid

20. I don't like people who

21. Before the war I

22. I think that married life is

23. My family treats me as if

24. Those with whom I work

25. My mother and I

26. My greatest mistake was

27. I wish that my father

28. My greatest weakness is

29. My secret ambition in life

30. One of these days I

31. If only I could be afraid no more

32. The people I like best

33. If I were small again

34. If I had sexual relations

35. Most families I know

36. I like to work with people who

37. I think that most mothers

38. When I was younger I felt guilty about

39. I think that my father

40. When my luck is bad

41. What I want most of life

42. When I will be older

43. People who I think are above me

44. Because of my fears I sometimes have to

45. When I'm not near them, my friends

46. My clearest childhood memory

47. My sex life

48. When I was a small child my family

49. People with whom I work are mostly

50. I like my mother, but

51. The worst thing that I did in my life

References

Alon, M. The youth society. In A. I. Rabin & B. Hazan (Eds.), *Collective education in the kibbutz*. New York: Springer Publishing Company, 1973.

Altman, I., Taylor, D., & Wheeler, L. Ecological aspects of group behavior in social isolation. *Journal of Applied Social Psychology*, 1971, *1* (1), 76-100.

Amir, Y. The effectiveness of the kibbutz-born soldier in the Israel defense forces. *Human Relations*, 1969, *22* (4), 333-334.

Aronoff, J. *Psychological needs and culture systems—A case study*. Princeton: Van Nostrand, 1967.

Avgar, A., Bronfenbrenner, U., & Henderson, C. R., Jr. Socialization practices of parents, teachers, and peers in Israel: Kibbutz, moshav, and city. *Child Development*, 1977, *48*, 1219-1227.

Bandura, A., & Huston, A. Identification as a process of incidental learning. *Journal of Abnormal and Social Psychology*, 1961, *63*, 311-318.

Barry, H., III, & Paxson, L. M. Infancy and early child-hood: Cross-cultural codes 2. *Ethnology*, 1971, *10*, 466-508.

Beit-Hallahmi, B. Identification and identity integration in therapy with university students. *Journal of Contemporary Psychotherapy*, 1973, *5*, 140-145.

Beit-Hallahmi, B. Identity integration, self-image crisis, and "superego victory" in postadolescent university students. *Adolescence*, 1977, *45*, 57-64.

Beit-Hallahmi, B. The kibbutz family—revival or survival? Unpublished paper, Michigan State University, 1979.

Beit-Hallahmi, B., & Rabin, A. I. The kibbutz as a social experiment and as a child-rearing laboratory. *American Psychologist*, 1977, *32* (7), 532–541.

Bettelheim, B. *The children of the dream.* New York: Macmillan, 1969.

Blasi, J. R. *The communal future: The kibbutz and the utopian dilemma.* Norwood, Pa.: Norwood Editions, 1978.

Bowlby, J. *Maternal care and mental health.* Geneva: World Health Organization, 1951.

Bronfenbrenner, U. Identification and interpersonal perception. In P. Tagiuri & L. Petrullo (Eds.), *Person perception and interpersonal behavior.* Palo Alto: Stanford University Press, 1958.

Bronfenbrenner, U. Freudian theories of identification and their derivatives. *Child Development*, 1960, *31*, 15–40.

Buber, M. *Paths in Utopia.* Boston: Beacon Press, 1958.

Butcher, J. N., & Gur, R. Translation and standardization of the Hebrew MMPI. In N. Y. Butcher & P. A. Pancheri (Eds.), *Handbook of cross-cultural MMPI research.* Minneapolis: University of Minnesota Press, 1976.

Butcher, J. N., & Pancheri, P. *Handbook of cross national MMPI research.* Minneapolis: University of Minnesota Press, 1976.

Butcher, J. N., & Tellegen, A. Common methodological problems in MMPI research. *Journal of Consulting and Clinical Psychology*, 1978, *46* (4), 620–628.

Byrne, D., Barry, J., & Nelson, D. Relationship of the revised repression-sensitization scale to measures of self-description. *Psychological Reports*, 1963, *13*, 323–334.

Caldwell, A. B. MMPI critical items. Unpublished report, 1969. (Available from Caldwell Reports. 3122 Santa Monica Blvd., Los Angeles, CA 90004).

Caplan, G. Clinical observations on the emotional life of children in the communal settlements of Israel. In S. E. Senn (Ed.), *Problems of infancy and childhood.* New York: The Josiah Macy, Jr. Foundation, 1954.

Crandall, V. C., & Gozali, J. The social desirability responses of children of four religious-cultural groups. *Child Development*, 1969, *40*, 751–762.

Dana-Engelstein, N. Repression-sensitization and interpersonal relationships among adults in the kibbutz and in the moshav. Unpublished master's thesis, The University of Haifa, 1978 [Hebrew].

Davis, K. *Human Society.* New York: Macmillan, 1937.

Devereux, E. C., Jr., Shouval, R., Bronfenbrenner, U., Rodgers, R. R., Kav-Venaki, S., Kiely, E., & Karson, E. Socialization practices of parents, teachers, and peers in Israel: The kibbutz versus the city. *Child Development*, 1974, *45*, 269–281.

Diamond, S. Kibbutz and shtetl: The history of an idea. *Social Problems*, 1957, *5*, 71–99. (a)

Diamond, S. The kibbutz: Utopia in crisis. *Dissent*, 1957, *4*, 132–140. (b)

Diamond, S. Personality dynamics in an Israeli collective: A psychohistorical analysis of two generations. *History of Childhood Quarterly*, 1975, *3*, 1–41.

Eden, D., Shirom, A., Kellerman, J. L., Aronson, J., & French, J. R. P., Jr. Stress, anxiety and coronary risk in a supportive society. In C. Spielberger (Ed.), *Stress and anxiety* (Vol. 4). Washington: Hemisphere, 1977.

Eisenstadt, S. N. *From generation to generation*. Glencoe, Ill.: Free Press, 1956.

Eisenstadt, S. N., Weintraub, D., & Toren, N. *Analysis of processes of role change*. Jerusalem: Israel Universities Press, 1967.

Endleman, R. Familistic social change in the Israeli kibbutz. *Annals of the New York Academy of Sciences*, 1977, *285*, 605–611.

Erikson, E. *Childhood and society*. New York: Norton, 1950.

Etzioni, A. Solidaric work-groups in collective settlements (Kibbutzim). *Human Organization*, 1957, *16*, 2–6.

Eylon, Y. Warmth, competence and identification. *Canadian Journal of Behavioral Science*, 1974, *6* (1), 45–58.

Farran, D. C., & Ramey, C. T. Infant day care and attachment behaviors toward mothers and teachers. *Child Development*, 1977, *48*, 1112–1116.

Fenichel, O. *The psychoanalytic theory of neurosis*. New York: Norton, 1945.

Ferguson, E. D. The use of early recollections for assessing life style and diagnosing psychopathology. *Journal of Projective Techniques and Personality Assessment*, 1964, *28* (4), 402–411.

Fiedler, F. E. Interpersonal perception and group effectiveness. In P. Tagiuri & L. Petrullo (Eds.), *Person perception and interpersonal behavior*. Palo Alto: Stanford University Press, 1958.

Fisher, S., & Cleveland, S. E. *Body image and personality*. New York: Dover, 1968.

Fox, N. Attachment of kibbutz infants to mother and metapelet. *Child Development*, 1977, *48*, 1228–1239.

Freud, S. *New introductory lectures on psychoanalysis*. New York: Norton, 1933. (Originally published, 1915.)

Freud, S. *Group psychology and the analysis of the ego*. London: Hogarth Press, 1948.

Fried, Y. Psychomotor development of kibbutz children. *Ofakim*, 1960, *14*, 303–312 [Hebrew].

Gerson, M. On the stability of the family in the kibbutz. *Megamot*, 1966, *14* (4), 395–408 [Hebrew].

Gerson, M. *On education and the family in the kibbutz*. Merchaviah, Israel: Hakibbutz Haartzi, 1968.

Gerson, M. Women in the kibbutz. *American Journal of Orthopsychiatry*, 1971, *41*, 566–573.

Gerson, M. *Family, women, and socialization in the kibbutz.* Lexington, Mass.: Heath, 1978.

Gewirtz J. L. The course of infant smiling in four child-rearing environments in Israel. In B. M. Foss (Ed.), *Determinants of infant behavior* (Vol. 3). New York: Wiley, 1965.

Gewirtz, J. L., & Gewirtz, H. B. Stimulus conditions, infant behavior and social learning in four Israeli child-rearing environments. In B. M. Foss (Ed.), *Determinants of infant behavior* (Vol. 3). New York: Wiley, 1965.

Gilford, R., & Bengston, V. Measuring marital satisfaction in three generations: Positive and negative dimensions. *Journal of Marriage and the Family*, 1979, *41*, 387–398.

Giovacchini, P. L. Symbiosis and intimacy. *International Journal of Psycho-analytic Psychotherapy*, 1976, *5*, 413–436.

Goell, Y. Kibbutz jubilee. *The Jerusalem Post-Independence Day Supplement*, April 20, 1977, *21*.

Golan, S. *Communal education.* Merhavia: Sifriat Poalim, 1961 [Hebrew].

Goldfarb, W. Emotional and intellectual consequences of psychological deprivation in infancy: A reevaluation. In P. Hoch & P. Zubin (Eds.), *Psychopathology of childhood.* New York: Grune & Stratton, 1955.

Goldstein, I., & Borus, J. F. Kibbutz and city children: A comparative study of syntactic and articulatory abilities. *Journal of Speech and Hearing Disorders*, 1976, *41* (1), 10–15.

Golomb, N., & Katz, D. *The kibbutzim as open social systems.* Israel: Ruppin Institute, 1970 (mimeo).

Graham, J. R. *The MMPI: A practical guide.* New York: Oxford University Press, 1977.

Gray, S. W., & Klaus, R. The measurement of parental identification. *Genetic Psychology Monographs*, 1956, *54*, 87-114.

Guilford, J. P. *Fundamental statistics in psychology and education.* New York: McGraw-Hill, 1965.

Haan, N. Coping and defense mechanisms related to personality inventories. *Journal of Consulting Psychology*, 1965, *29*, 373–378.

Hagen, H. Crew interaction during a thirty day simulated space flight. Unpublished manuscript, U.S. Air Force, School of Aerospace Medicine, June 1961.

Handel, A. Self concept of the adolescent in the kibbutz. *Megamot*, 1961, *11*, 142–159 [Hebrew].

Helm, B., Fromme, K. D., Murphy, P. J., & Scott, W. C. Experiencing double-bind conflict: A semantic differential assessment of interaction perception. *Journal of Research in Personality*, 1971, *10*, 166–176.

Hurvitz, E. The family in the kibbutz. In S. Wurm (Ed.), *Sefer Bussel.* Tel Aviv: Am Oved, 1960.

Irvine, E. E. Observations on the aims and methods of child-rearing in communal settlements in Israel. *Human Relations*, 1952, *5* (3), 247–276.

Irvine, E. E. Children in kibbutzim: Thirteen years after. *Journal of Child Psychology and Psychiatry*, 1966, *7*, 167–178.

Jarus, A., Marcus, J., Oren, J., & Rapaport, Ch. (Eds.), *Children and families in Israel: Some mental health perspectives.* New York: Gordon & Breach, 1970.

Jay, J., & Birney, R. C. Research findings on the kibbutz adolescent: A response to Bettelheim. *American Journal of Orthopsychiatry*, 1973, *43* (3), 347–354.

Kaffman, M. A. A comparison of psychopathology: Israeli children from kibbutz and from urban surroundings. *American Journal of Orthopsychiatry*, 1965, *35* (3), 509–530. (a)

Kaffman, M. Family diagnosis and therapy in child emotional pathology. *Family Process*, 1965, *4* (2). (b)

Kaffman, M. Survey of opinions and attitudes of kibbutz members toward mental illness: Preliminary report. *The Israel Annals of Psychiatry and Related Disciplines*, 1967, *5*, 17–31.

Kaffman, M. Characteristics of the emotional pathology of the kibbutz child. *American Journal of Orthopsychiatry*, 1972, *42*, 692–709. (a)

Kaffman, M. Family conflict in the psychopathology of the kibbutz child. *Family Process*, 1972, *XI*, 171–188. (b)

Kaffman, M. Toilet-training by multiple caretakers: Enuresis among kibbutz children. *Israel Annuals of Psychiatry and Related Disciplines*, 1972, *10* (4), 341–365. (c)

Kaffman, M. Sexual standards and behavior of the kibbutz adolescent. *American Journal of Orthopsychiatry*, 1977, *47* (2), 207–217.

Kaffman, M. Adolescent rebellion in the kibbutz. *Journal of the American Academy of Child Psychiatry*, 1978, *17* (1), 154–164.

Kaffman, M., & Elizur, E. Kibbutz adolescents today—changes and trends. *Israel Annals of Psychiatry and Related Disciplines*, 1976, *14*, 145–154.

Kaffman, M., Elizur, E., Katz, F., Levin, N., & Lichtenberg, J. Infants who become enuretics: A longitudinal study of 161 kibbutz children. *Monographs of the Society for Research in Child Development*, 1977, *42* (2, Serial No. 170), 1–61.

Kaffman, M., Weaver, S. J., & Weaver, A. Family relations test responses of retarded readers: Reliability and comparative data. *Journal of Personality Assessment*, 1972, *36*, 353–360.

Kagan, J., & Moss, H. *Birth to maturity.* New York: Wiley, 1962.

Kagan, J., Kearsley, R. B., & Zelazo, P. R. The effects of infant day care on psychological development. *Evaluation Quarterly*, 1977, *1*, 109–142.

Kaminer, H. The linkage between socialization and relationships of adults and their parents: A comparison between kibbutz and moshav. Unpublished master's thesis, University of Haifa, 1979.

Kaplan De-Nour, A., Moses, R., Rosenfeld, J., & Marcus, J. Psychopathology of children raised in the kibbutz: A critical review of the literature. *Israel Annals of Psychiatry and Related Disciplines*, 1970, *8*, 68–85.

Kardiner, A. The roads to suspicion, rage, apathy and social disintegration. In I. Galdston (Ed.), *Beyond the germ theory*. New York: Health Education Council, 1954.

Katz, F., & Lewin, G. Early childhood education. In A. I. Rabin & B. Hazan (Eds.), *Collective education in the kibbutz*. New York: Springer, 1973.

Knapp, C. W., & Harwood, B. T. Factors in the determination of intimate same-sex friendship. *Journal of Genetic Psychology*, 1977, *131*, 83–90.

Kohen-Raz, R. Mental and motor development of kibbutz, institutionalized, and home-reared infants in Israel. *Child Development*, 1968, *39*, 489–504.

Krasilowsky, D., Ginath, Y., Landau, R., & Bodenheimer, M. The significance of parent-role substitution by society in various social structures. *American Journal of Orthopsychiatry*, 1972, *42* (4), 710–717.

Kugelmass, S., & Breznitz, S. Perception of parents by kibbutz adolescents. *Human Relations*, 1966, *19*, 117–122.

Lazowick, L. M. On the nature of identification. *Journal of Abnormal and Social Psychology*, 1955, *51*, 175–183.

Lasch, C. *Haven in a heartless world: The family besieged*. New York: Basic Books, 1977.

Leon, D. *The kibbutz: Portrait from within*. London: Pergamon Press, 1969.

Levinson, D. J., Darrow, C. N., Klein, E. B., Levinson, M. H., & McKee, B. *The Seasons of a Man's Life*. New York: Knopf, 1978.

Loevinger, J., and Wessler, R. *Measuring ego development 1: Construction and use of a sentence completion test*. San Francisco: Jossly-Bass, 1970.

Luetgert, M. J., & Greenwald, B. S. Relation of emotional intimacy and parental dominance to adult identification. *Journal of Clinical Psychology*, 1975, *31*, 25–27.

Luria, Z., Goldwasser, M., & Goldwasser, A. Response to transgression in stories of Israeli children. *Child Development*, 1963, *34*, 271–280.

Maas, H. S. Preadolescent peer relations and adult intimacy. *Psychiatry*, 1968, *31*, 161–172.

Maccoby, E. E., & Feldman, S. S. Mother-attachment and stranger-reactions in the third year of life. *Monographs of the Society for Research in Child Development*, 1972, *37* (1, Serial No. 146), 1–83.

Madsen, M. C., & Shapira, A. Cooperation and challenge in four cultures. *Journal of Social Psychology*, 1977, *102*, 189–195.

Mandel, M., & Klein, M. Self-concept and social status of kibbutz children as related to the mutual appraisal of their parents. *Megamot*, 1977, *23* (2), 172–183.

Manen, G. C. The validity of parent–child socialization measures: A comparison of the use of assumed and real parent–child similarity with criterion variables. *Genetic Psychology Monographs*, 1973, *88*, 201–227.

Mannarino, A. P. Friendship patterns and altruistic behavior in preadolescent males. *Developmental Psychology*, 1976, *12* (6), 555–556.

Mannarino, A. P. Friendship patterns and self-concept development in pre-adolescent males. *The Journal of Genetic Psychology*, 1978, *133*, 105–110. (a)

Mannarino, A. P. The interactional process in preadolescent friendships. *Psychiatry*, 1978, *41* (3), 308–312. (b)

McClelland, D. C. *Power—the inner experience*. New York: Irvington Publishers, 1975.

Mead, M. A cultural anthropologist's approach to maternal deprivation. In M. D. Ainsworth et al. *Deprivation of maternal care*. Geneva: World Health Organization, 1962.

Mead, M. Kibbutz children. *Midstream*, 1966, *12* (8), 77–80.

Meares, R. The secret. *Psychiatry: Journal for the Study of Interpersonal Processes*, 1976, *39* (3), 258–265.

Middlebrook, P. N. *Social psychology and modern life*. New York: Knopf, 1974.

Minuchin, S. *Families and family therapy*. Cambridge: Harvard University Press, 1974.

Moulton, R. W., & Liberty, P. G. Patterning of parental affection and disciplinary dominance as a determinant of guilt and sex typing. *Journal of Personal and Social Psychology*, 1966, *4*, 356–363.

Murdock, G. P. *Social structure*. New York: Macmillan, 1949.

Murphy, H. B. M. The meaning of symptom check list in mental health surveys: A testing of multiple hypotheses. *Social Science and Medicine*, 1978, *12*, 67–75.

Murphy, L. B. Explorations in child personality. In A. I. Rabin et al. (Eds.), *Further exploration in personality*. New York: Wiley, 1981.

Mussen, P., & Distler, L. Child rearing antecedents of masculine identification in kindergarten boys. *Child Development*, 1960, 31, 89–100.

Nagler, S. Clinical observations on kibbutz children. *Israel Annals of Psychiatry and Related Disciplines*, 1963, *1* (2), 201–216.

Nahir, H. T., & Yussen, S. R. The performance of kibbutz and city-reared Israeli children on two role-taking tasks. *Developmental Psychology*, 1977, *13* (5), 450–455.

Nevo, B. Using biographical information to predict success of men and women in the army. *Journal of Applied Psychology*, 1976, *61* (1), 106–108.

Nevo, B. Personality differences between kibbutz born and city born adults. *The Journal of Psychology*, 1977, *96*, 303–308.

Osgood, C. E. The nature and measurement of meaning. *Psychological Bulletin*, 1952, *49*, 197–237.

Osgood, C. E. Exploration in semantic space: A personal diary. *Journal of Social Issues*, 1971, *27*, 4.

Osgood, C. E., Suci, G. J., & Tennenbaum, P. H. *The measurement of meaning*. Urbana: University of Illinois Press, 1957.

Phillips, L. *Human adaptation and its failures*. New York and London: Academic Press, 1968.

Pirojnikoff, L. A., Hadar, I., & Hadar, A. Dogmatism and social distance: A cross-cultural study. *The Journal of Social Psychology*, 1971, *85*, 187–193.

Portnoy, F. C., & Simmons, C. H. Day care and attachment. *Child Development*, 1978, *49* (1), 239–242.

Preale, S., Amir, Y., & Sharon, S. Perceptual articulation and test effectiveness in several Israeli sub-cultures. *Journal of Personal and Social Psychology*, 1970, *15*, 180–195.

Rabin, A. I. The Israeli kibbutz as a 'laboratory' for testing psychodynamic hypotheses. *Psychological Records*, 1957, 7, 111–115. (a)

Rabin, A. I. Personality maturity of kibbutz and non-kibbutz children as reflected in Rorschach findings. *Journal of Projective Techniques*, 1957, *21*, 148–153. (b)

Rabin, A. I. Culture components as a significant factor in child development: II, Kibbutz adolescents. *American Journal of Orthopsychiatry*, 1961, *31*, 493–504. (a)

Rabin, A. I. Personality study in Israeli kibbutzim. In B. Kaplan (Ed.), *Studying personality cross-culturally*. Evanston: Row, Peterson & Co., 1961. (b)

Rabin, A. I. Kibbutz mothers view collective education. *American Journal of Orthopsychiatry*, 1964, *34* (1), 140–142.

Rabin, A. I. *Growing up in the kibbutz*. New York: Springer Publishing Co., 1965.

Rabin, A. I. The sexes-ideology and reality in the Israeli kibbutz. In G. H. Seward and R. C. Williamson (Eds.), *Sex roles in a changing society*. New York: Random House, 1970.

Rabin, A. I. *Kibbutz studies: a digest of books and articles on the kibbutz by social scientists, educators and others*. East Lansing: Michigan State University Press, 1971.

Rabin, A. I. Enduring sentiments: The continuity of personality over time. *Journal of Personality Assessment*, 1977, *41* (6), 564–572.

Rabin, A. I., & Goldman, H. The relationship of severity of guilt to intensity of identification in kibbutz and non-kibbutz children. *Journal of Social Psychology*, 1966, *69* (1), 159–163.

Rabin, A. I., & Hazan, B. (Eds.). *Collective education in the kibbutz from infancy to maturity*. New York: Springer, 1973.

Rapaport, D. The study of the kibbutz education and its bearing on the theory of development. *American Journal of Orthopsychiatry*, 1958, *28*, 587–597.

Regev, E. Affective moderation and diffusion in communal child-rearing. Unpublished M.A. thesis, University of Haifa, 1977.

Regev, E., Beit-Hallahmi, B., & Sharabany, R. Affective expression in kibbutz-communal, kibbutz-familial, and city raised children in Israel. *Child Development*, 1980, *51*, 232–237.

Rettig, K. S. Relation of social systems to intergenerational changes in moral attitudes. *Journal of Personality and Social Psychology*, 1966, *4* (4), 409–414.

Rosner, M., Ben-David, J., Avnat, A., Cohen, N., & Levitan, U. *The second generation: Continuity and change in the kibbutz.* Tel Aviv: Sifriat Poalim, 1978 [Hebrew].

Sacks, J. M., & Levi, S. The sentence completion test. In L. E. Abt & L. Bellak (Eds.), *Projective psychology.* New York: Knopf, 1950.

Scher, D., Nevo, B., & Beit-Hallahmi, B. Beliefs about equal rights for men and women among Israeli and American students. *Journal of Social Psychology*, 1979, *109*, 11–15.

Schlesinger, B. Family life in the kibbutz of Israel: Utopia gained or paradise lost? *International Journal of Comparative Psychology*, 1970, *11*, 251–271.

Sears, R. R., Maccoby, E. E., & Levine, H. *Patterns of child rearing.* Evanston, Ill.: Row-Peterson, 1957.

Shapira, A. Developmental differences in competitive behavior of kibbutz and city children in Israel. *Journal of Social Psychology*, 1976, *98* (1), 19–26.

Sharabany, R. *Intimate friendship among kibbutz and city children and its measurement.* Doctoral dissertation, Cornell University, 1974.

Sharabany, R. Socialization in the kibbutz-bibliography. *JSAS Catalogue of Selected Documents in Psychology*, 1975 (Win.), *5*, 185 (Ms. N. 847).

Shepher, J. Familism and social structure: The case of the kibbutz. *Journal of Marriage and the Family*, 1969, *31*, 568–573.

Shepher, J. Mate selection among second generation kibbutz adolescents and adults: Incest avoidance and negative imprinting. *Archives of Sexual Behavior*, 1971, *1* (4), 293–307.

Shlonsky, 1961, Interview in Bamahaneh, 10.26.71 [Hebrew].

Shorter, E. *The making of the modern family.* New York: Basic Books, 1975.

Shouval, R., Kav-Venaki, S., Bronfenbrenner, U., Devereux, E. C., & Kiely, E. Anomalous reactions to social pressure of Israeli and Soviet children raised in family versus collective settings. *Journal of Personality and Social Psychology*, 1975, *32* (3), 477–489.

Shur, S., Beit-Hallahmi, B., Blasi, J. R., & Rabin, A. I. *The kibbutz: a bibliography of scientific and professional publications in English.* Darby, Pa.: Norwoood Editions, 1981.

Skinner, B. F. *Walden two.* New York: Macmillan, 1948.

Spiro, M. Education in a communal village in Israel. *American Journal of Orthopsychiatry*, 1953, *23*, 120–130.

Spiro, M. E. Is the family universal? *American Anthropologist*, 1954, *56*, 839–846.

Spiro, M. E. *Venture in utopia.* Cambridge: Harvard University Press, 1956.

Spiro, M. E. *Children of the kibbutz.* Cambridge: Harvard University Press, 1958.

Spochak, A. L. Parental identification and tendencies toward disorder as measured by the MMPI. *Journal of Abnormal and Social Psychology*, 1952, *47*, 159–165.

Srole, L., Langner, T. S., Michael, S. T., Opler, M. K., & Rennie, T. A. C. *Mental health in the metropolis: The Midtown Manhattan study.* New York: McGraw-Hill, 1962.

Stoke, S. M. An inquiry into the concept of identification. *Journal of Genetic Psychology*, 1950, *76*, 163–189.

Strommen, E. A. Friendship. In E. Donelson, & J. Gullahorn (Eds.), *Women: A psychological perspective.* New York: Wiley, 1977.

Sullivan, H. S. *The interpersonal theory of psychiatry.* New York: Norton, 1953.

Tal, A. Learning conditions, personality factors, and achievement among city and kibbutz high school students. Unpublished M.A. thesis, Tel-Aviv University, 1978 [Hebrew].

Talmon-Garber, Y. *The Family in Cooperative and Collective Settlements.* Rome: Transactions of the World Population Conference, 1954.

Talmon-Garber, Y. The family and the collective socialization in the kibbutz. *Niv Hakvutza*, 1959, *13*, 2–52 [Hebrew]. (a)

Talmon, Y. Social structure and family size. *Human Relations*, 1959, *12*, 121–146. (b)

Talmon-Garber, Y. The family in revolutionary movement. In M. Nimkoff (Ed.), *Comparative family systems.* New York: Houghton-Mifflin, 1970. (a)

Talmon-Garber, Y. *The kibbutz: Sociological studies.* Jerusalem: Magnes Press, 1970. (b)

Talmon-Garber, Y. *Family and community in the kibbutz.* Cambridge: Harvard University Press, 1972.

Terman, L. M. Buttenwieser, P., Ferguson, L. W., Johnson, W. B., & Wilson, D. P. *Psychological factors in marital happiness.* New York: McGraw-Hill, 1938.

Thibaut, J. W., & Kelly, H. H. *The social psychology of groups.* New York: Wiley, 1959.

Tiger, L., & Shepher, J. *Women of the kibbutz.* New York: Harcourt, Brace, Jovanovich, 1975.

Troll, L. The family of later life: A decade review. In I. Broderick (Ed.), *A decade of family research and action.* Minneapolis: National Council of Family Relations, 1971.

Troll, L. E., and Smith, J. Attachment through the life span: Some questions about dyadic bonds among adults. *Human Development*, 1976, *19*, 156–170.

Uzgiris, I. C., & Hunt, J. McY. *Assessment in infancy.* Urbana: University of Illinois Press, 1975.

Walker, L. S., & Wright, P. H. Self-disclosure in friendship. *Perceptual and Motor Skills*, 1976, *42*, 735–742.

Weintraub, D., Lissak, M., & Azmon. Y. *Moshava, kibbutz and moshav.* Ithaca and London: Cornell University Press, 1969.

Winch, R. F. *Identification and its familial determinants.* Indianapolis: Bobs-Merrill, 1962.

Winett, R. A., Fuchs, W. L., Moffatt, S. A., and Nerviano, V. J. A cross-sectional study of children and their families in different child care environments: Some date and conclusions. *Journal of Community Psychology,* 1977, *5* (2), 149–159.

Winnik, H. Z. Milestones in the development of psychoanalysis in Israel. *Israel Annals of Psychiatry and Related Disciplines,* 1977, *15* (2), 85–91.

Worthy, A., Gary, L., & Kahn, G. M. Self-disclosure as an exchange process. *Journal of Personality and Social Psychology,* 1969, *13,* 59–64.

Wylie, R. C. *The self-concept: A review of methodological considerations and measuring instruments.* Lincoln: University of Nebraska Press, 1974.

Yarrow, L. J., Rubenstein, J. L., & Pedersen, F. A. *Infant and environment.* Washington, D.C.: Hemisphere, 1975.

Yinon, Y., & Freedman, N. The social needs of kibbutz and urban Israeli youth. *The Journal of Social Psychology,* 1977, *103,* 319–320.

Zak, I. *Non-cognitive factors in secondary teachers.* Research report published by the Research and Consultation Center for Educational Personnel, School of Education, Tel-Aviv University, 1976 [Hebrew].

Ziller, R. C. *The social self.* New York: Pergamon Press, 1973.

Index